A CASEBOOK

REFERENCE

CASEBOOKS IN CRITICISM
RECENT TITLES

Ralph Ellison's *Invisible Man:* A Casebook
Edited by John F. Callahan

Orson Welles's *Citizen Kane:* A Casebook
Edited by James Naremore

Alfred Hitchcock's *Psycho:* A Casebook
Edited by Robert Kolker

D. H. Lawrence's *Sons and Lovers:* A Casebook
Edited by John Worthen and Andrew Harrison

D. H. Lawrence's *Women in Love:* A Casebook
Edited by Richard Peace

Cervantes' *Don Quixote:* A Casebook
Edited by Roberto González Echevarría

Fyodor Dostoevsky's *Crime and Punishment:* A Casebook
Edited by Richard Peace

Charlotte Brontë's *Jane Eyre:* A Casebook
Edited by Elsie B. Michie

Laurence Sterne's *Tristam Shandy:* A Casebook
Edited by Thomas Keymer

William Wordsworth's *The Prelude:* A Casebook
Edited by Stephen Gill

Ezra Pound's *Cantos:* A Casebook
Edited by Peter Makin

Jane Austen's *Emma:* A Casebook
Edited by Fiona Stafford

Geoffrey Chaucer's *The Canterbury Tales:* A Casebook
Edited by Lee Patterson

HARRIET BEECHER STOWE'S

Uncle Tom's Cabin

◆ ◆ ◆

A CASEBOOK

Edited by
Elizabeth Ammons

OXFORD
UNIVERSITY PRESS
2007

OXFORD

UNIVERSITY PRESS

Oxford University Press, Inc., publishes works that further
Oxford University's objective of excellence
in research, scholarship, and education.

Oxford   New York

Auckland   Cape Town   Dar es Salaam   Hong Kong   Karachi
Kuala Lumpur   Madrid   Melbourne   Mexico City   Nairobi
New Delhi   Shanghai   Taipei   Toronto

With offices in

Argentina   Austria   Brazil   Chile   Czech Republic   France   Greece
Guatemala   Hungary   Italy   Japan   Poland   Portugal   Singapore
South Korea   Switzerland   Thailand   Turkey   Ukraine   Vietnam

Copyright © 2007 by Oxford University Press, Inc.

Published by Oxford University Press, Inc.
198 Madison Avenue, New York, New York 10016

www.oup.com

Oxford is a registered trademark of Oxford University Press

Library of Congress Cataloging-in-Publication Data
Harriet Beecher Stowe's Uncle Tom's cabin : a casebook / edited
by Elizabeth Ammons.
p. cm.—(Casebooks in criticism)
Includes bibliographical references.
ISBN 978-0-19-516695-8; 978-0-19-516696-5 (pbk.)
1. Stowe, Harriet Beecher, 1811–1896. Uncle Tom's cabin.
2. Uncle Tom (Fictitious character).   3. Southern States—In literature.
4. African Americans in literature.   5. Plantation life in literature.
6. Slavery in literature.   I. Ammons, Elizabeth.
PS2954.U6H36 2007
813'.3—dc22   2006038210

Printed in the United States of America
on acid-free paper

ACKNOWLEDGMENTS

Thank you to William Andrews for asking me to edit this volume, Abigail Manzella for excellent research assistance, and Shannon McLachlan for helpful editorial support.

Credits

◆ ◆ ◆

The editor and publisher are grateful to the authors and publishers listed below for permission to reprint the essays in this volume.

Ammons, Elizabeth. "*Uncle Tom's Cabin,* Empire, and Africa," in Elizabeth Ammons and Susan Belasco, eds. *Approaches to Teaching Stowe's* Uncle Tom's Cabin. New York: The Modern Language Association of America Press, 2000. 68–73. Copyright by The Modern Language Association of America. Used by permission of The Modern Language Association.

Baldwin, James. "Everybody's Protest Novel," in *Notes of a Native Son.* Boston: Beacon Press, 1955. Copyright 1955, renewed 1983, by James Baldwin. Reprinted by permission of Beacon Press, Boston.

Bellin, Joshua D. "Up to Heaven's Gate, Down in Earth's Dust: The Politics of Judgment in *Uncle Tom's Cabin.*" *American Literature* 65 (1993). 275–95. Copyright 1993 by Duke University Press. All rights reserved. Used by permission of the publisher.

Brown, Gillian. "Getting in the Kitchen with Dinah: Domestic Politics in *Uncle Tom's Cabin.*" *American Quarterly* 36 (1984), 503–23. Copyright by The American Studies Association. Reprinted with permission of The Johns Hopkins University Press.

Cantave, Sophia. "Who Gets to Create the Lasting Images? The Problem of Black Representation in *Uncle Tom's Cabin,*" in Elizabeth Ammons and Susan Belasco, eds. *Approaches to Teaching Stowe's* Uncle Tom's Cabin. New York: The Modern Language

Contents

✦ ✦ ✦

Harriet Beecher Stowe's
Uncle Tom's Cabin

A CASEBOOK

Introduction

ELIZABETH AMMONS

❖ ❖ ❖

UNCLE TOM'S CABIN HAS always stirred debate. When the novel came out in 1852, it enraged white Southerners, who called it libelous and Stowe a liar. In the *Southern Literary Messenger,* George F. Holmes accused her of vilifying Southern whites and planting "seeds of strife and violence" (Holmes [1852] 631), a charge he escalated the next year when he reviewed *A Key to Uncle Tom's Cabin* (1853), the book Stowe published to defend her novel. Holmes exclaimed: "The woman's rights Conventions, which have rendered the late years infamous, have unsexed in great measure the female mind, and shattered the temple of feminine delicacy and moral graces; and the result is before us in these dirty insinuations of Mrs. Stowe." Most outrageous in Holmes's view—and he was not alone—was a Yankee woman's presuming to tell men what to think. He blazoned across the page these words from the New Testament: "Let the woman learn in silence with all subjection. *But I suffer not a woman to teach, nor to usurp authority over the man, but to be in silence*" (Holmes [1853] 322–23). No less incensed, William Gilmore Simms wrote of *A Key to* Uncle Tom's Cabin in the *Southern Quarterly Review:* "Mrs. Stowe betrays a malignity so remarkable that the petticoat lifts of itself, and we see the hoof of the beast under the table" (Simms 226).

If *Uncle Tom's Cabin* angered pro-slavery whites, it prompted mixed reactions from abolitionists, black and white. Most embraced the book. The famous white poet and abolitionist John Greenleaf Whittier offered: "Ten thousand thanks for this immortal book," and Henry Wadsworth Longfellow called it "one of the greatest triumphs in recorded literary history, to say nothing of the higher triumph of its moral effect" (Stowe 162, 161). In France, George Sand referred to her review of the novel as an "homage" and said Stowe has "penetrated our hearts with emotion" (Fields 152). In the United States, William G. Allen declared in a letter to the editor of *Frederick Douglass' Paper,* a black abolitionist periodical: "What a book! It is, in its line, the wonder of wonders. How its descriptions stir the blood, indeed almost make it leap out of the heart!" (Allen 3). An in-house communication for the same paper stated: "The friends of freedom owe the Authoress a large debt of gratitude for this essential service rendered by her to the cause they love" (Levine 74). The paper's creator and editor, Frederick Douglass, though he would differ with Stowe on some things over the years, praised the novel warmly: "The word of Mrs. Stowe is addressed to the soul of universal humanity" (Gossett 172).

For many abolitionists, however, including Douglass, *Uncle Tom's Cabin* from the beginning posed problems, especially on the subjects of race, gradualism as a strategy for ending slavery, colonization of Liberia by free blacks, and the whole issue of whites speaking for African Americans. For example, Allen, despite his praise for the novel, had reservations about Stowe's representations of black people; he remarked in his letter to the editor that "if any man had too much piety, Uncle Tom was that man" (Allen 3). Fellow African American critic George T. Downing agreed, finding in George Harris "the only one that really portrays any other than the subservient, submissive Uncle Tom spirit, which has been the cause of so much disrespect for the colored man" (Gossett 173). Similarly, William J. Watkins, arguing in 1853 for the right of African Americans such as himself to join the Massachusetts state militia, deplored Stowe's portrait of Tom. He sarcastically told his white audience that Tom played into their fantasies of heaven as a place where "you shall play forever upon golden harps, and the colored people, if they, like Uncle Tom, submit to your indignities with Christian meekness [and] with becoming resignation, shall be permitted, from the Negro pew, to peep into the glory of your . . . heaven to all eternity" (Gossett 173). Equally outspoken, black abolitionist and author Martin Delany categorically denounced Stowe's endorsement of black colonization of Liberia and declared: "Mrs. Stowe knows nothing about us" (Gossett 174).

Many white abolitionists also were critical. The most famous, William Lloyd Garrison, admired aspects of *Uncle Tom's Cabin* but rejected Stowe's endorsement of African colonization and agreed entirely with black criticisms of Tom's nonviolence, not because Garrison advocated violence—in fact, he fiercely championed just the opposite—but because of Stowe's double standard. "We are curious to know," Garrison asked with heavy irony, "whether Mrs. Stowe is a believer in the duty of non-resistance for the white man, under all possible outrage and peril, as well as for the black man; whether . . . she impartially disarms all mankind in the name of Christ, be the danger of suffering what it may" (Gossett 170)—or is it only blacks who are supposed to turn the other cheek? Anticipating some later critics, the famous white abolitionist Wendell Phillips worried that the emotional power of *Uncle Tom's Cabin* was no guarantee of social action. "There is many a man who weeps over Uncle Tom," he observed, "and swears by the [pro-slavery New York] *Herald.*" Staunch abolitionist Lydia Maria Child found the novel's Calvinism overbearing and counterproductive (Gossett 168, 171). But most upsetting to white abolitionists, like black ones, was Stowe's endorsement of African colonization. It represented, in most antislavery advocates' views, a step backward for the cause of justice.

All of these reservations, however, made no difference. Met mostly by overwhelmingly positive reviews and hugely popular as soon as it appeared in book form, *Uncle Tom's Cabin* sold like no other work of fiction before or for decades after. The reading public in the United States and Britain, and then rapidly around the world, bought more copies of Stowe's novel than of any other book except the Bible, and its obscure author became an international celebrity virtually overnight.

But fame was not Harriet Beecher Stowe's goal when she wrote *Uncle Tom's Cabin.* Born in Connecticut in 1811, she was the middle-aged mother of six living children when she created the narrative as a serial in 1851–52 for a small antislavery newspaper called the *National Era,* and she wrote the book because political and religious convictions compelled her. As the daughter, sister, and wife of ministers, she inhabited a world alive with moral questions and evangelical zeal, as most of her writing illustrates; in fact, it is safe to say that if middle-class white women had been allowed to train for the ministry in the first half of the nineteenth century, she almost certainly would have entered that profession. Instead, she married a minister, Calvin Stowe, in 1836 in Cincinnati, Ohio, where she had moved from New England with her family in 1832. Before writing *Uncle Tom's Cabin,* she had published a few things (some stories and essays and two books: one a geography for children, the other a collection of sketches), but she had no reputation to speak of in either literary or antislavery circles. Certain members of her family were well known. Her father, Lyman Beecher, served as the president of Lane Seminary in

Cincinnati. Her brother Henry Ward Beecher was a celebrated New York City minister (who would end up charged with adultery in a scandalous case). Her sister Catharine Ward Beecher distinguished herself as an educator and pioneering theorist of what would later be called domestic science. By contrast, Harriet Beecher Stowe, though every bit as brilliant as her father and famous siblings, was at the time she started writing *Uncle Tom's Cabin* in 1851 a relatively unknown, overwrought, overworked mother of six: the struggling wife of a low-paid professor at Bowdoin College in Maine, where the Stowes had moved from Cincinnati in 1850.

Although she never emphasized the fact, Stowe's years in Cincinnati from 1832 to 1850 clearly played a major role in the creation of *Uncle Tom's Cabin*. With only the Ohio River between the city and the slave-holding state of Kentucky, Cincinnati was the scene of intense and often violent pro- and anti-slavery agitation. The region teemed with slave catchers, armed whites hunting down fugitives—and kidnapping free blacks—to sell South, and abolitionists in and around the city aided escaped slaves as they followed the Underground Railroad north to Canada. Bloody confrontations, race riots, and furious debates were not unusual in the 1830s and 1840s, especially because the white power structure in Cincinnati sided with slavery. Early in the century, Ohio had passed racist laws requiring free blacks to put up bond money to prove they were free and would cause no trouble, and three years before the Beecher family arrived in 1832, the elected leaders in Cincinnati, ten percent of which was African American, decreed that blacks had thirty days to post that bond or leave town. The edict encouraged mobs of whites to attack black people on the street while city authorities did nothing, and the terrorism forced more than eleven hundred African Americans—perhaps many more—to flee for their lives (Gossett 32).

Into this highly charged political environment Harriet Beecher moved thirty years before the Civil War because her father had accepted the position of president of Lane Seminary, where her future husband, Calvin Stowe, worked as a professor. Equivocal in his stand on slavery, Lyman Beecher as president of the seminary complied with the trustees' moratorium on debate about the issue. Preaching noninvolvement, gradualism, and distancing oneself from abolitionists, he instructed his grown children not to take a position one way or the other. Moreover, he belonged to the American Colonization Society, an organization that promoted emigration of free blacks to Liberia, an idea most African Americans and antislavery whites considered a plot to rid the United States of black people. When Beecher supported the trustees' demand that students not be allowed to discuss abolition, much less advocate it, the outraged students went on strike. Most of them left the institution and never returned.

All of this turmoil over slavery in Cincinnati had an impact on Harriet Beecher Stowe. In addition, her own personal struggles with poverty as the wife of a low-paid seminary teacher, her poor health caused by anxiety and too much childbearing, and the trauma she felt over the death of one of her children, Charlie, during a cholera epidemic in 1849 fed the passion that went into *Uncle Tom's Cabin*. But bringing all of these stresses to a crisis and literally causing her to put pen to paper was the Fugitive Slave Act of 1850.

The Fugitive Slave Act required all free people, North or South, to turn over escaped slaves directly to slave agents, thereby making active participation in the institution of slavery a Northern as well as a Southern reality. Harboring a fugitive in the North—indeed, even knowing the whereabouts of an escaped slave and failing to report it—was now an enforced federal crime. This new law had two powerful effects. First, it declared open season on African Americans. Kidnapping blacks—fugitives or free people, it made no difference—became more lucrative than ever before, which increased outrage and resistance in the antislavery and free black communities. As J. W. Loguen, an escaped slave who had become a minister, vehemently declared at a meeting in Syracuse, New York, in which he denounced the law along with its supporters, President Fillmore and Senator Daniel Webster:

> The time has come to change the tones of submission into tones of defiance—and to tell Mr. Fillmore and Mr. Webster, if they propose to execute this measure upon us, to send on their blood-hounds.... I don't respect this law—I don't fear it—I won't obey it! It outlaws me, and I outlaw it.... I will not live a slave, and if force is employed to re-enslave me, I shall make preparations to meet the crisis as becomes a man.... Your decision tonight in favor of resistance will give vent to the spirit of liberty, and it will break the bands of party, and shout for joy all over the North. (Zinn 181)

Second, and unforeseen to lawmakers, the Fugitive Slave Act activated many uncommitted Northern whites because it brought the slave trade right to their doorstep. It showed them firsthand the horrors of the system *and* required them to participate. As a result, it forced into the ranks of abolition many who had previously stood aloof, Northern whites who had been able to avoid or deny their complicity in the enslavement of blacks.

Harriet Beecher Stowe wrote *Uncle Tom's Cabin* because of the Fugitive Slave Act. Opposed to slavery but not active on the issue, she received a letter from her sister-in-law in the wake of the Fugitive Slave Act begging her to write against the institution. Like other Northern whites, Stowe now had to face her involvement in slavery. As she recalled in a letter to one of her children twenty-five years later, she wrote the novel out of her need to take action. "I well remember the winter you were a baby and I was writing 'Uncle Tom's Cabin,'" she explained. "My heart was bursting with the anguish excited by the cruelty and injustice our nation was showing to the slave, and praying God to let me do a little and to cause my cry for them to be heard. I remember many a night weeping over you as you lay sleeping beside me, and I thought of the slave mothers whose babes were torn from them" (Stowe 149). Driven by empathy with slave mothers brutally separated from their children, by religious conviction, and by political outrage, Stowe sent the first chapter of *Uncle Tom's Cabin* to the *National Era* in April 1851.

Although the 1851–52 serialized version of the novel attracted little attention, appearing as it did in a small antislavery newspaper that reached, for the most part, the already converted, the published book instantly became a phenomenon in 1852. More than three thousand copies sold the first day, fourteen power presses ran day and night to keep up with demand, and within a year there were 120 editions and 300,000 copies sold. Translations proliferated—eventually the book could be read in more than forty languages—and reviewers competed for superlatives to heap on the novel. While the narrative was still running as a serial in the *National Era,* the small Boston publisher John P. Jewett approached the Stowes about book publication and proposed that they help pay production costs and then share equally in the profits. But Calvin Stowe did not have money to contribute; anyway, he knew the proceeds would be small (antislavery literature always sold poorly). So he worked out a counterdeal that gave his wife ten percent of the profits— enough, he believed, as the well-known story goes, to allow her to buy a new dress. The novel, of course, bought far more than one dress, and it made the firm of John P. Jewett rich as well.

Trying to account for *Uncle Tom's Cabin*'s enormous popularity, one of Stowe's sons looked back late in the nineteenth century and theorized that the book "aroused the public sentiment of the world by presenting in the concrete that which had been a mere series of abstract propositions." People "understand pictures better than words," he explained, and to illustrate he argued:

> Someone rushes into your dining-room while you are at breakfast and cries out, "Terrible railroad accident, forty killed and wounded, six were burned alive."
>
> "Oh, shocking! dreadful!" you exclaim, and yet go quietly on with your rolls and coffee. But suppose you stood at that instant by the

wreck, and saw the mangled dead, and heard the piercing shrieks of the wounded, you would be faint and dizzy with the intolerable spectacle.

So "Uncle Tom's Cabin" made the crack of the slavedriver's whip, and the cries of the tortured blacks ring in every household in the land, till human hearts could endure it no longer. (Stowe 154–55)

Participating in the respected nineteenth-century literary tradition of sentimentalism, which held that art should actively churn up readers' emotions, *Uncle Tom's Cabin* was written to produce intense reactions of fear, anger, pity, horror, shame, hope. Congressman Horace Greeley had to disembark from a train because he was weeping so copiously as he read the book, and his response was typical. For many readers, as Stowe's son pointed out, *Uncle Tom's Cabin* made slavery immediate and opposition imperative.

As one consequence of its unprecedented popularity, Stowe's novel spawned a veritable industry of mass-culture images and consumer products. Mugs, figurines, wallpaper, candles, songs, imitative novels, rebuttal novels, and theatrical performances flooded the marketplace to agree or disagree with Stowe but in every case to capitalize on her success. Indeed, the novel inaugurated the pattern of consumer goods accompanying a blockbuster movie or best-selling novel that now seems normal.

The most lasting of these by-products, of course, have been the racist stereotypes generated by the book and its surrounding consumer culture: Uncle Tom, the toothy, grinning sycophant who loves white folks; Aunt Chloe, the jolly mammy who can't resist adorable white children; Topsy, the witless pickaninny. These stereotypes, some argue, do not reflect Stowe's novel but, instead, distort her characterization of Tom as a martyr willing to die to protect fellow slaves, Chloe as a canny co-conspirator in Eliza's escape, and Topsy as an incarnation of profound child abuse. Not the novel, this point of view maintains, but minstrelesque perversions of it, which Stowe condemned, give us the damaging stereotypes. Others, however, find in the novel—not outside and extraneous to it—precisely the racist attitudes and traditions, including elements of blackface minstrelsy, that have been picked up and mined by U.S. mass culture racism from 1852 to the present.

However one decides this issue—and it speaks to the continuing power of the text that debate persists—it cannot be denied that *Uncle Tom's Cabin* reproduces mainstream, white, nineteenth-century, racist ideas about black people. In contrast to how we view race today, Harriet Beecher Stowe, like most people in the United States in the mid-nineteenth century, regarded race as a biologically determined reality that endowed each racial group with innate characteristics. Further, like almost all other whites at the time, including the overwhelming majority of white abolitionists, the innate characteristics she ascribed to blacks stereotyped and denigrated them while elevating white Anglo Saxons. This racism, not invented by Stowe but certainly promulgated by her novel, has endured. It animates racist best-sellers derived from *Uncle Tom's Cabin,* such as Margaret Mitchell's *Gone with the Wind* (1936) and the popular movie it inspired. Before that, it shaped Thomas Dixon's best-selling 1905 racist novel, *The Clansman,* which generated the first blockbuster movie, D. W. Griffith's *The Birth of a Nation* (1915). That Ku Klux Klan recruiting film laid the foundation for the Hollywood movie industry and was the first film shown in the White House, although, as Michael Rogin explains, most books and academic courses on film ignore that history. And a glance at television shows or comedy club performances today shows that racist stereotypes continue to thrive not only in the United States but also, because television programming represents a major national export, around the world.

This legacy of racism inspired by *Uncle Tom's Cabin* has also produced an unbroken history of rebuttal by black writers and artists. From Harriet Wilson's *Our Nig* in 1859 to Wallace Thurman's *The Blacker the Berry* in 1929 to Toni Morrison's *The Bluest Eye* in 1970, African American authors have countered Stowe's Topsy narrative (see, e.g., Ammons and Hébert). And reactions to Stowe's story of Tom are so numerous that only a few can be mentioned. Although various nineteenth- and early-twentieth-century authors such as Frances Ellen Harper and Langston Hughes refer to Stowe's text positively, classics of the mid-twentieth century such as Richard Wright's *Native Son* (1940) and, even more obviously, his 1938 *Uncle Tom's Children* and Ralph Ellison's *Invisible Man* (1952) engage Stowe's text more complexly, especially her representation of black manhood. Nor have revisions abated in the contemporary era. As Sarah Meer summarizes:

> LeRoi Jones created an "Alternate Ending" to *Uncle Tom's Cabin* that barely seems to relate to the novel at all, itself perhaps a refutation of Stowe's story and her right to tell it. Ishmael Reed made the book and its author (and even her legend) surreal in *Flight to Canada* [1976]. Robert Alexander produced a coruscating take on the *Tom* play in *I Ain't Yo' Uncle* [1996], while the dancer Bill T. Jones's parodic, disturbing, and sometimes affectionate piece "Last Supper at Uncle Tom's Cabin/ The Promised Land" [1995] was designed, he claims, to reflect a reading of the novel that found it "hokum, misinformation[,] . . . moving, infuriating, beautiful, embarrassing, and important." (Meer 255)

As these responses to *Uncle Tom's Cabin* underscore, the novel—powerful and controversial in its own day—continues to prompt strong and often complicated reactions.

The chapters in this book address many of these issues about *Uncle Tom's Cabin* and race. They also give some sense of the trajectory of modern interest in the novel, which was dismissed in the New Critical mid-twentieth century as sentimental and too popular to be taken seriously but has since then enjoyed significant critical attention because of the advent of feminist, historicist, race-focused, poststructural, and postcolonial critical approaches to literature.

The opening pieces foreground Stowe's own views, beginning with three letters. The first Stowe wrote to the famous African American abolitionist Frederick Douglass to seek his help in contacting escaped slaves who might provide firsthand information about slavery. In it, she also argues her view that the church in America, though far from perfect, can play an important role in shaping antislavery commitment. The second, written to the equally famous white abolitionist William Lloyd Garrison, attempts to intervene in the hostility between Garrison and Douglass. Stowe criticizes Garrison for precipitating and participating in such divisiveness among allies and expresses regret that she was pulled into the discord herself. The third, addressed to Mrs. Follen, a white poet, is more personal. Stowe describes her domestic situation when she wrote *Uncle Tom's Cabin* and speaks with passion about what she learned in Cincinnati of the horrors of slavery from formerly enslaved African American women whom she employed to help with household and childrearing tasks.

The last two selections by Stowe come from her 1853 volume, *A Key to* Uncle Tom's Cabin, written to authenticate the novel by providing factual material and clear antislavery arguments in a nonfiction format. Both excerpts show her brilliance as a tough-minded, rigorous thinker, skilled at marshaling facts, attacking fallacious arguments, and building strong rhetorical appeals to both reason and emotion. "Does Public Opinion Protect the Slave?" counters the widespread argument that pro-slavery laws in the South and North were not a problem because people of good will would not tolerate mistreatment of slaves. Stowe condemns such thinking as blatantly racist and points out that whites would never accept such arguments with reference to fellow white people, even denigrated whites such as the Irish; she presents specific court cases illustrating her position (as she does throughout the *Key*), and she specifically exposes the moral hypocrisy of a supposedly benevolent white Southern minister, using his own words against him. Similarly grounded in Christian scripture, "What Is to Be Done?" gives practical activist advice to allies in the struggle against slavery. Stowe talks of the need to take a stand against racism locally, the importance of not giving in to denial or avoidance, and the imperative of healing divisions within the movement so that energy is not wasted on internal quarrels and differences. When Stowe wrote all of these pieces in the 1850s, she did not know whether, when, or how slavery would end in the United States. Her words come from the midst of the struggle.

The essays that follow these selections from Stowe offer various critical readings of *Uncle Tom's Cabin*. Written in the mid-twentieth century by the famous African American novelist and essayist James Baldwin, "Everybody's Protest Novel" has become a classic in Stowe scholarship. Baldwin attacks the racism of *Uncle Tom's Cabin*, particularly Stowe's emasculation of Tom, and characterizes the novel's sentimentalism as a blatant appeal to prurient fascination with darkness, both theological and racial. Publishing in the same era and equally disdainful of nineteenth-century sentimentalism, the well-known white male critic Leslie A. Fiedler reads *Uncle Tom's Cabin* psychoanalytically in the piece titled here "Love and Death in *Uncle Tom's Cabin*." Discussing the heterosexual dynamics of the novel, Fiedler suggests that a pornographic fascination with the erotics of death in the figure of the virginal girl-child Eva may explain the extraordinary impact of the novel.

Taking issue with such criticism of Stowe's sentimentalism, Jane P. Tompkins's "Sentimental Power: *Uncle Tom's Cabin* and the Politics of Literary History," like Baldwin's essay, now stands as a classic in Stowe scholarship. Written by a prominent white feminist, the essay defends and reinterprets Stowe's sentimentalism as literarily effective, intellectually complex, and politically salient. Tompkins challenges male-dominated definitions of art and reads the novel's appeal to emotion as a key element in Stowe's feminist antislavery argument, which Tompkins argues is grounded in nineteenth-century domestic ideology and maternal values. Pursuing this line of white feminist thinking even further in "Getting in the Kitchen with Dinah: Domestic Politics in *Uncle Tom's Cabin*," Gillian Brown interprets Stowe's novel as a brief for mother rule in the United States. Brown presents the novel as a radical text that advocates the replacement of patriarchy with matriarchy and the widespread adoption of domestic ideology, including in the public sphere.

Also contextualizing the novel historically but concentrating on race rather than gender, Robert B. Stepto in "Sharing the Thunder: The Literary Exchanges of Harriet Beecher Stowe, Henry Bibb, and Frederick Douglass" places *Uncle Tom's Cabin* in conversation with two black-authored texts of the period, Bibb's autobiographical slave narrative and Douglass's novella, *The Heroic Slave*. Stepto's detailed examination reveals a number of shared outlooks but also important areas of difference, most of them centering on issues of black heroism, the role of Christianity in the struggle for emancipation, and African colonization. Sarah Meer in "Topsy and the End Man: Blackface in *Uncle Tom's Cabin*" likewise locates Stowe's novel in U.S. racial and cultural history. Meer investigates the text's debt to and manipulation of blackface minstrelsy to argue that Stowe effectively uses the well-known device of end-man/interlocuter dialogue in exchanges between Topsy and Miss Ophelia. This essay argues that Stowe adapts minstrel stage tropes to antislavery ends while also recognizing that readers can and have misappropriated the text's rhetorical maneuvers to support racist agendas.

P. Gabrielle Foreman's "'This Promiscuous Housekeeping': Death, Transgression, and Homoeroticism in *Uncle Tom's Cabin*" returns to sexuality and sexually charged themes such as those discussed by James Baldwin and Leslie A. Fiedler, as well as Hortense J. Spillers in her well-known essay, "Changing the Letter: The Yokes, the Jokes of Discourse, or, Mrs. Stowe, Mr. Reed." Foreman illuminates interracial homoerotic desire and anxiety in the novel and, focusing especially on the relationships between Adolph and Augustine St. Clare and Tom and Legree, asks how repressed homosexual desire functions in Stowe's book. Sophia Cantave's "Who Gets to Create the Lasting Images? The Problem of Black Representation in *Uncle Tom's Cabin*," written from a black feminist point of view, addresses head-on the problematic issue of the novel's continuing racist power in American culture. Much as Stepto places Stowe's novel in conversation with texts by two African American male contemporaries, Cantave juxtaposes *Uncle Tom's Cabin* and Harriet E. Wilson's *Our Nig,* plus, to a lesser degree, the personal narrative of Mary Prince, to ask why Stowe's text has become *the* text about slavery, blackness, and race relations in the United States. Especially in the classroom, what are the persistent negative effects of this 150-year legacy?

Concluding the volume are two essays that examine ideologies and contradictions that simultaneously advance and undermine Stowe's vision of social justice in *Uncle Tom's Cabin.* Joshua D. Bellin's "Up to Heaven's Gate, Down in Earth's Dust: The Politics of Judgment in *Uncle Tom's Cabin*" embeds Stowe's theological and moral arguments about slavery in the mainstream white Christian beliefs and debates of her day to show how the novel struggles with the question at the core of much antislavery thought at the time. Does the answer for abolitionists lie in trusting in God for a solution or in trusting in human agency and action, including violent action? My own essay, "Freeing the Slaves and Banishing the Blacks: Racism, Empire, and Africa in *Uncle Tom's Cabin*," with which the volume ends, critiques Stowe's endorsement of Liberian colonization in *Uncle Tom's Cabin.* I explain the origins and agenda of the American Colonization Society, as well as the opposition to colonization voiced by most abolitionists, black and white, and locate Stowe's racism in mid-nineteenth-century biologistic theories of race. In asking us to think about the intertwining of racism and colonialism in Stowe's novel, I argue for reading *Uncle Tom's Cabin* not only in terms of its national narrative but also in terms of its global and imperialist designs.

Works Cited

Allen, William G. "Letter to the Editor." *Frederick Douglass' Paper.* 20 May 1852: 3.

Ammons, Elizabeth. "Stowe's Dream of the Mother-Savior: *Uncle Tom's Cabin* and American Women Writers before the 1920s." *New Essays on* Uncle Tom's Cabin, ed. Eric J. Sundquist. Cambridge: Cambridge University Press, 1986: 155–95.

Fields, Annie, ed. *Life and Letters of Harriet Beecher Stowe.* Boston: Houghton Mifflin, 1898.

Gossett, Thomas F. Uncle Tom's Cabin *and American Culture.* Dallas, TX: Southern Methodist University Press, 1985.

Hébert, Kimberly G. "Acting the Nigger: Topsy, Shirley Temple, and Toni Morrison's Pecola." *Approaches to Teaching Stowe's* Uncle Tom's Cabin, ed. Elizabeth Ammons and Susan Belasco. New York: Modern Language Association, 2000: 184–98.

Holmes, George F. "Review of *A Key to Uncle Tom's Cabin.*" *Southern Literary Messenger* 19 (1853): 322–23.

———. "Review of *Uncle Tom's Cabin.*" *Southern Literary Messenger* 18 (1852): 631.

Levine, Robert S. "*Uncle Tom's Cabin* in *Frederick Douglass' Paper:* An Analysis of Reception." *American Literature* 64 (1992): 71–93.

Meer, Sarah. *Uncle Tom Mania: Slavery, Minstrelsy and Transatlantic Culture in the 1850s.* Athens: University of Georgia Press, 2005.

Rogin, Michael. "'The Sword Became a Flashing Vision': D. W. Griffith's *The Birth of a Nation.*" *Representations* 9 (1985): 150–95.

Simms, William Gilmore. "Review of *A Key to Uncle Tom's Cabin.*" *Southern Quarterly Review* 7 (1853): 226.

Spillers, Hortense. "Changing the Letter: The Yokes, the Jokes of Discourse, or, Mrs. Stowe, Mr. Reed," *Slavery and the Literary Imagination,* ed. Deborah McDowell and Arnold Rampersad. Baltimore: Johns Hopkins University Press, 1989: 25–61.

Stowe, Charles Edward. *Life of Harriet Beecher Stowe Compiled from Her Letters and Journals.* Boston: Houghton, Mifflin, 1890.

Zinn, Howard. *A People's History of the United States, 1492–Present.* New York: HarperCollins, 2003.

Letter to Frederick Douglass

HARRIET BEECHER STOWE

◆ ◆ ◆

Brunswick, July 9, 1851.

Frederick Douglass, Esq.:

SIR,—YOU MAY PERHAPS have noticed in your editorial readings a series of articles that I am furnishing for the "Era" under the title of "Uncle Tom's Cabin, or Life among the Lowly."

In the course of my story the scene will fall upon a cotton plantation. I am very desirous, therefore, to gain information from one who has been an actual laborer on one, and it occurred to me that in the circle of your acquaintance there might be one who would be able to communicate to me some such information as I desire. I have before me an able paper written by a Southern planter, in which the details and *modus operandi* are given from his point of sight. I am anxious to have something more from another standpoint. I wish to be able to make a picture that shall be graphic and true to nature in its details. Such a person as Henry Bibb, if in the country, might give me just the kind of information I desire. You may possibly know of some other person. I will subjoin to this letter a list of questions, which in that case you will do me a favor by inclosing to the individual, with the request that he will at earliest convenience answer them.

For some few weeks past I have received your paper through the mail, and have read it with great interest, and desire to return my acknowledgments for it. It will be a pleasure to me at some time when less occupied to contribute something to its columns. I have noticed with regret your sentiments on two subjects—the church and African colonization, . . . with the more regret because I think you have a considerable share of reason for your feelings on both these subjects; but I would willingly, if I could, modify your views on both points.

In the first place you say the church is "pro-slavery." There is a sense in which this may be true. The American church of all denominations, taken as a body, comprises the best and most conscientious people in the country. I do not say it comprises none but these, or that none such are found out of it, but only if a census were taken of the purest and most high principled men and women of the country, the majority of them would be found to be professors of religion in some of the various Christian denominations. This fact has given to the church great weight in this country—the general and predominant spirit of intelligence and probity and piety of its majority has given it that degree of weight that it has the power to decide the great moral questions of the day. Whatever it unitedly and decidedly sets itself against as moral evil it can put down. In this sense the church is responsible for the sin of slavery. Dr. Barnes has beautifully and briefly expressed this on the last page of his work on slavery, when he says: "Not all the force out of the church could sustain slavery an hour if it were not sustained in it." It then appears that the church has the power to put an end to this evil and does not do it. In this sense she may be said to be pro-slavery. But the church has the same power over intemperance, and Sabbath-breaking, and sin of all kinds. There is not a doubt that if the moral power of the church were brought up to the New Testament standpoint it is sufficient to put an end to all these as well as to slavery. But I would ask you, Would you consider it a fair representation of the Christian church in this country to say that it is pro-intemperance, pro-Sabbath-breaking, and pro everything that it might put down if it were in a higher state of moral feeling? If you should make a list of all the abolitionists of the country, I think that you would find a majority of them in the church—certainly some of the most influential and efficient ones are ministers.

I am a minister's daughter, and a minister's wife, and I have had six brothers in the ministry (one is in heaven); I certainly ought to know something of the feelings of ministers on this subject. I was a child in 1820 when the Missouri question was agitated, and one of the strongest and deepest impressions on my mind was that made by my father's sermons and prayers, and the anguish of his soul for the poor slave at that time. I remember his preaching drawing tears down the hardest faces of the old farmers in his congregation.

I well remember his prayers morning and evening in the family for "poor, oppressed, bleeding Africa," that the time of her deliverance might come; prayers offered with strong crying and tears, and which indelibly impressed my heart and made me what I am from my very soul, the enemy of all slavery. Every brother I have has been in his sphere a leading anti-slavery man. One of them was to the last the bosom friend and counselor of Lovejoy. As for myself and husband, we have for the last seventeen years lived on the border of a slave State, and we have never shrunk from the fugitives, and we have helped them with all we had to give. I have received the children of liberated slaves into a family school, and taught them with my own children, and it has been the influence that we found in the church and by the altar that has made us do all this. Gather up all the sermons that have been published on this offensive and unchristian Fugitive Slave Law, and you will find that those against it are numerically more than those in its favor, and yet some of the strongest opponents have not published their sermons. Out of thirteen ministers who meet with my husband weekly for discussion of moral subjects, only three are found who will acknowledge or obey this law in any shape.

After all, my brother, the strength and hope of your oppressed race does lie in the church—in hearts united to Him of whom it is said, "He shall spare the souls of the needy, and precious shall their blood be in his sight." Everything is against you, but Jesus Christ is for you, and He has not forgotten his church, misguided and erring though it be. I have looked all the field over with despairing eyes; I see no hope but in Him. This movement must and will become a purely religious one. The light will spread in churches, the tone of feeling will rise, Christians North and South will give up all connection with, and take up their testimony against, slavery, and thus the work will be done.

H. B. Stowe

Letter to William Lloyd Garrison

HARRIET BEECHER STOWE

◆ ◆ ◆

Cabin, December 19, 1853.

Mr. Garrison

DEAR SIR,—AFTER SEEING YOU, I enjoyed the pleasure of a personal interview with Mr. Douglass, and I feel bound in justice to say that the impression was far more satisfactory than I had anticipated.

There did not appear to be any deep underlying stratum of bitterness; he did not seem to me malignant or revengeful. I think it was only a temporary excitement and one which he will outgrow.

I was much gratified with the growth and development both of his mind and heart. I am satisfied that his change of sentiment was not a mere political one but a genuine growth of his own conviction. A vigorous reflective mind like his cast among those who nourish these new sentiments is naturally led to modified views.

At all events, he holds no opinion which he cannot defend, with a variety of richness of thought and expression and an aptness of illustration which shows it to be a growth from the soil of his own mind with a living root, and not a twig broken off other men's thoughts and stuck down to subserve a temporary purpose.

His plans for the elevation of his own race are manly, sensible, comprehensive; he has evidently observed closely and thought deeply and will, I trust, act efficiently.

You speak of him as an apostate. I cannot but regard this language as unjustly severe. Why is he any more to be called an apostate for having spoken ill-tempered things of former friends than they for having spoken severely and cruelly as they have of him? Where is this work of excommunication to end? Is there but one true anti-slavery church and all others infidels? Who shall declare which it is? I feel bound to remonstrate with this—for the same reason that I do with slavery—because I think it an injustice. I must say still

19

farther, that if the first allusion to his family concerns was unfortunate this last one is more unjustifiable still. I am utterly surprised at it. As a friend to you and to him, I view it with the deepest concern and regret.

What Douglass *is* really, time will show. I trust that he will make no farther additions to the already unfortunate controversial literature of the cause. *Silence* in this case will be eminently—*golden.*

I must indulge the hope you will see reason at some future time to alter your opinion and that what you now cast aside as worthless shall yet appear to be a treasure. There is abundant room in the anti-slavery field for him to perform a work without crossing the track or impeding the movements of his old friends, and perhaps in some future time, meeting each other from opposite quarters of a victorious field, you may yet shake hands together.

I write this note, because in the conversation I had with you, and also with Miss Weston, I admitted so much that was unfavorable to Mr. Douglass that I felt bound in justice to state the more favorable views which had arisen to my mind.

Very sincerely your friend,

H. B. Stowe

Letter to Mrs. Follen

HARRIET BEECHER STOWE

◆ ◆ ◆

Andover, February 16, 1853.

My dear madam,—I hasten to reply to your letter, to me the more interesting that I have long been acquainted with you, and during all the nursery part of my life made daily use of your poems for children.

I used to think sometimes in those days that I would write to you, and tell you how much I was obliged to you for the pleasure which they gave us all.

So you want to know something about what sort of a woman I am! Well, if this is any object, you shall have statistics free of charge. To begin, then, I am a little bit of a woman,—somewhat more than forty, about as thin and dry as a pinch of snuff; never very much to look at in my best days, and looking like a used-up article now.

I was married when I was twenty-five years old to a man rich in Greek and Hebrew, Latin and Arabic, and, alas! rich in nothing else. When I went to housekeeping, my entire stock of china for parlor and kitchen was bought for eleven dollars. That lasted very well for two years, till my brother was married and brought his bride to visit me. I then found, on review, that I had neither plates nor teacups to set a table for my father's family; wherefore I thought it best to reinforce the establishment by getting me a tea-set that cost ten dollars more, and this, I believe, formed my whole stock in trade for some years.

But then I was abundantly enriched with wealth of another sort.

I had two little, curly-headed twin daughters to begin with, and my stock in this line has gradually increased, till I have been the mother of seven children, the most beautiful and the most loved of whom lies buried near my Cincinnati residence. It was at his dying bed and at his grave that I learned what a poor slave mother may feel when her child is torn away from her. In those depths of sorrow which seemed to me immeasurable, it was my only prayer to God that such anguish might not be suffered in vain. There were circumstances about his death of such peculiar bitterness, of what seemed almost cruel suffering, that I felt that I could never be consoled for it, unless this crushing of my own heart might enable me to work out some great good to others. . . .

I allude to this here because I have often felt that much that is in that book ("Uncle Tom") had its root in the awful scenes and bitter sorrows of that summer. It has left now, I trust, no trace on my mind, except a deep compassion for the sorrowful, especially for mothers who are separated from their children.

During long years of struggling with poverty and sickness, and a hot, debilitating climate, my children grew up around me. The nursery and the kitchen were my principal fields of labor. Some of my friends, pitying my trials, copied and sent a number of little sketches from my pen to certain liberally paying "Annuals" with my name. With the first money that I earned in this way I bought a feather-bed! for as I had married into poverty and without a dowry, and as my husband had only a large library of books and a great deal of learning, the bed and pillows were thought the most profitable investment. After this I thought that I had discovered the philosopher's stone. So when a new carpet or mattress was going to be needed, or when, at the close of the year, it began to be evident that my family accounts, like poor Dora's, "wouldn't add up," then I used to say to my faithful friend and factotum Anna, who shared all my joys and sorrows, "Now, if you will keep the babies and attend to the things in the house for one day, I'll write a piece, and then we shall be out of the scrape." So I became an author,—very modest at first, I do assure you, and remonstrating very seriously with the friends who had thought it best to put my name to the pieces by way of getting up a reputation; and if you ever see a woodcut of me, with an immoderately long nose, on the cover of all the U.S. Almanacs, I wish you to take notice, that I have been forced into it contrary to my natural modesty by the imperative solicitations of my dear five thousand friends and the public generally. One thing I must say with regard to my life at the West, which you will understand better than many English women could.

I lived two miles from the city of Cincinnati, in the country, and domestic service, not always you know to be found in the city, is next to an impossibility to obtain in the country, even by those who are willing to give the highest wages; so what was to be expected for poor me, who had very little of this world's goods to offer?

Had it not been for my inseparable friend Anna, a noble-hearted English girl, who landed on our shores in destitution and sorrow, and clave to me as Ruth to Naomi, I had never lived through all the trials which this uncertainty and want of domestic service imposed on both: you may imagine, therefore, how glad I was when, our seminary property being divided out into small lots which were rented at a low price, a number of poor families settled in our vicinity, from whom we could occasionally obtain domestic service. About a dozen families of liberated slaves were among the number, and they became my favorite resort in cases of emergency. If anybody wishes to have a black face look handsome, let them be left, as I have been, in feeble health in oppressive hot weather, with a sick baby in arms, and two or three other little ones in the nursery, and not a servant in the whole house to do a single turn. Then, if they could see my good old Aunt Frankie coming with her honest, bluff, black face, her long, strong arms, her chest as big and stout as a barrel, and her hilarious, hearty laugh, perfectly delighted to take one's washing and do it at a fair price, they would appreciate the beauty of black people.

My cook, poor Eliza Buck,—how she would stare to think of her name going to England!—was a regular epitome of slave life in herself; fat, gentle, easy, loving and lovable, always calling my very modest house and door-yard "The Place," as if it had been a plantation with seven hundred hands on it. She had lived through the whole sad story of a Virginia-raised slave's life. In her youth she must have been a very handsome mulatto girl. Her voice was sweet, and her manners refined and agreeable. She was raised in a good family as a nurse and seamstress. When the family became embarrassed, she was suddenly sold on to a plantation in Louisiana. She has often told me how, without any warning, she was suddenly forced into a carriage, and saw her little mistress screaming and stretching her arms from the window towards her as she was driven away. She has told me of scenes on the Louisiana plantation, and she has often been out at night by stealth ministering to poor slaves who had been mangled and lacerated by the lash. Hence she was sold into Kentucky, and her last master was the father of all her children. On this point she ever maintained a delicacy and reserve that always appeared to me remarkable. She always called him her husband; and it was not till after she had lived with me some years that I discovered the real nature of the connection. I shall never forget how sorry I felt for her, nor my feelings at her humble apology, "You know, Mrs. Stowe, slave women cannot help themselves." She had two very pretty quadroon daughters, with her beautiful hair and eyes, interesting children, whom I had instructed in the family school with my children. Time would fail to tell you all that I learned incidentally of the slave system in the history of various slaves who came into my family, and of the underground railroad which, I may say, ran through our house. But the letter is already too long.

You ask with regard to the remuneration which I have received for my work here in America. Having been poor all my life and expecting to be poor the rest of it, the idea of making money by a book which I wrote just because I could not help it, never occurred to me. It was therefore an agreeable surprise to receive ten thousand dollars as the first-fruits of three months' sale. I presume as much more is now due. Mr. Bosworth in England, the firm of Clarke & Co., and Mr. Bentley, have all offered me an interest in the sales of their editions in London. I am very glad of it, both on account of the value of what they offer, and the value of the example they set in this matter, wherein I think that justice has been too little regarded.

I have been invited to visit Scotland, and shall probably spend the summer there and in England.

I have very much at heart a design to erect in some of the Northern States a normal school, for the education of colored teachers in the United States and in Canada. I have very much wished that some permanent memorial of good to the colored race might be created out of the proceeds of a work which promises to have so unprecedented a sale. My own share of the profits will be less than that of the publishers', either English or American; but I am willing to give largely for this purpose, and I have no doubt that the publishers, both American and English, will unite with me; for nothing tends more immediately to the emancipation of the slave than the education and elevation of the free.

I am now writing a work which will contain, perhaps, an equal amount of matter with "Uncle Tom's Cabin." It will contain all the facts and documents on which that story was founded, and an immense body of facts, reports of trials, legal documents, and testimony of people now living South, which will more than confirm every statement in "Uncle Tom's Cabin."

I must confess that till I began the examination of facts in order to write this book, much as I thought I knew before, I had not begun to measure the depth of the abyss. The law records of courts and judicial proceedings are so incredible as to fill me with amazement whenever I think of them. It seems to me that the book cannot but be felt, and, coming upon the sensibility awaked by the other, do something.

I suffer exquisitely in writing these things. It may be truly said that I write with my heart's blood. Many times in writing "Uncle Tom's Cabin" I thought my health would fail utterly; but I prayed earnestly that God would help me till I got through, and still I am pressed beyond measure and above strength.

This horror, this nightmare abomination! can it be in my country! It lies like lead on my heart, it shadows my life with sorrow; the more so that I feel, as for my own brothers, for the South, and am pained by every horror I am obliged to write, as one who is forced by some awful oath to disclose in court some family disgrace. Many times I have thought that I must die, and yet I pray God that I may live to see something done. I shall in all probability be in London in May: shall I see you?

It seems to me so odd and dream-like that so many persons desire to see me, and now I cannot help thinking that they will think, when they do, that God hath chosen "the weak things of this world."

If I live till spring I shall hope to see Shakespeare's grave, and Milton's mulberry-tree, and the good land of my fathers,—old, old England! May that day come!

Yours affectionately,

H. B. Stowe

Does Public Opinion Protect the Slave?

HARRIET BEECHER STOWE

◆ ◆ ◆

THE UTTER INEFFICIENCY of the law to protect the slave in any respect has been shown.

But it is claimed that, precisely because the law affords the slave no protection, therefore public opinion is the more strenuous in his behalf.

Nothing more frequently strikes the eye, in running over judicial proceedings in the Courts of slave States, than announcements of the utter inutility of the law to rectify some glaring injustice towards this unhappy race, coupled with congratulatory remarks on that beneficent state of *public sentiment* which is to supply entirely this acknowledged deficiency of the law.

On this point it may, perhaps, be sufficient to ask the reader, whether North or South, to review in his own mind the judicial documents which we have presented, and ask himself what inference is to be drawn, as to the state of public sentiment, from the cases there presented—from the pleas of lawyers, the decisions of judges, the facts sworn to by witnesses, and the general style and spirit of the whole proceedings.

In order to appreciate this more fully, let us compare a trial in a free State with a trial in a slave State.

In the free State of Massachusetts, a man of standing, learning, and high connexions, murdered another man. He did not torture him, but with one blow sent him in a moment from life. The murderer had every advantage of position, of friends; it may be said, indeed, that he had the sympathy of the whole United States; yet how calmly, with what unmoved and awful composure, did the judicial examination proceed! The murderer was condemned to die. What a sensation shook the country! Even sovereign States assumed the attitude of petitioners for him.

There was a voice of entreaty, from Maine to New Orleans. There were remonstrances, and there were threats; but still, with what passionless calmness retributive justice held on her way! Though the men who were her instruments were men of merciful and bleeding hearts, yet they bowed in silence to her sublime will. In spite of all that influence, and wealth, and power could do, a cultivated and intelligent man, from the first rank of society, suffered the same penalty that would fall on any other man who violated the sanctity of human life.

Now, compare this with a trial in a slave State. In Virginia, Souther also murdered a man; but he did not murder him by one merciful blow, but by twelve hours of torture so horrible that few readers could bear even the description of it. It was a mode of death which, to use the language that Cicero in his day applied to crucifixion, "ought to be for ever removed from the sight, hearing, and from the very thoughts of mankind." And to this horrible scene two white men were WITNESSES!

Observe the mode in which these two cases were tried, and the general sensation they produced. Hear the lawyers, in this case of Souther, coolly debating whether it can be considered any crime at all. Hear the decision of the inferior Court, that it is murder in the *second degree,* and apportioning as its reward five years of imprisonment. See the horrible butcher coming up to the superior Court in the attitude of an injured man! See the case recorded as that of *Souther* VERSUS *The Commonwealth,* and let us ask any intelligent man, North or South, what sort of public sentiment does this show?

Does it show a belief that the negro is a man? Does it not show decidedly that he is *not* considered as a man? Consider further the horrible principle which, re-affirmed in the case, is the law of the land in Virginia. *It is the policy of the law, in respect to the relation of master and slave, and for the sake of securing proper subordination on the part of the slave, to protect the master from prosecution in all such cases, even if the whipping and punishment be malicious, cruel, and excessive!*

When the most cultivated and intelligent men in the State formally, calmly, and without any apparent perception of saying anything inhuman, utter such an astounding decision as this, what *can* be thought of it? If they do not consider this cruel, what is cruel? And, if their feelings are so blunted as to see no cruelty in such a decision, what hope is there of any protection to the slave?

This law is a plain and distinct permission to such wretches as Souther to inflict upon the helpless slave any torture they may choose, without any accusation or impeachment of crime. It distinctly tells Souther, and the white witnesses who saw his deed, and every other low, unprincipled man in the Court, that it is the policy of the law to protect him in malicious, cruel, and excessive punishments.

What sort of an education is this for the intelligent and cultivated men of a State to communicate to the lower and less-educated class? Suppose it to be solemnly announced in Massachusetts, with respect to free labourers or apprentices, that it is the policy of the law, for the sake of producing subordination, to protect the master in inflicting any punishment, however cruel, malicious, and excessive, short of death. We cannot imagine such a principle declared, without a rebellion and a storm of popular excitement to which that of Bunker Hill was calmness itself; but, supposing the State of Massachusetts were so "twice dead and plucked up by the roots" as to allow such a decision to pass without comment concerning her working classes—suppose it did pass, and become an active, operative reality, what kind of an educational influence would it exert upon the commonwealth? What kind of an estimate of the working classes would it show in the minds of those who make and execute the law?

What an immediate development of villainy and brutality would be brought out by such a law, avowedly made to protect men in cruelty! Cannot men be cruel enough, without all the majesty of law being brought into operation to sanction it, and make it reputable?

And suppose it were said, in vindication of such a law, "Oh, of course, no respectable, humane man would ever think of taking advantage of it!" Should we not think the old State of Massachusetts sunk very low, to have on her legal records direct assurances of protection to deeds which no decent man would ever do?

And, when this shocking permission is brought in review at the judgment-seat of Christ, and the awful Judge shall say to its makers, aiders, and abettors, Where is thy brother?—when all the souls that have called from under the altar, "How long, O Lord, dost thou not judge and avenge our blood," shall arise around the judgment-seat as a great cloud of witnesses, and the judgment is set and the books are opened—what answer will be made for such laws and decisions as these?

Will they tell the great Judge that it was necessary to preserve the slave system—that it could not be preserved without them?

Will they dare look upon those eyes, which are as a flame of fire, with any such avowal?

Will he not answer, as with a voice of thunder, "Ye have killed the poor and needy, and ye have forgotten that the Lord was his helper?"

The deadly sin of slavery is its denial of humanity to man. This has been the sin of oppression, in every age. To tread down, to vilify and crush the image of God, in the person of the poor and lowly, has been the great sin of man since the creation of the world. Against this sin all the prophets of ancient times poured forth their thunders. A still stronger witness was borne against this sin, when God in Jesus Christ took human nature, and made each human being a brother of the Lord. But the last and most sublime witness shall be borne when a MAN shall judge the whole earth—a Man who shall acknowledge for His brother the meanest slave, equally with the proudest master.

In most singular and affecting terms it is asserted in the Bible that the Father hath committed all judgment to the Son, BECAUSE HE IS THE SON OF MAN. That human nature, which, in the person of the poor slave, has been despised and rejected, scoffed and scorned, scourged and tortured, shall in that day be glorified; and it shall appear the most fearful of sins to have made light of the sacredness of humanity, as these laws and institutions of slavery have done. The fact is, that the whole system of slave-law, and the whole practice of the slave-system, and the public sentiment that is formed by it, are alike based on the greatest of all heresies, *a denial of equal human brotherhood.* A whole race has been thrown out of the range of human existence, their immortality disregarded, their dignity as children of God scoffed at, their brotherhood with Christ treated as a fable, and all the law and public sentiment and practice with regard to them such as could be justified only on supposition that they were a race of inferior animals.

It is because the negro is considered an *inferior animal,* and not worthy of any better treatment, that the system which relates to him and the treatment which falls to him are considered humane.

Take any class of white men, however uneducated, and place them under the same system of laws, and make their civil condition in all respects like that of the negro, and would it not be considered the most outrageous cruelty?

Suppose the slave-law were enacted with regard to all the Irish in our country, and they were parcelled off as the property of any man who had money enough to buy them. Suppose their right to vote, their right to bring suit in any case, their right to bear testimony in courts of justice, their right to contract a legal marriage, their right to hold property or to make contracts of any sort, were all by one stroke of law blotted out. Furthermore, suppose it was forbidden to teach them to read and write, and that their children to all ages were "doomed to live without knowledge." Suppose that, in judicial proceedings, it were solemnly declared, with regard to them, that the *mere beating* of an Irishman, "apart from any circumstances of cruelty, or any attempt to kill," was no offence against the peace of the State. Suppose that it were declared that, for the better preservation of subjection among them, the law would protect the master in any kind of punishment inflicted, even if it should appear to be malicious, cruel, and excessive; and suppose that monsters like Souther, in availing themselves of this permission, should occasionally torture Irishmen to death, but still this circumstance should not be deemed of sufficient importance to call for any restriction on the part of the master. Suppose it should be coolly said, "Oh, yes, Irishmen are occasionally tortured to death, we know; but it is not by any means a *general* occurrence; in fact, no men of position in society would do it; and when cases of the kind do occur, they are indignantly frowned upon."

Suppose it should be stated that the reason that the law restraining the power of the master cannot be made any more stringent is, that the general system cannot be maintained without allowing this extent of power to the master.

Suppose that, having got all the Irishmen in the country down into this condition, they should maintain that such was the public sentiment of humanity with regard to them as abundantly to supply the want of all legal rights, and to make their condition, on the whole, happier than if they were free. Should we not say that a public sentiment which saw no cruelty in thus depriving a whole race of every right dear to manhood could see no cruelty in anything, and had proved itself wholly unfit to judge upon the subject? What man would not rather see his children in the grave than see them slaves? What man, who, should he wake to-morrow morning in the condition of an American slave, would not wish himself in the grave? And yet all the defenders of slavery start from the point that this legal condition is not *of itself* a cruelty! They would hold it the last excess of cruelty with regard to themselves, or any white man; why do they call it no cruelty at all with regard to the negro?

The writer in defence of slavery in *Fraser's Magazine* justifies this depriving of a whole class of any legal rights, by urging that "the good there is in human nature will supply the deficiencies of human legislation." This remark is one most significant, powerful index of the state of public sentiment, produced even in a generous mind, by the slave-system. This writer thinks the good there is in human nature will supply the absence of all legal rights to thousands and millions of human beings. He thinks it right to risk their bodies and their souls on the good there is in human nature; yet this very man would not send a fifty-dollar bill through the post-office, in an unsealed letter, trusting to "the good there is in human nature."

Would this man dare to place his children in the position of slaves, and trust them to "the good in human nature"?

Would he buy an estate from the most honourable man of his acquaintance, and have no legal record of the deed, trusting to "the good in human nature"? And if "the good in human nature" will not suffice for him and his children, how will it suffice for his brother and his brother's children? Is his happiness of any more importance in God's sight than his brother's happiness, that his must be secured by legal bolts, and bonds, and bars, and his brother's left to "the good there is in human nature"? Never are we so impressed with the utter deadness of public sentiment to protect the slave, as when we see such opinions as these uttered by men of a naturally generous and noble character.

The most striking and the most painful examples of the perversion of public sentiment, with regard to the negro race, are often given in the writings of men of humanity, amiableness, and piety.

That devoted labourer for the slave, the Rev. Charles C. Jones, thus expresses his sense of the importance of one African soul:—

> Were it now revealed to us that the most extensive system of instruction which we could devise, requiring a vast amount of labour and protracted through ages, would result in the tender mercy of our God in the salvation of the soul of one poor African, we should feel warranted in cheerfully entering upon our work, with all its costs and sacrifices.

What a noble, what a sublime spirit, is here breathed! Does it not show a mind capable of the very highest impulses?

And yet, if we look over his whole writings, we shall see painfully how the moral sense of the finest mind may be perverted by constant familiarity with such a system.

We find him constructing an appeal to masters to have their slaves *orally* instructed in religion. In many passages he speaks of oral instruction as confessedly an imperfect species of instruction, very much inferior to that which results from personal reading and examination of the word of God. He says in one place, that in order to do much good it must be begun very early in life; and intimates that people in advanced years can acquire very little from it; and yet he decidedly expresses his opinion that slavery is an institution with which no Christian has cause to interfere.

The slaves, according to his own showing, are cut off from the best means for the salvation of their souls, and restricted to one of a very inferior nature. They are placed under restriction which makes their souls as dependent upon others for spiritual food as a man without hands is dependent upon others for bodily food. He recognises the fact, which his own experience must show him, that the slave is at all times liable to pass into the hands of those who will not take the trouble thus to feed his soul; nay, if we may judge from his urgent appeals to masters, he perceives around him many who, having spiritually cut off the slave's hands, refuse to feed him. He sees that, by the operation of this law as a matter of fact, thousands are placed in situations where the perdition of the soul is almost certain, and yet he declares that he does not feel called upon at all to interfere with their civil condition!

But if the soul of every poor African is of that inestimable worth which Mr. Jones believes, does it not follow that he ought to have the very best means for getting to heaven which it is possible to give him? And is not he who can read the Bible for himself in a better condition than he who is dependent upon the reading of another? If it be said that such teaching cannot be afforded, because it makes them unsafe property, ought not a clergyman like Mr. Jones to meet this objection in his own expressive language?—

> Were it now revealed to us that the most extensive system of instruction which we could devise, requiring a vast amount of labour and protracted through ages, would result in the tender mercy of our God in the salvation of the soul of one poor African, we should feel warranted in cheerfully entering upon our work, with all its costs and sacrifices.

Should not a clergyman like Mr. Jones tell masters that they should risk the loss of all things seen and temporal, rather than incur the hazard of bringing eternal ruin on these souls? All the arguments which Mr. Jones so eloquently used with masters to persuade them to give their slaves oral instruction, would apply with double force to show their obligation to give the slave the power of reading the Bible for himself.

Again, we come to hear Mr. Jones telling masters of the power they have over the souls of their servants, and we hear him say—

> We may, according to the power lodged in our hands, forbid religious meetings and religious instruction on our own plantations; we may forbid our servants going to church at all, or only to such churches as we may select for them. We may literally shut up the kingdom of heaven against men, and suffer not them that are entering to go in.

And when we hear Mr. Jones say all this, and then consider that he must see and know this awful power is often lodged in the hands of wholly irreligious men, in the hands of men of the most profligate character, we can account for his thinking such a system right only by attributing it to that blinding, deadening influence which the public sentiment of slavery exerts even over the best-constituted minds.

Neither Mr. Jones nor any other Christian minister would feel it right that the eternal happiness of their own children should be thus placed in the power of any man who should have money to pay for them. How, then, can they think it right that this power be given in the case of their African brother?

Does this not show that, even in the case of the most humane and Christian people, who theoretically believe in the equality of all souls before God, a constant familiarity with slavery works a practical infidelity on this point; and that they give their assent to laws which practically declare that the salvation of the servant's soul is of less consequence than the salvation of the property relation?

Let us not be thought invidious or uncharitable in saying, that where slavery exists there are so many causes necessarily uniting to corrupt public sentiment with regard to the slave, that the best-constituted minds cannot trust themselves in it. In the Northern and free States public sentiment has been, and is to this day, fatally infected by the influence of a past and the proximity of a present system of slavery. Hence the injustice with which the negro in many of our States is treated. Hence, too, those apologies for slavery, and defences of it, which issue from Northern presses, and even Northern pulpits. If even at the North the remains of slavery can produce such baleful effects in corrupting public sentiment, how much more must this be the case where this institution is in full force!

The whole American nation is, in some sense, under a paralysis of public sentiment on this subject. It was said by a heathen writer, that the gods gave us a fearful power when they gave us the faculty of becoming accustomed to things. This power has proved a fearful one indeed in America. We have got used to things which might stir the dead in their graves.

When but a small portion of the things daily done in America has been told in England, and France, and Italy, and Germany, there has been a perfect shriek and outcry of horror. America alone remains cool, and asks, "What is the matter?"

Europe answers back, "Why, we have heard that men are *sold* like cattle in your country."

"Of course they are," says America; "but what then?"

"We have heard," says Europe, "that millions of men are forbidden to read and write in your country."

"We know that," says America; "but what is this outcry about?"

"We have heard," says Europe, "that Christian girls are sold to shame in your markets!"

"That isn't quite as it should be," says America; "but still what is this *excitement* about?"

"We hear that three millions of your people can have no legal marriageties," says Europe.

"Certainly, that is true," returns America; "but you made such an outcry, we thought you saw some great *cruelty* going on."

"And you profess to be a free country!" says indignant Europe.

"Certainly, we are the freest and most enlightened country in the world! What are you talking about?" says America.

"You send your missionaries to Christianise us," says Turkey; "and our religion has abolished this horrible system."

"You! you are all heathen over there—what business have you to talk?" answers America.

Many people seem really to have thought that nothing but horrible exaggerations of the system of slavery could have produced the sensation which has recently been felt in all modern Europe. They do not know that the thing they have become accustomed to, and handled so freely in every discussion, seems to all other nations the sum and essence of villainy. Modern Europe, opening her eyes and looking on the legal theory of the slave system, on the laws and interpretations of law which define it, says to America, in the language of the indignant Othello, If thou wilt justify a thing like this—

> Never pray more; abandon all remorse;
> On Horror's head horrors accumulate;
> Do deeds to make Heaven weep, all earth amazed;
> For nothing canst thou to damnation add
> Greater than this.

There is an awful state of familiarity with evil which the apostle calls being "dead in trespasses and sins," where truth has been resisted, and evil perseveringly defended, and the convictions of conscience stifled, and the voice of God's Holy Spirit bidden to depart. There is an awful paralysis of the moral sense, when deeds unholiest and crimes most fearful cease any longer to affect the nerve. That paralysis, always a fearful indication of the death and dissolution of nations, is a doubly-dangerous disease in a republic whose only power is in intelligence, justice, and virtue.

What Is to Be Done?

HARRIET BEECHER STOWE

◆　◆　◆

T**HE THING TO** be done, of which I shall chiefly speak, is, that the whole American Church, of all denominations, should unitedly come up, not *in form,* but *in fact,* to the noble purpose avowed by the Presbyterian Assembly of 1818, to seek the *entire abolition of slavery throughout America and throughout Christendom.*

To this noble course the united voice of Christians in all other countries is urgently calling the American Church. Expressions of this feeling have come from Christians of all denominations in England, in Scotland, in Ireland, in France, in Switzerland, in Germany, in Persia, in the Sandwich Islands, and in China. All seem to be animated by one spirit. They have loved and honoured this American Church. They have rejoiced in the brightness of her rising. Her prosperity and success have been to them as their own, and they have had hopes that God meant to confer inestimable blessings through her upon all nations. The American Church has been to them like the rising of a glorious sun, shedding healing from his wings, dispersing mists and fogs, and bringing songs of birds and voices of cheerful industry, and sounds of gladness, contentment, and peace. But lo ! in this beautiful orb is seen a disastrous spot of dim eclipse, whose gradually widening shadow threatens a total darkness. Can we wonder that the voice of remonstrance comes to us from those who have so much at stake in our prosperity and success? We have sent out our missionaries to all quarters of the globe; but how shall they tell their heathen converts the things that are done in Christianised America? How shall our missionaries in Mahometan countries hold up their heads, and proclaim the superiority of our religion, when we tolerate barbarities which they have repudiated?

A missionary among the Karens, in Asia, writes back that his course is much embarrassed by a suspicion that is afloat among the Karens that the Americans intend to steal and sell them. He says.—

> I dread the time when these Karens will be able to read our books, and get a full knowledge of all that is going on in our country. Many of them are very inquisitive now, and often ask me questions that I find it very difficult to answer.

No, there is no resource. The Church of the United States is shut up, in the providence of God, to one work. She can never fulfil her mission till this is done. So long as she neglects this, it will lie in the way of everything else which she attempts to do.

She must undertake it for another reason—because she alone can perform the work peaceably. If this fearful problem is left to take its course as a mere political question, to be ground out between the upper and nether millstones of political parties, then what will avert agitation, angry collisions, and the desperate rending of the Union? No, there is no safety but in making it a religious enterprise, and pursuing it in a Christian spirit, and by religious means.

If it now be asked what means shall the Church employ, we answer, this evil must be abolished by the same means which the apostles first used for the spread of Christianity, and the extermination of all the social evils which then filled a world lying in wickedness. Hear the apostle enumerate them: "*By pureness, by knowledge, by long-suffering, by the Holy Ghost, by love unfeigned, by the armour of righteousness on the right hand and on the left.*"

We will briefly consider each of these means.

First, "by Pureness." Christians in the Northern free States must endeavour to purify themselves and the country from various malignant results of the system of slavery; and, in particular, they must endeavour to abolish that which is the most sinful—the unchristian prejudice of caste.

In Hindustan there is a class called the Pariahs, with which no other class will associate, eat, or drink. Our missionaries tell the converted Hindoo that this prejudice is unchristian; for God hath made of one blood all who dwell on the face of the earth, and all mankind are brethren in Christ. With what face shall they tell this to the Hindoo, if he is able to reply, "In your own Christian country there is a class of Pariahs who are treated no better than we treat ours. You do not yourselves believe the things you teach us."

Let us look at the treatment of the free negro at the North. In the States of Indiana and Illinois, the most oppressive and unrighteous laws have been passed with regard to him. No law of any slave State could be more cruel in its spirit than that recently passed in Illinois, by which every free negro coming into the State is taken up and sold for a certain time, and then, if he do not leave the State, is sold again.

With what face can we exhort our Southern brethren to emancipate their slaves, if we do not set the whole moral power of the Church at the North against such abuses as this? Is this course justified by saying that the negro is vicious and idle? This is adding insult to injury.

What is it these Christian States do? To a great extent they exclude the coloured population from their schools; they discourage them from attending their churches by invidious distinctions; as a general fact, they exclude them from their shops, where they might learn useful arts and trades; they crowd them out of the better callings where they might earn an honourable livelihood; and having thus discouraged every elevated aspiration, and reduced them to almost inevitable ignorance, idleness, and vice, they fill up the measure of iniquity by making cruel laws to expel them from their States, thus heaping up wrath against the day of wrath.

If we say that every Christian at the South who does not use his utmost influence against the iniquitous slave-laws is guilty, as a republican citizen, of sustaining those laws, it is no less true that every Christian at the North who does not do what in him lies to procure the repeal of such laws in the free States, is, so far, guilty for their existence. Of late years we have had abundant quotations from the Old Testament to justify all manner of oppression. A Hindoo, who knew nothing of this generous and beautiful book, except from such pamphlets as Mr. Smylie's, might possibly think it was a treatise on piracy, and a general justification of robbery. But let us quote from it the directions which God gives for the treatment of the stranger: "If a stranger sojourn with you in your land, ye shall not vex him. But the stranger that dwelleth among you shall be as one born among you; thou shalt love him as thyself." How much more does this apply when the stranger has been brought into our land by the injustice and cruelty of our fathers!

We are happy to say, however, that the number of States in which such oppressive legislation exists is small. It is also a matter of encouragement and hope that the unphilosophical and unchristian prejudice of caste is materially giving way, in many parts of our country, before a kinder and more Christian spirit.

Many of our schools and colleges are willing to receive the coloured applicant on equal terms with the white. Some of the Northern free States accord to the coloured freeman full political equality and privileges. Some of the coloured people, under this encouragement, have, in many parts of our country, become rich and intelligent. A very fair proportion of educated men is rising among them. There are among them respectable editors, eloquent orators, and laborious and well-instructed clergymen. It gives us pleasure to say that, among intelligent and Christian people, these men are treated with the consideration they deserve; and, if they meet with insult and ill-treatment, it is commonly from the less-educated class, who, being less enlightened, are always longer under the influence of prejudice. At a recent ordination at one of the largest and most respectable churches in New York, the moderator of the Presbytery was a black man, who began life as a slave; and it was undoubtedly a source of gratification to all his Christian brethren to see him presiding in this capacity. He put the questions to the candidates in the German language, the church being in part composed of Germans. Our Christian friends in Europe may, at least, infer from this that, if we have had our faults in times past, we have, some of us, seen and are endeavouring to correct them.

To bring this head at once to a practical conclusion, the writer will say to every individual Christian, who wishes to do something for the abolition of slavery, Begin by doing what lies in your power for the coloured people in your vicinity. Are there children excluded from schools by unchristian prejudice? Seek to combat that prejudice by fair arguments, presented in a right spirit. If you cannot succeed, then endeavour to provide for the education of these children in some other manner. As far as in you lies, endeavour to secure for them, in every walk of life, the ordinary privileges of American citizens. If they are excluded from the omnibus and railroad-car in the place where you reside, endeavour to persuade those who have the control of these matters to pursue a more just and reasonable course. Those Christians who are heads of mechanical establishments can do much for the cause by receiving coloured apprentices. Many masters excuse themselves for excluding the coloured apprentice by saying that, if they receive him, all their other hands will desert them. To this it is replied, that if they do the thing in a Christian temper and for a Christian purpose, the probability is that, if their hands desert at first, they will return to them at last—all of them, at least, whom they would care to retain.

A respectable dressmaker in one of our towns has, as a matter of principle, taken coloured girls for apprentices; thus furnishing them with a respectable means of livelihood. Christian mechanics, in all the walks of life, are earnestly requested to consider this subject, and see if, by offering their hand to raise this poor people to respectability, and knowledge, and competence, they may not be performing a service which the Lord will accept as done unto himself.

Another thing which is earnestly commended to Christians is the raising and comforting of those poor Churches of coloured people, who have been discouraged, dismembered, and disheartened by the operation of the Fugitive Slave Law.

In the city of Boston is a Church which, even now, is struggling with debt and embarrassment, caused by being obliged to buy its own deacons, to shield them from the terrors of that law.

Lastly, Christians at the North, we need not say, should abstain from all *trading in slaves*, whether direct or indirect, whether by partnership with Southern houses or by receiving immortal beings as security for debt. It is not necessary to expand this point. It speaks for itself.

By all these means the Christian Church at the North must secure for itself purity from all complicity with the sin of slavery, and from the unchristian customs and prejudices which have resulted from it.

The second means to be used for the abolition of slavery is "Knowledge."

Every Christian ought thoroughly, carefully, and prayerfully to examine this system of slavery. He should regard it as one upon which he is bound to have right views and right opinions, and to exert a right influence in forming and concentrating a powerful public sentiment, of all others the most efficacious remedy. Many people are deterred from examining the statistics on this subject, because they do not like the men who have collected them. They say they do not like abolitionists, and therefore they will not attend to those facts and figures which they have accumulated. This, certainly, is not wise or reasonable. In all other subjects which deeply affect our interests, we think it best to take information where we can get it, whether we like the persons who give it to us or not.

Every Christian ought seriously to examine the extent to which our national government is pledged and used for the support of slavery. He should thoroughly look into the statistics of slavery in the District of Columbia, and, above all, into the statistics of that awful system of legalised piracy and oppression by which hundreds and thousands are yearly torn from home and friends, and all that heart holds dear, and carried to be sold like beasts in the markets of the South. The smoke from this bottomless abyss of injustice puts out the light of our Sabbath suns in the eyes of all nations. Its awful groans and wailings drown the voice of our psalms and religious melodies. All nations know these things of us, and shall we not know them of ourselves? Shall we not have courage, shall we not have patience, to investigate thoroughly our own bad case, and gain a perfect knowledge of the length and breadth of the evil we seek to remedy?

The third means for the abolition of slavery is by "Long-suffering."

Of this quality there has been some lack in the attempts that have hitherto been made. The friends of the cause have not had patience with each other, and have not been able to treat each other's opinions with forbearance. There have been many painful things in the past history of this subject; but is it not time when all the friends of the slave should adopt the motto, "*forgetting* the things that are behind, and reaching forth unto those which are before"? Let not the believers of immediate abolition call those who believe in gradual emancipation time-servers and traitors; and let not the upholders of gradual emancipation call the advocates of immediate abolition fanatics and incendiaries. Surely some more brotherly way of convincing good men can be found, than by standing afar off on some Ebal and Gerizim, and cursing each other. The truth spoken in love will always go further than the truth spoken in wrath; and, after all, the great object is to persuade our Southern brethren to admit the idea of *any* emancipation at all. When we have succeeded in persuading them that *anything* is necessary to be done, then will be the time for bringing up the question whether the object shall be accomplished by an immediate or a gradual process. Meanwhile, let our motto be, "Whereto we have already attained, let us walk by the same rule, let us mind the same things; and if any man be otherwise minded, God shall reveal even this unto him." "Let us receive even him that is weak in the faith, but not to doubtful disputations." Let us not reject the good there is in any, because of some remaining defects.

We come now to the consideration of a power without which all others must fail—"the Holy Ghost."

The solemn creed of every Christian Church, whether Roman, Greek, Episcopal, or Protestant, says, "*I believe in the Holy Ghost.*" But how often do Christians, in all these denominations, live and act, and even conduct their religious affairs as if they had "never so much as heard whether there be any Holy Ghost." If we trust to our own reasonings, our own misguided passions, and our own blind self-will, to effect the reform of abuses, we shall utterly fail. There is a power, silent, convincing, irresistible, which moves over the dark and troubled heart of man, as of old it moved over the dark and troubled waters of Chaos, bringing light out of darkness, and order out of confusion.

Is it not evident to everyone who takes enlarged views of human society that a gentle but irresistible influence is pervading the human race, prompting groanings, and longings, and dim aspirations for some coming era of good? Worldly men read the signs of the times, and call this power the *Spirit of the Age*—but should not the Church acknowledge it as the Spirit of God?

Let it not be forgotten, however, that the gift of his most powerful regenerating influence, at the opening of the Christian dispensation, was conditioned on prayer. The mighty movement that began on the day of Pentecost was preceded by united, fervent, persevering prayer. A similar spirit of prayer must precede the coming of the divine Spirit, to effect a revolution so great as that at which we aim. The most powerful instrumentality which God has delegated to man, and around which cluster all his glorious promises, is prayer. All past prejudices and animosities on this subject must be laid aside, and the whole Church unite as one man in earnest, fervent prayer. Have we forgotten the promise of the Holy Ghost? Have we forgotten that He was to abide with us for ever? Have we forgotten that it is He who is to convince the world of sin, of righteousness, and of judgment? O divine and Holy Comforter! thou promise of the Father! thou only powerful to enlighten, convince, and renew! return, we beseech thee, and visit this vine and this vineyard of thy planting! With thee nothing is impossible; and what we, in our weakness, can scarcely conceive, thou canst accomplish!

Another means for the abolition of slavery is "Love unfeigned."

In all moral conflicts, that party who can preserve, through every degree of opposition and persecution, a divine, unprovokable spirit of love, must finally conquer. Such are the immutable laws of the moral world. Anger, wrath, selfishness, and jealousy have all a certain degree of vitality. They often produce more show, more noise, and temporary result than love. Still, all these passions have in themselves the seeds of weakness. Love, and love only, is immortal; and when all the grosser passions of the soul have spent themselves by their own force, love looks forth like the unchanging star, with a light that never dies.

In undertaking this work, we must love both the slaveholder and the slave. We must never forget that both are our brethren. We must expect to be misrepresented, to be slandered, and to be hated. How can we attack so powerful an interest without it? We must be satisfied simply with the pleasure of being true friends, while we are treated as bitter enemies.

This holy controversy must be one of principle, and not of sectional bitterness. We must not suffer it to degenerate, in our hands, into a violent prejudice against the South; and, to this end, we must keep continually before our minds the more amiable features and attractive qualities of those with whose principles we are obliged to conflict. If they say all manner of evil against us, we must reflect that we expose them to great temptation to do so when we assail institutions to which they are bound by a thousand ties of interest and early association, and to whose evils habit has made them in a great degree insensible. The apostle gives us this direction in cases where we are called upon to deal with offending brethren, "Consider thyself, lest thou also be tempted." We may apply this to our own case, and consider that if we had been exposed to the temptations which surround our friends at the South, and received the same education, we might have felt, and thought, and acted as they do. But, while we cherish all these considerations, we must also remember that it is no love to the South to countenance and defend a pernicious system; a system which is as injurious to the master as to the slave; a system which turns fruitful fields to deserts; a system ruinous to education, to morals, and to religion and social progress; a system of which many of the most intelligent and valuable men at the South are weary, and from which they desire to escape, and by emigration are yearly escaping. Neither must we concede the rights of the slave; for he is also our brother, and there is a reason why we should speak for him which does not exist in the case of his master. He is poor, uneducated, and ignorant, and cannot speak for himself. We must, therefore, with greater jealousy, guard his rights. Whatever else we compromise, we must not compromise the rights of the helpless, nor the eternal principles of rectitude and morality.

We must never concede that it is an honourable thing to deprive working-men of their wages, though, like many other abuses, it is customary, reputable, and popular, and though amiable men, under the influence of old prejudices, still continue to do it. Never, not even for a moment, should we admit the thought that an heir of God and a joint heir of Jesus Christ may lawfully be sold upon the auction-block, though it be a common custom. We must repudiate, with determined severity, the blasphemous doctrine of property in human beings.

Some have supposed it an absurd refinement to talk about separating principles and persons, or to admit that he who upholds a bad system can be a good man. All experience proves the contrary. Systems most unjust and despotic have been defended by men personally just and humane. It is a melancholy consideration, but no less true, that there is almost no absurdity and no injustice that has not, at some period of the world's history, had the advantage of some good man's virtues in its support.

It is a part of our trial in this imperfect life—were evil systems only supported by the evil, our moral discipline would be much less severe than it is, and our course in attacking error far plainer.

On the whole, we cannot but think that there was much Christian wisdom in the remark, which we have before quoted, of a poor old slave-woman, whose whole life had been darkened by this system, that we must *"hate the sin, but love the sinner."*

The last means for the abolition of slavery is the armour of righteousness on the right hand and on the left.

By this we mean an earnest application of all straightforward, honourable, and just measures, for the removal of the system of slavery. Every man, in his place, should remonstrate against it. All its sophistical arguments should be answered, its biblical defences unmasked, by correct reasoning and interpretation. Every mother should teach the evil of it to her children. Every clergyman should fully and continually warn his Church against any complicity with such a sin. It is said that this would be introducing politics into the pulpit. It is answered that, since people will have to give an account of their political actions in the day of judgment, it seems proper that the minister should instruct them somewhat as to their political responsibilities. In that day Christ will ask no man whether he was of this or that party; but he certainly will ask him whether he gave his vote in the fear of God, and for the advancement of the kingdom of righteousness.

It is often objected that slavery is a distant sin, with which we have nothing to do. If any clergyman wishes to test this fact, let him once plainly and faithfully preach upon it. He will probably, then, find that the roots of the poison-tree have run under the very hearthstone of New England families, and that in his very congregation are those in complicity with this sin.

It is no child's play to attack an institution which has absorbed into itself so much of the political power and wealth of this nation; and they who try it will soon find that they wrestle "not with flesh and blood." No armour will do for this warfare but the "armour of righteousness."

To our brethren in the South, God has pointed out a more arduous conflict. The very heart shrinks to think what the faithful Christian must endure who assails this institution on its own ground; but it *must be done.* How was it at the North? There was a universal effort to put down the discussion of it here by mob law. Printing-presses were broken, houses torn down, property destroyed. Brave men, however, stood firm; martyr blood was shed for the right of free opinion in speech; and so the right of discussion was established. Nobody tries that sort of argument now—its day is past. In Kentucky, also, they tried to stop the discussion by similar means. Mob violence destroyed a printing-press, and threatened the lives of individuals. But there were brave men there, who feared not violence or threats of death; and emancipation is now open for discussion in Kentucky. The fact is, the South *must* discuss the matter of slavery. She *cannot* shut it out, unless she lays an embargo on the literature of the whole civilised world. If it be, indeed, divine and God-appointed, why does she so tremble to have it touched? If it be of God, all the free inquiry in the world cannot overthrow it. Discussion must and will come. It only requires courageous men to lead the way.

Brethren in the South, there are many of you who are truly convinced that slavery is a sin, a tremendous wrong; but if you confess your sentiments, and endeavour to propagate your opinions, you think that persecution, affliction, and even death await you. How can we ask you, then, to come forward? *We* do not ask it. Ourselves weak, irresolute, and worldly, shall we ask you to do what perhaps we ourselves should not dare? But we will beseech *Him* to speak to you, who dared and endured more than this for your sake, and who can strengthen you to dare and endure for His. He can raise you above all temporary and worldly considerations. He can inspire you with that love to himself which will make you willing to leave father and mother, and wife and child, yea, to give up life itself, for his sake. And if ever he brings you to that place where you and this world take a final farewell of each other, where you make up your mind solemnly to give all up for his cause, where neither life nor death, nor things present, nor things to come, can move you from this purpose—then will you know a joy which is above all other joy, a peace constant and unchanging as the eternal God from whom it springs.

Dear brethren, is this system to go on for ever in your land? Can you think these slave-laws anything but an abomination to a just God? Can you think this internal slave-trade to be anything but an abomination in his sight?

Look, we beseech you, into those awful slave-prisons which are in your cities. Do the groans and prayers which go up from those dreary mansions promise well for the prosperity of our country?

Look, we beseech you, at the mournful march of the slave-coffles; follow the bloody course of the slave-ships on your coast. What, suppose you, does the Lamb of God think of all these things? He whose heart was so tender that he wept, at the grave of Lazarus, over a sorrow that he was so soon to turn into joy—what does he think of this constant, heart-breaking, yearly-repeated anguish? What does he think of Christian wives forced from their husbands, and husbands from their wives? What does he think of Christian daughters, whom his Church first educates, indoctrinates, and baptises, and then leaves to be sold as merchandise?

Think you such prayers as poor Paul Edmondson's, such death-bed scenes as Emily Russell's, are witnessed without emotion by that generous Saviour, who regards what is done to his meanest servant as done to himself?

Did it never seem to you, O Christian! when you have read the sufferings of Jesus, that you would gladly have suffered with him? Does it never seem almost ungenerous to accept eternal life as the price of such anguish on his part, while you bear no cross for him? Have you ever wished you could have watched with him in that bitter conflict at Gethsemane, when even his chosen slept? Have you ever wished that you could have stood by him when all forsook him and fled—that you could have owned when Peter denied—that you could have honoured him when buffeted and spit upon? Would you think it too much honour? Could you, like Mary, have followed him to the cross, and stood a patient sharer of that despised, unpitied agony? *That* you cannot do. That hour is over. Christ now is exalted, crowned, glorified; all men speak well of him, rich churches rise to him, and costly sacrifice goes up to him. What chance have you, among the multitude, to prove your love—to show that you would stand by him discrowned, dishonoured, tempted, betrayed, and suffering? Can you show it in any way but by espousing the cause of his suffering poor? Is there a people among you despised and rejected of men, heavy with oppression, acquainted with grief, with all the power of wealth and fashion, of political and worldly influence, arrayed against their cause? Christian, you can acknowledge Christ in them!

If you turn away indifferent from this cause—"if thou forbear to deliver them that are drawn unto death, and those that be ready to be slain; if thou sayest, Behold, we knew it not, doth not he that pondereth the heart consider it? and he that keepeth the soul, doth he not know it? Shall he not render to every man according to his works?"

In the last judgment will he not say to you, "I have been in the slave-prison—in the slave-coffle; I have been sold in your markets; I have toiled for naught in your fields; I have been smitten on the mouth in your courts of justice; I have been denied a hearing in my own Church, and ye cared not for it. Ye went, one to his farm, and another to his merchandise." And if ye shall answer, "*When,* Lord?" He shall say unto you, "Inasmuch as ye have done it to the least of these my brethren, ye have done it unto me."

Everybody's Protest Novel

JAMES BALDWIN

◆　◆　◆

IN UNCLE TOM'S CABIN, that cornerstone of American social protest fiction, St. Clare, the kindly master, remarks to his coldly disapproving Yankee cousin, Miss Ophelia, that, so far as he is able to tell, the blacks have been turned over to the devil for the benefit of the whites in this world—however, he adds thoughtfully, it may turn out in the next. Miss Ophelia's reaction is, at least, vehemently right-minded: "This is perfectly horrible!" she exclaims. "You ought to be ashamed of yourselves!"

Miss Ophelia, as we may suppose, was speaking for the author; her exclamation is the moral, neatly framed, and incontestable like those improving mottoes sometimes found hanging on the walls of furnished rooms. And, like these mottoes, before which one invariably flinches, recognizing an insupportable, almost an indecent glibness, she and St. Clare are terribly in earnest. Neither of them questions the medieval morality from which their dialogue springs: black, white, the devil, the next world—posing its alternatives between heaven and the flames—were realities for them as, of course, they were for their creator. They spurned and were terrified of the darkness, striving mightily for the light; and considered from this aspect, Miss Ophelia's exclamation, like Mrs. Stowe's novel, achieves a bright, almost a lurid significance, like the light from a fire which consumes a witch. This is the more striking as one considers the novels of Negro oppression written in our own, more enlightened day, all of which say only: "This is perfectly horrible! You ought to be ashamed of yourselves!" (Let us ignore, for the moment, those novels of oppression written by Negroes, which add only a raging near-paranoiac postscript to this statement and actually reinforce, as I hope to make clear later, the principles which activate the oppression they decry.)

Uncle Tom's Cabin is a very bad novel, having, in its self-righteous, virtuous sentimentality, much in common with *Little Women*. Sentimentality, the ostentatious parading of excessive and spurious emotion, is the mark of dishonesty, the inability to feel; the wet eyes of the sentimentalist betray his aversion to experience, his fear of life, his arid heart; and it is always, therefore, the signal of secret and violent inhumanity, the mask of cruelty. *Uncle Tom's Cabin*—like its multitudinous, hard-boiled descendants—is a catalogue of violence. This is explained by the nature of Mrs. Stowe's subject matter, her laudable determination to flinch from nothing in presenting the complete picture; an explanation which falters only if we pause to ask whether or not her picture is indeed complete; and what constriction or failure of perception forced her to so depend on the description of brutality—unmotivated, senseless—and to leave unanswered and unnoticed the only important question: what it was, after all, that moved her people to such deeds.

But this, let us say, was beyond Mrs. Stowe's powers; she was not so much a novelist as an impassioned pamphleteer; her book was not intended to do anything more than prove that slavery was wrong; was, in fact, perfectly horrible. This makes material for a pamphlet but it is hardly enough for a novel; and the only question left to ask is why we are bound still within the same constriction. How is it that we are so loath to make a further journey than that made by Mrs. Stowe, to discover and reveal something a little closer to the truth?

But that battered word, truth, having made its appearance here, confronts one immediately with a series of riddles and has, moreover, since so many gospels are preached, the unfortunate tendency to make one belligerent. Let us say, then, that truth, as used here, is meant to imply a devotion to the human being, his freedom and fulfillment; freedom which cannot be legislated, fulfillment which cannot be charted. This is the prime concern, the frame of reference; it is not to be confused with a devotion to Humanity which is too easily equated with a devotion to a Cause; and Causes, as we know, are notoriously bloodthirsty. We have, as it seems to me, in this most mechanical and interlocking of civilizations, attempted to lop this creature down to the status of a time-saving invention. He is not, after all, merely a member of a Society or a Group or a deplorable conundrum to be explained by Science. He is—and how old-fashioned the words sound!—something more than that, something resolutely indefinable, unpredictable. In overlooking, denying, evading his complexity—which is nothing more than the disquieting complexity of ourselves—we are diminished and we perish; only within this web of ambiguity, paradox, this hunger, danger, darkness, can we find at once ourselves and the power that will free us from ourselves. It is this power of revelation which is the business of the novelist, this journey toward a more vast reality which must take precedence over all other claims. What is today parroted as his Responsibility—which seems to mean that he must make formal declaration that he is involved in, and affected by, the lives of other people and to say something improving about this somewhat self-evident fact—is, when he believes it, his corruption and our loss; moreover, it is rooted in, interlocked with and intensifies this same mechanization. Both *Gentlemen's Agreement* and *The Postman Always Rings Twice* exemplify this terror of the human being, the determination to cut him down to size. And in *Uncle Tom's Cabin* we may find foreshadowing of both: the formula created by the necessity to find a lie more palatable than the truth has been handed down and memorized and persists yet with a terrible power.

It is interesting to consider one more aspect of Mrs. Stowe's novel, the method she used to solve the problem of writing about a black man at all. Apart from her lively procession of field-hands, house-niggers, Chloe, Topsy, etc.—who are the stock, lovable figures presenting no problem—she has only three other Negroes in the book. These are the important ones and two of them may be dismissed immediately, since we have only the author's word that they are Negro and they are, in all other respects, as white as she can make them. The two are George and Eliza, a married couple with a wholly adorable child—whose quaintness, incidentally, and whose charm, rather puts one in mind of a darky boot-black doing a buck and wing to the clatter of condescending coins. Eliza is a beautiful, pious hybrid, light enough to pass—the heroine of *Quality* might, indeed, be her reincarnation—differing from the genteel mistress who has overseered her education only in the respect that she is a servant. George is darker, but makes up for it by being a mechanical genius, and is, moreover, sufficiently un-Negroid to pass through town, a fugitive from his master, disguised as a Spanish gentleman, attracting no attention whatever beyond admiration. They are a race apart from Topsy. It transpires by the end of the novel, through one of those energetic, last-minute convolutions of the plot, that Eliza has some connection with French gentility. The figure from whom the novel takes its name, Uncle Tom, who is a figure of controversy yet, is jet-black, wooly-haired, illiterate; and

he is phenomenally forbearing. He has to be; he is black; only through this
forbearance can he survive or triumph. (Cf. Faulkner's preface to *The Sound and
the Fury:* These others were not Compsons. They were black:—They endured.)
His triumph is metaphysical, unearthly; since he is black, born without the
light, it is only through humility, the incessant mortification of the flesh,
that he can enter into communion with God or man. The virtuous rage of
Mrs. Stowe is motivated by nothing so temporal as a concern for the relationship of men to one another—or, even, as she would have claimed, by a concern for their relationship to God—but merely by a panic of being hurled into
the flames, of being caught in traffic with the devil. She embraced this merciless doctrine with all her heart, bargaining shamelessly before the throne of
grace: God and salvation becoming her personal property, purchased with the
coin of her virtue. Here, black equates with evil and white with grace; if, being
mindful of the necessity of good works, she could not cast out the blacks—
a wretched, huddled mass, apparently, claiming, like an obsession, her inner
eye—she could not embrace them either without purifying them of sin. She
must cover their intimidating nakedness, robe them in white, the garments of
salvation; only thus could she herself be delivered from ever-present sin, only
thus could she bury, as St. Paul demanded, "the carnal man, the man of the
flesh." Tom, therefore, her only black man, has been robbed of his humanity
and divested of his sex. It is the price for that darkness with which he has been
branded.

Uncle Tom's Cabin, then, is activated by what might be called a theological terror, the terror of damnation; and the spirit that breathes in this book,
hot, self-righteous, fearful, is not different from that spirit of medieval times
which sought to exorcize evil by burning witches; and is not different from
that terror which activates a lynch mob. One need not, indeed, search for
examples so historic or so gaudy; this is a warfare waged daily in the heart, a
warfare so vast, so relentless and so powerful that the interracial handshake
or the interracial marriage can be as crucifying as the public hanging or the
secret rape. This panic motivates our cruelty, this fear of the dark makes it
impossible that our lives shall be other than superficial; this, interlocked with
and feeding our glittering, mechanical, inescapable civilization which has put
to death our freedom.

This, notwithstanding that the avowed aim of the American protest novel
is to bring greater freedom to the oppressed. They are forgiven, on the strength
of these good intentions, whatever violence they do to language, whatever
excessive demands they make of credibility. It is, indeed, considered the sign
of a frivolity so intense as to approach decadence to suggest that these books
are both badly written and wildly improbable. One is told to put first things

first, the good of society coming before niceties of style or characterization. Even if this were incontestable—for what exactly is the "good" of society?—it argues an insuperable confusion, since literature and sociology are not one and the same; it is impossible to discuss them as if they were. Our passion for categorization, life neatly fitted into pegs, has led to an unforeseen, paradoxical distress; confusion, a breakdown of meaning. Those categories which were meant to define and control the world for us have boomeranged us into chaos; in which limbo we whirl, clutching the straws of our definitions. The "protest" novel, so far from being disturbing, is an accepted and comforting aspect of the American scene, ramifying that framework we believe to be so necessary. Whatever unsettling questions are raised are evanescent, titillating; remote, for this has nothing to do with us, it is safely ensconced in the social arena, where, indeed, it has nothing to do with anyone, so that finally we receive a very definite thrill of virtue from the fact that we are reading such a book at all. This report from the pit reassures us of its reality and its darkness and of our own salvation; and "As long as such books are being published," an American liberal once said to me, "everything will be all right."

But unless one's ideal of society is a race of neatly analyzed, hardworking ciphers, one can hardly claim for the protest novel the lofty purpose it claims for itself or share the present optimism concerning them. They emerge for what they are: a mirror of our confusion, dishonesty, panic, trapped and immobilized in the sunlit prison of the American dream. They are fantasies, connecting nowhere with reality, sentimental; in exactly the same sense that such movies as *The Best Years of Our Lives* or the works of Mr. James M. Cain are fantasies. Beneath the dazzling pyrotechnics of these current operas one may still discern, as the controlling force, the intense theological preoccupations of Mrs. Stowe, the sick vacuities of *The Rover Boys*. Finally, the aim of the protest novel becomes something very closely resembling the zeal of those alabaster missionaries to Africa to cover the nakedness of the natives, to hurry them into the pallid arms of Jesus and thence into slavery. The aim has now become to reduce all Americans to the compulsive, bloodless dimensions of a guy named Joe.

It is the peculiar triumph of society—and its loss—that it is able to convince those people to whom it has given inferior status of the reality of this decree; it has the force and the weapons to translate its dictum into fact, so that the allegedly inferior are actually made so, insofar as the societal realities are concerned. This is a more hidden phenomenon now than it was in the days of serfdom, but it is no less implacable. Now, as then, we find ourselves bound, first without, then within, by the nature of our categorization. And escape is not effected through a bitter railing against this trap; it is as though this very striving were the only motion needed to spring the trap upon us. We take our shape, it is true, within and against that cage of reality bequeathed us at our birth; and yet it is precisely through our dependence on this reality that we are most endlessly betrayed. Society is held together by our need; we bind it together with legend, myth, coercion, fearing that without it we will be hurled into that void, within which, like the earth before the Word was spoken, the foundations of society are hidden. From this void—ourselves—it is the function of society to protect us; but it is only this void, our unknown selves, demanding, forever, a new act of creation, which can save us—"from the evil that is in the world." With the same motion, at the same time, it is this toward which we endlessly struggle and from which, endlessly, we struggle to escape.

It must be remembered that the oppressed and the oppressor are bound together within the same society; they accept the same criteria, they share the same beliefs, they both alike depend on the same reality. Within this cage it is romantic, more, meaningless, to speak of a "new" society as the desire of the oppressed, for that shivering dependence on the props of reality which he shares with the *Herrenvolk* makes a truly "new" society impossible to conceive. What is meant by a new society is one in which inequalities will disappear, in which vengeance will be exacted; either there will be no oppressed at all or the oppressed and the oppressor will change places. But, finally, as it seems to me, what the rejected desire is, is an elevation of status, acceptance within the present community. Thus, the African, exile, pagan, hurried off the auction block and into the fields, fell on his knees before that God in Whom he must now believe; who had made him, but not in His image. This tableau, this impossibility, is the heritage of the Negro in America: *Wash me,* cried the slave to his Maker, *and I shall be whiter, whiter than snow!* For black is the color of evil; only the robes of the saved are white. It is this cry, implacable on the air and in the skull, that he must live with. Beneath the widely published catalogue of brutality—bringing to mind, somehow, an image, a memory of church-bells burdening the air—is this reality which in the same nightmare notion, he both flees and rushes to embrace. In America, now, this country devoted to the death of the paradox—which may, therefore, be put to death by one—his lot is as ambiguous as a tableau by Kafka. To flee or not, to move or not, it is all the same, his doom is written on his forehead, it is carried in his heart. In *Native Son,* Bigger Thomas stands on a Chicago street corner watching airplanes flown by white men racing against the sun and "Goddamn" he says, the bitterness bubbling up like blood, remembering a million indignities, the terrible, rat-infested house, the humiliation of home-relief, the intense, aimless, ugly bickering, hating it; hatred smoulders through these pages like sulphur fire. All of Bigger's life is controlled, defined by his hatred and his fear. And later, his fear drives him to murder and his hatred to rape; he dies, having come, through this violence, we are told, for the first time, to a kind of life, having for the first time redeemed his manhood. Below the surface of this novel there lies, as it seems to me, a continuation, a complement of that monstrous legend it was written to destroy. Bigger is Uncle Tom's descendant, flesh of his flesh, so exactly opposite a portrait that, when the books are placed together, it seems that the contemporary Negro novelist and the dead New England woman are locked together in a deadly, timeless battle; the one uttering merciless exhortations, the other shouting curses. And, indeed, within this web of lust and fury, black and white can only thrust and counter-thrust, long for each other's slow, exquisite death; death by torture, acid, knives and burning; the thrust, the counter-thrust, the longing making the heavier that cloud which blinds and suffocates them both, so that they go down into the pit together. Thus has the cage betrayed us all, this moment, our life, turned to nothing through our terrible attempts to insure it. For Bigger's tragedy is not that he is cold or black or hungry, not even that he is American, black; but that he has accepted a theology that denies him life, that he admits the possibility of his being sub-human and feels constrained, there-fore, to battle for his humanity according to those brutal criteria bequeathed him at his birth. But our humanity is our burden, our life; we need not battle for it; we need only do what is infinitely more difficult, that is, accept it. The failure of the protest novel lies in its rejection of life, the human being, the denial of his beauty, dread, power, in its insistence that it is his categorization alone which is real and which cannot be transcended.

Love and Death in *Uncle Tom's Cabin*

LESLIE A. FIEDLER

◆ ◆ ◆

THE GREATEST OF ALL novels of sentimental protest is, however, dedicated not to the problem of drink but to that of slavery, though its author was a total abstainer, who would appear at literary luncheons only if promised that no wine would be served. The novel, of course, is Harriet Beecher Stowe's *Uncle Tom's Cabin,* which she read in installments to her children as she composed it in 1851 and 1852. They wept as they listened; and she wept, too, returned to each installment at such a pitch of frenzy that she began after a while to feel as if the volume were being dictated rather than invented. "The Lord himself wrote it!" she insisted later; and if He had, indeed, written and autographed it, it could not have sold better—some 300,000 copies in the very first year of publication, and millions in the following years, perhaps outstripping even *The Last of the Mohicans.* It is an astonishingly various and complex book, simplified in the folk mind, which has remembered in its place the dramatic version in which Mrs. Stowe had no hand and which she saw, secretly, only once.

In *Uncle Tom's Cabin,* there are two contrasting studies of marriage: one between an opportunistic, morally lax husband and an enduring Christian wife; another between a hypochondriacal, self-pitying shrew—an acute but cruel caricature of the Southern lady—and a gentle, enduring husband. The latter relationship between the St. Clares, who are mother and father to Little

Eva, is from a purely novelistic point of view the most skillfully executed section of the book; but it is scarcely remembered by *Uncle Tom's* admirers. No more do the really erotic episodes stick in the collective memory of America: neither Legree's passionate relationship with the half-mad slave girl, Cassy, nor his breathless, ultimately frustrated attempt to violate the fifteen-year-old quadroon, Emmeline. The story of the decline of Cassy from a protected Creole childhood, in which she is scarcely aware that she is a Negro, through her lush bondage to a chivalrous white New Orleans lover, in which she is scarcely aware she is a slave, to the point where she is pawed publicly in the slave market and degraded to the level of becoming Legree's unwilling mistress is fictional material of real interest; merely sketched in by Mrs. Stowe, it has recently been worked out in great detail by R. P. Warren in *Band of Angels.* Yet it fades from the mind even just after we have read *Uncle Tom.* It is not essential to the book which became part of our childhood. Of the complex novel created by Mrs. Stowe (or God!), America has chosen to preserve only the child's book.

Though we *know* Emmeline and Cassy are cowering in the attic at the moment that Quimbo and Sambo under Legree's direction are beating Uncle Tom to death, it is only the latter scene which we *feel.* We respond to the suffering and the triumph and the distressingly tearful arrival, just too late, of Marse George, the boy who has loved and remembered Tom and who is our surrogate in the book. All the conventional loves and romances of the book slip away, precisely because they are conventional, but also because they are irrelevant: the boy-girl all-white love of Eva and her cousin Henrique; and even, though it is a unifying thread joining the first volume of the novel to the second, the separation, the individual flights, and the joyous reunion in Canada of Eliza and George. We remember Eliza and the bloodhound, Eliza on the ice; we have to check the text to discover what happened to her after she left the floes behind, to remember that with her husband she emigrated to Liberia! Poor George—his existence is fictional only, not mythic. Unlettered Negroes to this day will speak of a pious compromiser of their own race, who urges Christian forbearance rather than militancy, as a "Tom" or "Uncle Tom"; it has become a standard term of contempt. But no one speaks of the advocate of force who challenges him as a "George," though Mrs. Stowe's protagonist of that name was a very model for the righteous use of force against force.

Only Uncle Tom and Topsy and Little Eva have archetypal stature; only the loves of the black man for the little white girl, of the white girl for the black, of the white boy for the slave live the lives of myths. Mrs. Stowe's laudable effort to establish a counter-stereotype to the image of the black rapist that haunts the mind of the South was a failure. We do not remember the turncoat Puritan Legree squeezing the virginal breast of Emmeline, eyeing her lustfully; he is frozen forever, the last enduring myth of the book, in his role of slave-driver, at his purest moment of passion, himself the slave of his need to destroy the Christian slave Tom: "There was one hesitating pause, one irresolute relenting thrill, and the spirit of evil came back with sevenfold vehemence; and Legree, foaming with rage, smote his victim to the ground." It is at this moment that Legree seems the archetypal Seducer, ready for the final violation which the reader has all along feared and awaited with equal fervor.

For all the false rhetoric of Mrs. Stowe's description, that blow has an impact as wide in its significance as the assault of Lovelace, the attack of Cain; in it, the white man seals his guilt against the black, confesses his complicity in an act at once predestined and free. This is the moment that stays with us always, balanced against the counter-moment in which George grasps the hand of the dying Tom—*too late,* for Mrs. Stowe cannot help telling the truth—and weeps. The fact of brutality, the hope of forgiveness and mutual love: these are the twin images of guilt and reconciliation that represent for the popular mind of America the truth of slavery. How oddly they undercut the scenes of separated families, of baffled mother-love, at which Mrs. Stowe worked so hard—feeling perhaps that to her bourgeois readers slavery would stand condemned only if it were proved an offense against the sacred family and the suffering mother.

The chief pleasures of *Uncle Tom's Cabin* are, however, rooted not in the moral indignation of the reformer but in the more devious titillations of the sadist; not love but death is Mrs. Stowe's true Muse. For its potential readers, the death of Uncle Tom, the death of Little Eva, the almost-death of Eliza are the big scenes of *Uncle Tom's Cabin,* for they find in the fact and in the threat of death the thrill once provided by the fact or threat of sexual violation. Death is the supreme rapist who threatens when all other Seducers have been banished to the semi-pornographic pulps. And it is the sexless child who comes to seem his proper victim, after the nubile Maiden is considered too ambiguous and dangerous a subject for polite literature. The aroma of sexuality clings to this Maiden, innocent as she may be; and Eliza, for instance, caught by her pursuers, might easily become the object not of bloodlust, which is considered safe, but of quite specific sexual desire. Mrs. Stowe was Puritan enough not to flinch from such problems, but most of her readers were not; and they selected from her gallery of abused females the sexless child to remember and revere.

Little Eva seemed the answer to a particularly vexing genteel dilemma. To save the female for polite readers who wanted women but not sex was not an easy matter. The only safe woman is a dead woman; but even she, if young and beautiful, is only half safe, as any American knows, recalling the necrophilia of Edgar Allan Poe. The only *safe,* safe female is a pre-adolescent girl dying or dead. But this, of course, is Little Eva, the pre-pubescent corpse as heroine, model for all the protagonists of a literature at once juvenile and genteelly gothic.

Though the essential theme of the novel is, as we have come to see, love, it has never been forbidden the spice of death; and in its beginnings, it presented both in one, though both in terms of a fully adult world. In the earliest bourgeois fiction, we remember, the reader was permitted to assist at the last moments of the betrayed woman, no more excluded from the deathbed than from the marriage bed or the couch of sexual betrayal. In the later, more genteel stages of the novel, however, when it was no longer considered permissible to witness female sexual immorality, the reader was banned from the bedrooms of mature women even at the moment of their deaths. He had to content himself with the spectacle of the immaculate child winning her father to God by her courage in the face of a premature end.

Little Eva is the classic case in America, melting the obdurate though kindly St. Clare from skepticism to faith. What an orgy of approved pathos such scenes provided in the hands of a master like Harriet Beecher Stowe, or the later Louisa May Alcott, who in *Little Women* reworked the prototype of Mrs. Stowe into a kind of fiction specifically directed at young girls! Here is the *locus classicus* from *Uncle Tom's Cabin.*

"Dear papa," said the child, with a last effort, throwing her arms about his neck. In a moment they dropped again; and, as St. Clare raised his head, he saw a spasm of mortal agony pass over the face—she struggled for breath, and threw up her little hands.

"O God, this is dreadful," he said, turning away in agony, and wringing Tom's hand. . . . "O, Tom, my boy, it is killing me!" . . .

The child lay panting on her pillows, as one exhausted—the large clear eyes rolled up and fixed. Ah, what said those eyes, that spoke so much of heaven? Earth was past, and earthly pain; but so solemn, so mysterious, was the triumphant brightness of that face, that it checked even the sobs of sorrow. . . .

The bed was draped in white; and there, beneath the drooping angel-figure, lay a little sleeping form—sleeping never to waken!

If there seems something grotesque in such a rigging of the scene, so naked a relish of the stiffening white body between the whiter sheets; if we find an especially queasy voyeurism in this insistence on entering the boudoirs of immature girls, it is perhaps the fault of our post-Freudian imaginations, incapable of responding sentimentally rather than analytically to such images. The bed we know is the place of deflowering as well as dying, and in the bridal bed, a young girl, still virgin, dies to be replaced by the woman, mourning forever the white thing she once was. At least, so an age of innocence dreamed the event; they did not have to *understand* what they dreamed. With no sense of indecorum, they penetrated, behind Mrs. Stowe, the bedroom of the Pure Young Thing and participated in the kill. To be allowed (vicariously) to murder the deflowered Clarissa of the earlier novel is, perhaps, satisfactory enough, since the appeasement of guilt, the hatred of sin lies at its root; but to murder (just as vicariously) the pre-adolescent Virgin is to be granted the supreme privilege of assaulting innocence, appeasing the hatred of virtue, which must surely have stirred uneasily before such atrociously immaculate examples. And it is all done without recourse to "sex," as sex was then quite narrowly defined—*cleanly* sadistic to an age in which no one suspected that the shadow of the Marquis de Sade might fall upon the social reformer. All was permitted the writer capable of combining such erotic evocations of death with attacks on slavery or demands for the reorganization of debtors' prisons, boys' schools, and almshouses.

The notion that Mrs. Stowe (whose blend of morality and prurience led her to expose the love life of Byron and his sister, when she had run out of material closer to home) might be a pornographer was as unthinkable to the great audience of her age as the fact that Dickens, her teacher in this regard, drew all his life on his own odd taste for pre-nubile girls. That Dickens' Little Nell is the model for Little Eva seems probable enough; though, indeed, the atmosphere of the era makes the simultaneous emergence of such archetypal small girls far from unlikely. It is Dickens, however, who first provides in *The Old Curiosity Shop* (1842) the iconography of the Holy Family of the genteel Protestant bourgeoisie. Not the Divine Boy but the Good Good Girl is imagined, cuddled not in the arms of the mother but in those of the father, and not at the moment of birth but at that of death. When *The Old Curiosity Shop* first appeared, critics spoke of the affiliation of Little Nell to Cordelia; and indeed, the final scenes of *King Lear* must have suggested to Dickens the form of what has been called the Protestant *Pietà*: the white-clad daughter, dying or dead, in the arms of the old man, tearful papa or grandfather or (in America) the woolly-haired slave.

It is the unendurable happy ending, as the white slip of a thing too good for this world prepares to leave it for the next, while readers and parents, lovers all, sob into their handkerchiefs. The Good Good Girl, blond, asexual goddess

of nursery or orphanage or old plantation house ("Always dressed in white,"
Mrs. Stowe writes of Eva, "she seemed to move like a shadow through all sorts
of places, without contracting spot or stain; and there was not a corner or
nook . . . where those fairy footsteps had not glided, and that visionary golden
head, with its deep blue eyes, fleeted along"), must die not only so we may
weep—and tears are, for the sentimentalist, the true baptism of the heart—
but also because there is nothing else for her to do. There lies before the Little
Evas of the world no course of action which would not sully them; allowed to
grow up, Little Eva could only become—since she is forbidden the nunnery by
the Protestant ethos and the role of the old maid is in our culture hopelessly
comic—wife, mother, or widow, tinged no matter how slightly with the stain
of sexuality, *suffered* perhaps rather than sought, but, in any case, *there*!

Sentimental Power

Uncle Tom's Cabin *and the Politics of Literary History*

JANE P. TOMPKINS

◆ ◆ ◆

ONCE, DURING A difficult period of my life, I lived in the basement of a house on Forest Street in Hartford, Connecticut, which had belonged to Isabella Beecher Hooker—Harriet Beecher Stowe's half-sister. This woman at one time in her life had believed that the millennium was at hand and that she was destined to be the leader of a new matriarchy.[1] When I lived in that basement, however, I knew nothing of Stowe, or of the Beechers, or of the utopian visions of nineteenth-century American women. I made a reverential visit to the Mark Twain house a few blocks away, took photographs of his study, and completely ignored Stowe's own house—also open to the public—which stood across the lawn. Why should I go? Neither I nor anyone I knew regarded Stowe as a serious writer. At the time I was giving my first lecture course in the American Renaissance—concentrated exclusively on Hawthorne, Melville, Poe, Emerson, Thoreau, and Whitman—and although *Uncle Tom's Cabin* was written in exactly the same period, and although it is probably the most influential book ever written by an American, I would never have dreamed of including it on my reading list. To begin with, its very popularity would have militated against it; as everybody knew, the classics of American fiction were, with a few exceptions, all *succès d'estime*.

In 1969, when I lived on Forest Street, the women's movement was just getting under way. It was several years before Kate Chopin's *The Awakening* and Charlotte Perkins Gilman's "The Yellow Wallpaper" would make it onto college reading lists, sandwiched in between Theodore Dreiser and Frank Norris. These women, like some of their male counterparts, had been unpopular in their own time and owed their reputations to the discernment of latter-day critics. Because of their work, it is now respectable to read these writers, who, unlike Nathaniel Hawthorne, had to wait several generations for their champions to appear in the literary establishment. But despite the influence of the women's movement, and despite the explosion of work in nineteenth-century American social history, and despite the new historicism that is infiltrating literary studies, the women, like Harriet Beecher Stowe, whose names were household words in the nineteenth century—women such as Susan Warner, Sarah J. Hale, Augusta Evans, Elizabeth Stuart Phelps, her daughter Mary, who took the same name, and Frances Hodgson Burnett—these women remain excluded from the literary canon. And while it has recently become fashionable to study their works as examples of cultural deformation, even critics who have invested their professional careers in that study and who declare themselves feminists still refer to their novels as trash.[2]

My principal target of concern, however, is not feminists who have written on popular women novelists of the nineteenth century but the male-dominated scholarly tradition that controls both the canon of American literature (from which these novelists are excluded) and the critical perspective that interprets the canon for society. For the tradition of Perry Miller, F. O. Matthiessen, Harry Levin, Richard Chase, R. W. B. Lewis, Yvor Winters, and Henry Nash Smith has prevented even committed feminists from recognizing and asserting the *value* of a powerful and specifically female novelistic tradition. The very grounds on which sentimental fiction has been dismissed by its detractors, grounds that have come to seem universal standards of aesthetic judgment, were established in a struggle to supplant the tradition of evangelical piety and moral commitment these novelists represent. In reaction against their world view, and perhaps even more against their success, twentieth-century critics have taught generations of students to equate popularity with debasement, emotionality with ineffectiveness, religiosity with fakery, domesticity with triviality, and all of these, implicitly, with womanly inferiority.

In this view, sentimental novels written by women in the nineteenth century were responsible for a series of cultural evils whose effects still plague us: the degeneration of American religion from theological rigor to anti-intellectual consumerism, the rationalization of an unjust economic order, the propagation of the debased images of modern mass culture, and the encouragement of self-indulgence and narcissism in literature's most avid readers—women.[3] To the extent that they protested the evils of society, their protest is seen as duplicitous, the product and expression of the very values they pretended to condemn. Unwittingly or not, so the story goes, they were apologists for an oppressive social order. In contrast to male authors like Thoreau, Whitman, and Melville, who are celebrated as models of intellectual daring and honesty, these women are generally thought to have traded in false stereotypes, dishing out weak-minded pap to nourish the prejudices of an ill-educated and underemployed female readership. Self-deluded and unable to face the harsh facts of a competitive society, they are portrayed as manipulators of a gullible public who kept their readers imprisoned in a dream world of self-justifying clichés. Their fight against the evils of their society was a fixed match from the start.[4]

The thesis I will argue in this essay is diametrically opposed to these. It holds that the popular domestic novel of the nineteenth century represents a monumental effort to reorganize culture from the woman's point of view; that this body of work is remarkable for its intellectual complexity, ambition, and resourcefulness; and that, in certain cases, it offers a critique of American society far more devastating than any delivered by better-known critics such as Hawthorne and Melville. Finally, it suggests that the enormous popularity of these novels, which has been cause for suspicion bordering on disgust, is a reason for paying close attention to them. *Uncle Tom's Cabin* was, in almost any terms one can think of, the most important book of the century. It was the first American novel ever to sell over a million copies, and its impact is generally thought to have been incalculable. Expressive of and responsible for the values of its time, it also belongs to a genre, the sentimental novel, whose chief characteristic is that it is written by, for, and about women. In this respect, *Uncle Tom's Cabin* is not exceptional but representative. It is the *summa theologica* of nineteenth-century America's religion of domesticity, a brilliant redaction of the culture's favorite story about itself: the story of salvation through motherly love. Out of the ideological materials they had at their disposal, the sentimental novelists elaborated a myth that gave women the central position of power and authority in the culture; and of these efforts *Uncle Tom's Cabin* is the most dazzling exemplar.

I have used words like "monumental" and "dazzling" to describe Stowe's novel and the tradition of which it is a part because they have for too long been the casualties of a set of critical attitudes that equate intellectual merit with certain kinds of argumentative discourse and certain kinds of subject matter. A long tradition of academic parochialism has enforced this sort of discourse through a series of cultural contrasts: light "feminine" novels versus tough-minded intellectual treatises; domestic "chattiness" versus serious thinking; and summarily, the "damned mob of scribbling women" versus a few giant intellects, unappreciated and misunderstood in their time, struggling manfully against a flood of sentimental rubbish.[5]

The inability of twentieth-century critics either to appreciate the complexity and scope of a novel like Stowe's or to account for its enormous popular success stems from their assumptions about the nature and function of literature. In modernist thinking, literature is by definition a form of discourse that has no designs on the world. It does not attempt to change things, but merely to represent them, and it does so in a specifically literary language whose claim to value lies in its uniqueness. Consequently, sequently, works whose stated purpose is to influence the course of history, and which therefore employ a language that is not only not unique but common and accessible to everyone, do not qualify as works of art. Literary texts such as the sentimental novel, which make continual and obvious appeals to the reader's emotions and use technical devices that are distinguished by their utter conventionality, epitomize the opposite of everything that good literature is supposed to be. "For the literary critic," writes J. W. Ward, summing up the dilemma posed by *Uncle Tom's Cabin,* "the problem is how a book so seemingly artless, so lacking in apparent literary talent, was not only an immediate success but has endured."[6]

How deep the problem goes is illustrated dramatically by George F. Whicher's discussion of Stowe's novel in *The Literary History of the United States.* Reflecting the consensus view on what good novels are made of, Whicher writes: "Nothing attributable to Mrs. Stowe or her handiwork can account for the novel's enormous vogue; its author's resources as a purveyor of Sunday-school fiction were not remarkable. She had at most a ready command of broadly conceived melodrama, humor, and pathos, and of these popular elements she compounded her book."[7] At a loss to understand how a book so compounded was able to "convulse a mighty nation," Whicher concludes—incredibly—that Stowe's own explanation, that "God wrote it," "solved the paradox." Rather than give up his bias against "melodrama," "pathos," and "Sunday-school fiction," Whicher takes refuge in a solution which, even according to his lights, is patently absurd.[8] And no wonder. The modernist literary aesthetic cannot account for the unprecedented and persistent popularity of a book like *Uncle Tom's Cabin,* for this novel operates according to principles quite other than those which have been responsible for determining the currently sanctified American literary classics.

It is not my purpose, however, to drag Hawthorne and Melville from their pedestals, nor to claim that the novels of Harriet Beecher Stowe, Fanny Fern, and Elizabeth Stuart Phelps are good in the same way that *Moby Dick* and *The Scarlet Letter* are; rather, I will argue that the work of the sentimental writers is complex and significant in ways *other than* those which characterize the established masterpieces. I will ask the reader to set aside some familiar categories for evaluating fiction—stylistic intricacy, psychological subtlety, epistemological complexity—and to see the sentimental novel, not as an artifice of eternity answerable to certain formal criteria and to certain psychological and philosophical concerns, but as a political enterprise, halfway between sermon and social theory, that both codifies and attempts to mold the values of its time.

The power of a sentimental novel to move its audience depends upon the audience's being in possession of the conceptual categories that constitute character and event. That storehouse of assumptions includes attitudes towards the family and towards social institutions, a definition of power and its relation to individual human feeling, notions of political and social equality, and above all, a set of religious beliefs that organize and sustain the rest. Once in possession of the system of beliefs that undergirds the patterns of sentimental fiction, it is possible for modern readers to see how its tearful episodes and frequent violations of probability were invested with a structure of meanings that fixed these works, for nineteenth-century readers, not in the realm of fairy tale or escapist fantasy, but in the very bedrock of reality. I do not say that we can read sentimental fiction exactly as Stowe's audience did—that would be impossible—but that we can and should set aside the modernist prejudices that consign this fiction to oblivion, in order to see how and why it worked for its readers, in its time, with such unexampled effect.

Let us consider the episode in *Uncle Tom's Cabin* most often cited as the epitome of Victorian sentimentalism—the death of little Eva—because it is the kind of incident most offensive to the sensibilities of twentieth-century academic critics. It is on the belief that this incident is nothing more than a sob story that the whole case against sentimentalism rests. Little Eva's death, so the argument goes, like every other sentimental tale, is awash with emotion but does nothing to remedy the evils it deplores. Essentially, it leaves the slave system and the other characters unchanged. This trivializing view of the episode is grounded in assumptions about power and reality so common that we are not even aware they have been invoked. Thus generations of critics have commented with condescending irony on little Eva's death. But in the system of belief that undergirds Stowe's enterprise, dying is the supreme form of heroism. In *Uncle Tom's Cabin,* death is the equivalent not of defeat but of victory; it brings an access of power, not a loss of it; it is not only the crowning achievement of life, it is life, and Stowe's entire presentation of little Eva is designed to dramatize this fact.

Stories like the death of little Eva are compelling for the same reason that the story of Christ's death is compelling: they enact a philosophy, as much political as religious, in which the pure and powerless die to save the powerful and corrupt, and thereby show themselves more powerful than those they save. They enact, in short, a *theory* of power in which the ordinary or "commonsense" view of what is efficacious and what is not (a view to which most modern critics are committed) is simply reversed, as the very possibility of social action is made dependent on the action taking place in individual hearts. Little Eva's death enacts the drama of which all the major episodes of the novel are transformations: the idea, central to Christian soteriology,[9] that the highest human calling is to give one's life for another. It presents one version of the ethic of sacrifice on which the entire novel is based and contains in some form all of the motifs that, by their frequent recurrence, constitute the novel's ideological framework.

Little Eva's death, moreover, is also a transformation of stories circulating in the culture at large. It may be found, for example, in a dozen or more versions in the evangelical sermons of the Reverend Dwight Lyman Moody when he preached in Great Britain and Ireland in 1875. In one version it is called "The Child Angel," and it concerns a beautiful golden-haired girl of seven, her father's pride and joy, who dies and, by appearing to him in a dream in which she calls to him from heaven, brings him salvation.[10] The tale shows that by dying even a child can be the instrument of redemption for others, since in death she acquires over those who loved her a spiritual power beyond what she possessed in life.

The power of the dead or the dying to redeem the unregenerate is a major theme of nineteenth-century popular fiction and religious literature. Mothers and children are thought to be uniquely capable of this work. In a sketch entitled "Children," published the year after *Uncle Tom* came out, Stowe writes: "Wouldst thou know, O parent, what is that faith which unlocks heaven? Go not to wrangling polemics, or creeds and forms of theology, but draw to thy bosom thy little one, and read in that clear trusting eye the lesson of eternal life."[11] If children through their purity and innocence can lead adults to God while living, their spiritual power when they are dead is greater still. Death, Stowe argues in a pamphlet entitled *Ministration of Departed Spirits,* enables the Christian to begin his "real work." God takes people from us sometimes so that their "ministry can act upon us more powerfully from the unseen world."[12]

> The mother would fain electrify the heart of her child. She yearns and burns in vain to make her soul effective on its soul, and to inspire it with a spiritual and holy life; but all her own weaknesses, faults and mortal cares, cramp and confine her till death breaks all fetters; and then, first

truly alive, risen, purified, and at rest, she may do calmly, sweetly, and certainly, what, amid the tempest and tossings of her life, she labored for painfully and fitfully.[13]

When the spiritual power of death is combined with the natural sanctity of childhood, the child becomes an angel endowed with salvific force.

Most often, it is the moment of death that saves, when the dying child, glimpsing for a moment the glory of heaven, testifies to the reality of the life to come. Uncle Tom knows that this will happen when little Eva dies, and explains it to Miss Ophelia as follows:

> "You know it says in Scripture, 'At midnight there was a great cry made. Behold the bridegroom cometh.' That's what I'm spactin now, every night, Miss Feely,—and I couldn't sleep out o' hearin' no ways."
>
> "Uncle Tom, what makes you think so?"
>
> "Miss Eva, she talks to me. The lord, he sends his messenger in the soul. I must be thar, Miss Feely; for when that ar blessed child goes into the kingdom, they'll open the door so wide, we'll all get a look in at the glory, Miss Feely."[14]

Little Eva does not disappoint them. At the moment when she passes "from death into life," she exclaims, "O, love!—joy!—peace!" And her exclamation echoes those of scores of children who die in Victorian fiction and sermon literature with heaven in their eyes. Dickens's Paul Dombey, seeing the face of his dead mother, dies with the words "The light about the head is shining on me as I go!" The fair, blue-eyed young girl in Lydia Sigourney's *Letters to Mothers*, "death's purple tinge upon her brow," when implored by her mother to utter one last word, whispers "Praise!"[15]

Of course, it could be argued by critics of sentimentalism that the prominence of stories about the deaths of children is precisely what is wrong with the literature of the period; rather than being cited as a source of strength, the presence of such stories in *Uncle Tom's Cabin* should be regarded as an unfortunate concession to the age's fondness for lachrymose scenes. But to dismiss such scenes as "all tears and flapdoodle" is to leave unexplained the popularity of the novels and sermons that are filled with them, unless we choose to believe that a generation of readers was unaccountably moved to tears by matters that are intrinsically silly and trivial. That popularity is better explained, I believe, by the relationship of these scenes to a pervasive cultural myth which invests the suffering and death of an innocent victim with just the kind of power that critics deny to Stowe's novel: the power to work in, and change, the world.

This is the kind of action that little Eva's death in fact performs. It proves its efficacy, not through the sudden collapse of the slave system, but through the conversion of Topsy, a motherless, godless black child who has up until that point successfully resisted all attempts to make her "good." Topsy will not be "good" because, never having had a mother's love, she believes that no one can love her. When Eva suggests that Miss Ophelia would love her if only she were good, Topsy cries out, "No, she can't bar me, cause I'm a nigger!—she'd as soon have a toad touch her! Ther can't nobody love niggers, and niggers can't do nothin'! I don't care."

> "O, Topsy, poor child, *I* love you!" said Eva with a sudden burst of feeling and laying her little thin, white hand on Topsy's shoulder; "I love you, because you haven't had any father, or mother, or friends;—because you've been a poor, abused child! I love you, and I want you to be good. I am very unwell, Topsy, and I think I shan't live a great while; and it really grieves me, to have you be so naughty. I wish you would try to be good, for my sake;—it's only a little while I shall be with you."
>   The round, keen eyes of the black child were overcast with tears:— large, bright drops rolled heavily down one by one, and fell on the little white hand. Yes, in that moment, a ray of real belief, a ray of heavenly love, had penetrated the darkness of her heathen soul! She laid her head down between her knees, and wept and sobbed,—while the beautiful child, bending over her, looked like the picture of some bright angel stooping to reclaim a sinner. (P. 283)

The rhetoric and imagery of this passage, its little white hand, its ray from heaven, bending angel, and plentiful tears, suggest a literary version of the kind of polychrome religious picture that hangs on Sunday school walls. Words like "kitsch," "camp," and "corny" come to mind. But what is being dramatized here bears no relation to these designations. By giving Topsy her love, Eva initiates a process of redemption whose power, transmitted from heart to heart, can change the entire world. And indeed, the process has begun. From that time on, Topsy is "different from what she used to be" (eventually she will go to Africa and become a missionary to her entire race), and Miss Ophelia, who overhears the conversation, is different too. When little Eva is dead and Topsy cries out, "Ther an't *nobody* left now," Miss Ophelia answers her in Eva's place:

> "Topsy, you poor child," she said, as she led her into her room, "don't give up! *I* can love you, though I am not like that dear little child. I hope

I've learnt something of the love of Christ from her. I can love you; I do, and I'll try to help you to grow up a good Christian girl."

Miss Ophelia's voice was more than her words, and more than that were the honest tears that fell down her face. From that hour, she acquired an influence over the mind of the destitute child that she never lost. (P. 300)

The tears of Topsy and of Miss Ophelia, which we find easy to ridicule, are the sign of redemption in *Uncle Tom's Cabin;* not words but the emotions of the heart bespeak a state of grace, and these are known by the sound of a voice, the touch of a hand, but chiefly, in moments of greatest importance, by tears. When Tom lies dying on the plantation on the Red River, the disciples to whom he has preached testify to their conversion by weeping.

Tears had fallen on that honest, insensible face,—tears of late repentance in the poor, ignorant heathen, whom his dying love and patience had awakened to repentance. . . . (P. 420)

Even the bitter and unregenerate Cassy, "moved by the sacrifice that had been made for her," breaks down; "moved by the few last words which the affectionate soul had yet strength to breathe. . . . the dark, despairing woman had wept and prayed" (p. 420). When George Shelby, the son of Tom's old master, arrives too late to free him, "tears which did honor to his manly heart fell from the young man's eyes as he bent over his poor friend." And when Tom realizes who is there, "the whole face lighted up, the hard hands clasped, and tears ran down the cheeks" (p. 420). The vocabulary of clasping hands and falling tears is one we associate with emotional exhibitionism, with the overacting that kills true feeling off through exaggeration. But the tears and gestures of Stowe's characters are not in excess of what they feel; if anything, they fall short of expressing the experiences they point to—salvation, communion, reconciliation.

If the language of tears seems maudlin and little Eva's death ineffectual, it is because both the tears and the redemption they signify belong to a conception of the world that is now generally regarded as naïve and unrealistic. Topsy's salvation and Miss Ophelia's do not alter the anti-abolitionist majority in the Senate or prevent Southern plantation owners and Northern investment bankers from doing business to their mutual advantage. Because most modern readers regard such political and economic facts as final, it is difficult for them to take seriously a novel that insists on religious conversion as the necessary precondition for sweeping social change. But in Stowe's understanding of what such change requires it is the *modern* view that is naïve. The political and economic measures that constitute effective action for us, she regards as superficial, mere extensions of the worldly policies that produced the slave system in the first place. Therefore, when Stowe asks the question that is in every reader's mind at the end of the novel, namely, "What can any individual do?" she recommends, not specific alterations in the current political and economic arrangements, but rather a change of heart.

> There is one thing that every individual can do—they can see to it that *they feel right.* An atmosphere of sympathetic influence encircles every human being; and the man or woman who *feels* strongly, healthily and justly, on the great interests of humanity, is a constant benefactor to the human race. See, then, to your sympathies in this matter! Are they in harmony with the sympathies of Christ? or are they swayed and perverted by the sophistries of worldly policy? (P. 448)

Stowe is not opposed to concrete measures such as the passage of laws or the formation of political pressure groups; it is just that by themselves, such actions would be useless. For if slavery *were* to be abolished by these means, the moral conditions that produced slavery in the first place would continue in force. The choice is not between action and inaction, programs and feelings; the choice is between actions that spring from "the sophistries of worldly policy" and those inspired by "the sympathies of Christ." Reality, in Stowe's view, cannot be changed by manipulating the physical environment; it can only be changed by conversion in the spirit because it is the spirit alone that is finally real.

The notion that historical change takes place only through religious conversion, which is a theory of power as old as Christianity itself, is dramatized and vindicated in *Uncle Tom's Cabin* by the novel's insistence that all human events are organized, clarified, and made meaningful by the existence of spiritual realities.[16] The novel is packed with references to the four last things— Heaven, Hell, Death, and Judgment—references which remind the reader constantly that historical events can only be seen for what they are in the light of eternal truths. When St. Clare stands over the grave of little Eva, unable to realize "that it was his Eva that they were hiding from his sight," Stowe interjects, "Nor was it!—not Eva, but only the frail seed of that bright immortal form in which she shall yet come forth, in the day of the Lord Jesus!" (p. 300). And when Legree expresses satisfaction that Tom is dead, she turns to him and says, "Yes, Legree; but who shall shut up that voice in thy soul? that soul, past repentance, past prayer, past hope, in whom the fire that never shall be quenched is already burning?" (p. 416). These reminders come thick and fast; they are present in Stowe's countless quotations from Scripture, introduced at every possible opportunity—in the narrative, in dialogue, in epigraphs, in quotations from other authors; they are present in the Protestant hymns that thread their way through scene after scene, in asides to the reader, in apostrophes to the characters, in quotations from religious poetry, sermons, and prayers, and in long stretches of dialogue and narrative devoted to the discussion of religious matters. Stowe's narrative stipulates a world in which the facts of Christ's death and resurrection and coming day of judgment are never far from our minds because it is only within this frame of reference that she can legitimately have Tom claim, as he dies, "I've got the victory."

The eschatological vision, by putting all individual events in relation to an order that is unchanging, collapses the distinctions between them so that they become interchangeable representations of a single timeless reality. Groups of characters blend into the same character, while the plot abounds in incidents that mirror one another. These features are the features, not of classical nineteenth-century fiction, but of typological narrative. It is this tradition rather than that of the English novel which *Uncle Tom's Cabin* reproduces and extends; for this novel does not simply quote the Bible, it rewrites the Bible as the story of a Negro slave. Formally and philosophically, it stands opposed to works like *Middlemarch* and *The Portrait of a Lady* in which everything depends on human action and decision unfolding in a temporal sequence that withholds revelation until the final moment. The truths that Stowe's narrative conveys can only be reembodied, never discovered, because they are already revealed from the beginning. Therefore, what seem from a modernist point of view to be gross stereotypes in characterization and a needless proliferation of incident are essential properties of a narrative aimed at demonstrating that human history is a continual reenactment of the sacred drama of redemption. It is the novel's reenactment of this drama that made it irresistible in its day.

Uncle Tom's Cabin retells the culture's central religious myth, the story of the crucifixion, in terms of the nation's greatest political conflict—slavery—and of its most cherished social beliefs—the sanctity of motherhood and the family. It is because Stowe is able to combine so many of the culture's central concerns in a narrative that is immediately accessible to the general population that she is able to move so many people so deeply. The novel's typological organization allows her to present political and social situations both as themselves and as transformations of a religious paradigm which interprets them in a way that readers can both understand and respond to emotionally. For the novel functions both as a means of describing the social world and as a means of changing it. It not only offers an interpretative framework for understanding the culture and, through the reinforcement of a particular code of values, recommends a strategy for dealing with cultural conflict, but it is itself an agent of that strategy, putting into practice the measures it prescribes. As the religious stereotypes of "Sunday school fiction" define and organize the elements of social and political life, so the "melodrama" and "pathos" associated with the underlying myth of crucifixion put the reader's heart in the right place with respect to the problems the narrative defines. Hence, rather than making the enduring success of *Uncle Tom's Cabin* inexplicable, these popular elements that puzzled Whicher and have puzzled so many modern scholars— melodrama, pathos, Sunday school fiction—are the *only* terms in which the book's success can be explained.

The nature of these popular elements also dictates the terms in which any full-scale analysis of *Uncle Tom's Cabin* must be carried out. As I have suggested, its distinguishing features, generically speaking, are not those of the realistic novel but of typological narrative. Its characters, like the figures in an allegory, do not change or develop but reveal themselves in response to the demands of a situation. They are not defined primarily by their mental and emotional characteristics—that is to say, psychologically—but soteriologically, according to whether they are saved or damned. The plot, likewise, does not unfold according to Aristotelian standards of probability but in keeping with the logic of a preordained design, a design that every incident is intended, in one way or another, to enforce.[17] The setting does not so much describe the features of a particular time and place as point to positions on a spiritual map. In *Uncle Tom's Cabin* the presence of realistic detail tends to obscure its highly programmatic nature and to lull readers into thinking that they are in an everyday world of material cause and effect. But what pass for realistic details—the use of dialect, the minute descriptions of domestic activity—are in fact performing a rhetorical function dictated by the novel's ruling paradigm; once that paradigm is perceived, even the homeliest details show up not as the empirically observed facts of human existence but as the expressions of a highly schematic intent.[18]

This schematization has what one might call a totalizing effect on the particulars of the narrative, so that every character in the novel, every scene, and every incident comes to be apprehended in terms of every *other* character, scene, and incident: all are caught up in a system of endless cross-reference in which it is impossible to refer to one without referring to all the rest. To demonstrate what I mean by this kind of narrative organization— a demonstration that will have to stand in lieu of a full-scale reading of the novel—let me show how it works in relation to a single scene. Eva and Tom are seated in the garden of St. Clare's house on the shores of Lake Pontchartrain.

It was Sunday evening, and Eva's Bible lay open on her knee. She read,—"And I saw a sea of glass, mingled with fire."

"Tom," said Eva, suddenly stopping, and pointing to the lake, "there 't is."

"What, Miss Eva?"

"Don't you see,—there?" said the child, pointing to the glassy water, which, as it rose and fell, reflected the golden glow of the sky. "There's a 'sea of glass, mingled with fire.'"

"True enough, Miss Eva," said Tom: and Tom sang—

> *"O, had I the wings of the morning,*
> *I'd fly away to Canaan's shore;*
> *Bright angels should convey me home,*
> *To the new Jerusalem."*

"Where do you suppose new Jerusalem is, Uncle Tom?" said Eva.

"O, up in the clouds, Miss Eva."

"Then I think I see it," said Eva. "Look in those clouds!—they look like great gates of pearl; and you can see beyond them—far, far off—it's all gold. Tom, sing about 'spirits bright.'"

Tom sang the words of a well-known Methodist hymn,

> *"I see a band of spirits bright,*
> *That taste the glories there;*
> *They are all robed in spotless white,*
> *And conquering palms they bear."*

"Uncle Tom, I've seen them." said Eva. . . . "They come to me sometimes in my sleep, those spirits;" and Eva's eyes grew dreamy, and she hummed, in a low voice,

> *"They are all robed in spotless white,*
> *And conquering palms they bear."*

"Uncle Tom," said Eva, "I'm going there."

"Where, Miss Eva?"

The child rose, and pointed her little hand to the sky; the glow of evening lit her golden hair and flushed cheek with a kind of unearthly radiance, and her eyes were bent earnestly on the skies.

"I'm going *there*," she said, "to the spirits bright, Tom; *I'm going, before long.*" (Pp. 261–62)

The iterative nature of this scene presents in miniature the structure of the whole novel. Eva reads from her Bible about a "sea of glass, mingled with fire," then looks up to find one before her. She reads the words aloud a second time. They remind Tom of a hymn that describes the same vision in a slightly different form (Lake Pontchartrain and the sea of glass become "Canaan's shore" and the "new Jerusalem"), and Eva sees what he has sung, this time in the clouds, and offers her own description. Eva asks Tom to sing again, and his hymn presents yet another form of the same vision, which Eva again says she has seen: the spirits bright come to her in her sleep. Finally, Eva repeats the last two lines of the hymn and declares that she is going "there"—to the place that has now been referred to a dozen times in this passage. Stowe follows with another description of the golden skies and then with a description of Eva as a spirit bright, and closes the passage with Eva's double reiteration that she is going "there."

The entire scene itself is a re-presentation of others that come before and after. When Eva looks out over Lake Pontchartrain, she sees the "Canaan of liberty" which Eliza saw on the other side of the Ohio River, and the "eternal shores" Eliza and George Harris will reach when they cross Lake Erie in the end. Bodies of water mediate between worlds: the Ohio runs between the slave states and the free; Lake Erie divides the United States from Canada, where runaway slaves cannot be returned to their masters; the Atlantic Ocean divides the North American continent from Africa, where Negroes will have a nation of their own; Lake Pontchartrain shows Eva the heavenly home to which she is going soon; the Mississippi River carries slaves from the relative ease of the Middle States to the grinding toil of the Southern plantations; the Red River carries Tom to the infernal regions ruled over by Simon Legree. The correspondences between the episodes I have mentioned are themselves based on correspondences between earth and heaven (or hell). Ohio, Canada, and Liberia are related to one another by virtue of their relationship to the one "bright Canaan" for which they stand; the Mississippi River and the Ohio are linked by the Jordan. (Ultimately, there are only three places to be in this story: heaven, hell, or Kentucky, which represents the earthly middle ground in Stowe's geography.)

Characters in the novel are linked to each other in exactly the same way that places are: with reference to a third term that is the source of their identity. The figure of Christ is the common term that unites all of the novel's good characters, who are good precisely in proportion as they are imitations of him. Eva and Tom head the list (she reenacts the Last Supper and he the crucifixion) but they are also linked to most of the slaves, women, and children in the novel by the characteristics they all share: piety, impressionability, spontaneous affection—and victimization.[19] In this scene, Eva is linked with the "spirits bright" (she later becomes a "bright immortal form") both because she can see them and is soon to join them and because she, too, always wears white and is elsewhere several times referred to as an "angel." When Eva dies, she will join her father's mother, who was also named Evangeline and who herself always wore white, and who, like Eva, is said to be "the direct and living embodiment of the New Testament." And this identification, in its turn, refers back to Uncle Tom, who is "all the moral and Christian virtues bound in black morocco complete." The circularity of this train of association is typical of the way the narrative doubles back on itself: later on, Cassy, impersonating the ghost of Legree's saintly mother, will wrap herself in a white sheet.[20]

The scene I have been describing is a node with a network of allusion in which every character and event in the novel has a place. The narrative's rhetorical strength derives in part from the impression it gives of taking every kind of detail in the world into account, from the preparation of breakfast to the orders of the angels, and investing those details with a purpose and a meaning that are both immediately apprehensible and finally significant. The novel reaches out into the reader's world and colonizes it for its own eschatology: that is, it not only incorporates the homely particulars of "Life Among the Lowly" into its universal scheme, but it gives them a power and a centrality in that scheme which turns the sociopolitical order upside down. The totalizing effect of the novel's iterative organization and its doctrine of spiritual redemption are inseparably bound to its political purpose, which is to bring in the day when the meek—that is to say, women—will inherit the earth.

The specifically political intent of the novel is apparent in its forms of address. Stowe addresses her readers not simply as individuals but as citizens of the United States: "to you, generous, noble-minded men and women of the South," "farmers of Massachusetts, of New Hampshire, of Vermont," "brave and generous men of New York," "and you, mothers of America." She speaks to her audience directly in the way the Old Testament prophets spoke to Israel, exhorting, praising, blaming, warning of the wrath to come. "This is an age of the world when nations are trembling and convulsed. Almighty influence is abroad, surging and heaving the world, as with an earthquake. And is America safe? . . . O, Church of Christ, read the signs of the times!" (p. 451). Passages like these, descended from the revivalist rhetoric of *Sinners in the Hands of an Angry God,* are intended, in the words of a noted scholar, "to direct an imperiled people toward the fulfillment of their destiny, to guide them individually towards salvation, and collectively toward the American city of God."[21]

These sentences are from Sacvan Bercovitch's *The American Jeremiad,* an influential work of modern scholarship which, although it completely ignores Stowe's novel, makes us aware that *Uncle Tom's Cabin* is a jeremiad in the fullest and truest sense. A jeremiad, in Bercovitch's definition, is "a mode of public exhortation . . . designed to join social criticism to spiritual renewal, public to private identity, the shifting 'signs of the times' to certain traditional metaphors, themes, and symbols."[22] Stowe's novel provides the most obvious and compelling instance of the jeremiad since the Great Awakening, and its exclusion from Bercovitch's book is a striking instance of how totally academic criticism has foreclosed on sentimental fiction; for, because *Uncle Tom's Cabin* is absent from the canon, it is not "there" to be referred to even when it fulfills a man's theory to perfection; hence its exclusion from critical discourse is perpetuated automatically, and absence begets itself in a self-confirming cycle of neglect. Nonetheless, Bercovitch's characterization of the jeremiad provides an excellent account of how *Uncle Tom's Cabin* actually worked: among its characters, settings, situations, symbols, and doctrines, the novel establishes a set of correspondences that unite the disparate realms of experience Bercovitch names—social and spiritual, public and private, theological and political—and, through the vigor of its representations, attempts to move the nation as a whole toward the vision it proclaims.

The tradition of the jeremiad throws light on *Uncle Tom's Cabin* because Stowe's novel was political in exactly the same way the jeremiad was: both were forms of discourse in which "theology was wedded to politics and politics to the progress of the kingdom of God."[23] The jeremiad strives to persuade its listeners to a providential view of human history which serves, among other things, to maintain the Puritan theocracy in power. Its fusion of theology and politics is not only doctrinal, in that it ties the salvation of the individual to the community's historical enterprise; it is practical as well, for it reflects the interests of Puritan ministers in their bid to retain spiritual and secular authority. The sentimental novel, too, is an act of persuasion aimed at defining social reality; the difference is that the jeremiad represents the interests of Puritan ministers, while the sentimental novel represents the interests of middle-class women. But the relationship between rhetoric and history in both cases is the same. In both cases it is not as if rhetoric and history stand opposed, with rhetoric made up of wish fulfillment and history made up of recalcitrant facts that resist rhetoric's onslaught. Rhetoric *makes* history by shaping reality to the dictates of its political design; it makes history by convincing the people of the world that its description of the world is the true one. The sentimental novelists make their bid for power by positing the kingdom of heaven on earth as a world over which women exercise ultimate control. If history did not take the course these writers recommended, it is not because they were not political, but because they were insufficiently persuasive.

Uncle Tom's Cabin, however, unlike its counterparts in the sentimental tradition, was spectacularly persuasive in conventional political terms: it induced a nation to go to war and to free its slaves. But in terms of its own conception of power, a conception it shares with other sentimental fiction, the novel was a political failure. Stowe conceived her book as an instrument for bringing about the day when the world would be ruled not by force but by Christian love. The novel's deepest political aspirations are expressed only secondarily in its devastating attack on the slave system; the true goal of Stowe's rhetorical undertaking is nothing less than the institution of the kingdom of heaven on earth. Embedded in the world of *Uncle Tom's Cabin,* which is the fallen world of slavery, there appears an idyllic picture, both utopian and Arcadian, of the form human life would assume if Stowe's readers were to heed her moral lesson. In this vision, described in the chapter entitled "The Quaker Settlement," Christian love fulfills itself not in war but in daily living, and the principle of sacrifice is revealed not in crucifixion but in motherhood. The form that society takes bears no resemblance to the current social order. Man-made institutions—the church, the courts of law, the legislatures, the economic system—are nowhere in sight. The home is the center of all meaningful activity, women perform the most important tasks, work is carried on in a spirit of mutual cooperation, and the whole is guided by a Christian woman who, through the influence of her "loving words," "gentle moralities," and "motherly loving kindness," rules the world.

> For why? for twenty years or more, nothing but loving words and gentle moralities, and motherly loving kindness, had come from that chair;— head-aches and heart-aches innumerable had been cured there,— difficulties spiritual and temporal solved there,—all by one good, loving woman, God bless her! (P. 136)

The woman in question *is* God in human form. Seated in her kitchen at the head of her table, passing out coffee and cake for breakfast, Rachel Halliday, the millenarian counterpart of little Eva, enacts the redeemed form of the Last Supper. This is Holy Communion as it will be under the new dispensation: instead of the breaking of bones, the breaking of bread. The preparation of breakfast exemplifies the way people will work in the ideal society; there will be no competition, no exploitation, no commands. Motivated by self-sacrificing love, and joined to one another by its cohesive power, people will perform their duties willingly and with pleasure: moral suasion will take the place of force.

> All moved obediently to Rachel's gentle "Thee had better," or more gentle "Hadn't thee better?" in the work of getting breakfast. . . . Everything went on sociably, so quietly, so harmoniously, in the great kitchen,—it seemed so pleasant to everyone to do just what they were doing, there was an atmosphere of mutual confidence and good fellowship everywhere. (Pp. 141–42)

The new matriarchy that Isabella Beecher Hooker[24] had dreamed of leading, pictured here in the Indiana kitchen ("for a breakfast in the luxurious valleys of Indiana is . . . like picking up the rose-leaves and trimming the bushes in Paradise"), constitutes the most politically subversive dimension of Stowe's novel, more disruptive and far-reaching in its potential consequences than even the starting of a war or the freeing of slaves. Nor is the ideal of matriarchy simply a daydream; Catharine Beecher, Stowe's elder sister, had offered a ground plan for the realization of such a vision in her *Treatise on Domestic Economy* (1841), which the two sisters republished in 1869 in an enlarged version entitled *The American Woman's Home.*[25] Dedicated "To the Women of America, in whose hands rest the real destinies of the republic," this is an instructional book on homemaking in which a wealth of scientific information and practical advice is pointed toward a millenarian goal. Centering on the home, for these women, is not a way of indulging in narcissistic fantasy, as critics have argued, or a turning away from the world into self-absorption and idle reverie; it is the prerequisite of world conquest, defined as the reformation of the human race through proper care and nurturing of its young. Like *Uncle Tom's Cabin, The American Woman's Home* situates the minutiae of domestic life in relation to their soteriological function: "What, then, is the end designed by the family state which Jesus Christ came into this world to secure? It is to provide for the training of our race . . . by means of the self-sacrificing labors of the wise and good . . . with chief reference to a future immortal existence."[26] "The family state," the authors announce at the beginning, "is the aptest earthly illustration of the heavenly kingdom, and . . . woman is its chief minister."[27] In the body of the text the authors provide women with everything they need to know for the proper establishment and maintenance of home and family, from the construction of furniture ("The bed frame is to be fourteen inches wide, and three inches in thickness. At the head, and at the foot, is to be screwed a notched two-inch board, three inches wide, as in Fig. 8"), to architectural plans, to chapters of instruction on heating, ventilation, lighting, healthful diet and preparation of food, cleanliness, the making and mending of clothes, the care of the sick, the organization of routines, financial management, psychological health, the care of infants, the managing of young children, home amusement, the care of furniture, the planting of gardens, the care of domestic animals, the disposal of waste, the cultivation of fruit, and providing for "the helpless, the homeless, and the vicious." After each of these activities has been treated in detail, they conclude by describing the ultimate aim of the domestic enterprise: the founding of a "truly 'Christian family'" will lead to the gathering of a "Christian neighborhood." This "cheering example," they continue,

> would soon spread, and ere long colonies from these prosperous and Christian communities would go forth to shine as "lights of the world" in all the now darkened nations. Thus the "Christian family" and "Christian neighborhood" would become the grand ministry, as they were designed to be, in training our whole race for heaven.[28]

The imperialistic drive behind the encyclopedism and determined practicality of this household manual flatly contradicts the traditional derogations of the American cult of domesticity as a "mirror-phenomenon," "self-immersed" and "self-congratulatory."[29]

The American Woman's Home is a blueprint for colonizing the world in the name of the "family state" under the leadership of Christian women. What is more, people like Stowe and Catharine Beecher were speaking not simply for a set of moral and religious values. In speaking for the home, they spoke for an economy—household economy—which had supported New England life since its inception. The home, rather than representing a retreat or a refuge from a crass industrial-commercial world, offers an economic *alternative* to that world, one which calls into question the whole structure of American society that was growing up in response to the increase in trade and manufacturing.[30] Stowe's image of a utopian community as presented in Rachel Halliday's kitchen is not simply a Christian dream of communitarian cooperation and harmony; it is a reflection of the real communitarian practices of village life, practices that had depended upon cooperation, trust, and a spirit of mutual supportiveness such as characterize the Quaker community of Stowe's novel.

One could argue, then, that for all its revolutionary fervor *Uncle Tom's Cabin* is a conservative book, because it advocates a return to an older way of life— household economy—in the name of the nation's most cherished social and religious beliefs. Even the woman's centrality might be seen as harking back to the "age of homespun" when the essential goods were manufactured in the home and their production was carried out and guided by women. But Stowe's very conservatism—her reliance on established patterns of living and traditional beliefs—is precisely what gives her novel its revolutionary potential. By pushing those beliefs to an extreme and by insisting that they be applied universally, not just to one segregated corner of civil life but to the conduct of all human affairs, Stowe means to effect a radical transformation of her society. The brilliance of the strategy is that it puts the central affirmations of a culture into the service of a vision that would destroy the present economic and social institutions; by resting her case, absolutely, on the saving power of Christian love and on the sanctity of motherhood and the family, Stowe relocates the center of power in American life, placing it not in the government, nor in the courts of law, nor in the factories, nor in the marketplace, but in the kitchen. And that means that the new society will not be controlled by men but by women. The image of the home created by Stowe and Catharine Beecher in their treatise on domestic science is in no sense a shelter from the stormy blast of economic and political life, a haven from reality divorced from fact which allows the machinery of industrial capitalism to grind on; it is conceived as a dynamic center of activity, physical and spiritual, economic and moral, whose influence spreads out in ever-widening circles. To this activity—and this is the crucial innovation—men are incidental. Although the Beecher sisters pay lip service on occasion to male supremacy, women's roles occupy virtually the whole of their attention and dominate the scene. Male provender is deemphasized in favor of female processing. Men provide the seed, but women bear and raise the children. Men provide the flour, but women bake the bread and get the breakfast. The removal of the male from the center to the periphery of the human sphere is the most radical component of this millenarian scheme, which is rooted so solidly in the most traditional values: religion, motherhood, home, and family. Exactly what position men will occupy in the millennium is specified by a detail inserted casually into Stowe's description of the Indiana kitchen. While the women and children are busy preparing breakfast, Simeon Halliday, the husband and father, stands "in his shirt-sleeves before a little looking-glass in the corner, engaged in the anti-patriarchal activity of shaving" (pp. 141–42).

With this detail, so innocently placed, Stowe reconceives the role of men in human history: while Negroes, children, mothers, and grandmothers do the world's primary work, men groom themselves contentedly in a corner. The scene, as critics have noted is often the case in sentimental fiction, is "intimate," the backdrop is "domestic," the tone at times is even "chatty";

but the import, as critics have failed to recognize, is world-shaking. The enterprise of sentimental fiction, as Stowe's novel attests, is anything but domestic, in the sense of being limited to purely personal concerns; its mission, on the contrary, is global and its interests identical with the interests of the race. If the fiction written in the nineteenth century by women whose works sold in the hundreds of thousands has seemed narrow and parochial to the critics of the twentieth century, that narrowness and parochialism belong not to these works nor to the women who wrote them; they are the beholders' share.[31]

Notes

1. Johanna Johnston, *Runaway to Heaven* (Garden City, N.Y.: Doubleday, 1963).

2. Edward Halsey Foster, for example, prefaces his book-length study of the work of Susan and Anna Warner by saying: "If one searches nineteenth century popular fiction for something that has literary value, one searches, by and large, in vain" (*Susan and Anna Warner* [Boston: G. K. Hall, 1978]). At the other end of the spectrum stands a critic like Sally Mitchell, whose excellent studies of Victorian women's fiction contain statements that, intentionally or not, condescend to the subject matter: e.g., "Thus, we should see popular novels as emotional analyses, rather than intellectual analyses, rather than intellectual analyses, of a particular society" ("Sentiment and Suffering: Women's Recreational Reading in the 1860's," *Victorian Studies* 21 [Fall 1977]: 34). The most typical move, however, is to apologize for the poor literary quality of the novels in a concessive clause—"melodramatic and simplistic though the plots may be, wooden and stereotyped as the characters may appear"—and then to assert that these texts are valuable on historical grounds.

3. Ann Douglas is the foremost of the feminist critics who have accepted this characterization of the sentimental writers, and it is to her formulation of the anti-sentimentalist position that my arguments throughout are principally addressed (*The Feminization of American Culture* [New York: Alfred A. Knopf, 1977]). Although her attitude toward the vast quantity of literature written by women between 1820 and 1870 is the one that the male-dominated tradition has always expressed—contempt—Douglas's book is nevertheless extremely important because of its powerful and sustained consideration of this long-neglected body of work. Because Douglas successfully focused critical attention on the cultural centrality of sentimental fiction, forcing the realization that it can no longer be ignored, it is now possible for other critics to put forward a new characterization of these novels and not be dismissed. For these reasons, it seems to me, her work is invaluable.

4. These attitudes are forcefully articulated by Douglas, ibid., p. 9.

5. The phrase "a damned mob of scribbling women," coined by Nathaniel Hawthorne in a letter he wrote to his publisher in 1855 and clearly the product of Hawthorne's own feelings of frustration and envy, comes embedded in a much-quoted passage that has set the tone for criticism of sentimental fiction ever since: "America is now wholly given over to a d****d mob of scribbling women, and I should have no chance of success while the public taste is occupied with their trash—and should be ashamed of myself if I did succeed. What is the mystery of these innumerable editions of *The Lamplighter,* and other books neither better nor worse? Worse they could not be, and better they need not be, when they sell by the hundred thousand." As quoted by Fred Lewis Pattee, *The Feminine Fifties* (New York: D. Appleton-Century, 1940), p. 110.

6. J. W. Ward, *Red, White, and Blue: Men, Books, and Ideas in American Culture* (New York: Oxford University Press, 1961), p. 75.

7. George F. Whicher, "Literature and Conflict," in *The Literary History of the United States,* ed. Robert E. Spiller et al., 3rd ed., rev. (New York: Macmillan, 1963), p. 583.

8. Ibid., p. 586. Edmund Wilson, despite his somewhat sympathetic treatment of Stowe in *Patriotic Gore,* seems to concur in this opinion, reflecting a characteristic tendency of commentators on the most popular works of sentimental fiction to regard the success of these women as some sort of mysterious eruption, inexplicable by natural causes (*Patriotic Gore: Studies in the Literature of the American Civil War* [New York: Oxford University Press, 1966], pp. 5, 32). Henry James gives this attitude its most articulate, though perhaps least defensible, expression in a remarkable passage from *A Small Boy and Others* (New York: Charles Scribner's Sons, 1913) where he describes Stowe's book as really not a book at all but "a fish, a wonderful 'leaping' fish"—the point being to deny Stowe any role in the process that produced such a wonder:

> Appreciation and judgment, the whole impression, were thus an effect for which there had been no process—any process so related having in other cases *had* to be at some point or other critical; nothing in the guise of a written book, therefore, a book printed, published, sold, bought and "noticed," probably ever reached its mark, the mark of exciting interest, without having at least groped for that goal *as* a book or by the exposure of some literary side. Letters, here, languished unconscious, and Uncle Tom, instead of making even one of the cheap short cuts through the medium in which books breathe, even as fishes in water, went gaily roundabout it altogether, as if a fish, a wonderful "leaping" fish, had simply flown in through the air. (pp. 159–60)

9. A branch of theology that deals with salvation as the effect of divine agency [*Editor*].

10. Reverend Dwight Lyman Moody, *Sermons and Addresses,* in *Narrative of Messrs. Moody and Sankey's Labors in Great Britain and Ireland with Eleven Addresses and Lectures in Full* (New York: Anson D. F. Randolph, 1875).

11. Harriet Beecher Stowe, "Children," in *Uncle Sam's Emancipation; Earthly Care, a Heavenly Discipline; and other sketches* (Philadelphia: W. P. Hazard, 1853), p. 83.

12. Harriet Beecher Stowe, *Ministration of Departed Spirits* (Boston: American Tract Society, n.d.), pp. 4, 3.

13. Ibid., p. 3.

14. Harriet Beecher Stowe, *Uncle Tom's Cabin; or, Life Among the Lowly* (New York: Harper & Row, 1965), pp. 295–96 [255]. This Harper Classic gives the text of the first edition originally published by John P. Jewett & Company of Boston and Cleveland in 1852. All future references to *Uncle Tom's Cabin* will be to this edition; page numbers are given in parentheses in the text. [Norton Critical Edition page numbers appear in brackets—*Editor*.]

15. Charles Dickens, *Dombey and Son* (Boston: Estes & Lauriat, 1882), p. 278; Lydia H. Sigourney, *Letters to Mothers* (Hartford, Conn.: Hudson & Skinner, 1838).

16. Religious conversion as the basis for a new social order was the mainspring of the Christian evangelical movement of the mid-nineteenth century. The emphasis on "feeling," which seems to modern readers to provide no basis whatever for the organization of society, was the key factor in the evangelical theory of reform. See Sandra Sizer's discussions of this phenomenon in *Gospel Hymns and Social Religion: The Rhetoric of Nineteenth-Century Revivalism* (Philadelphia: Temple University Press, 1979): "It is clear from the available literature that prayer, testimony, and exhortation were employed to create a *community* of intense *feeling,* in which individuals underwent similar experiences (centering on conversion) and would thenceforth unite with others in matters of moral decision and social behavior" (p. 52). "People in similar states of feeling, in short, would 'walk together,' would be agreed" (p. 59). "Conversion established individuals in a particular kind of relationship with God, by virtue of which they were automatically members of a social company, alike in interests and feelings" (pp. 70–71). Good order would be preserved by "relying on the spiritual and moral discipline provided by conversion, and on the company of fellow Christians, operating without the coercive force of government" (p. 72).

17. Angus Fletcher's *Allegory: The Theory of a Symbolic Mode* (Ithaca, N.Y.: Cornell University Press, 1964) discusses the characteristic features of allegory in such a way as to make clear the family resemblance between sentimental fiction and the allegorical mode. See, particularly, his analysis of character (pp. 35, 60), symbolic action (pp. 150 ff., 178, 180, 182), and imagery (p. 171).

18. Fletcher's comment on the presence of naturalistic detail in allegory is pertinent here:

> The apparent surface realism of an allegorical agent will recede in importance, as soon as he is felt to take part in a magical plot, as soon as his causal relations to others in that plot are seen to be magically based. This is an important point because there has often been confusion as to the function of the naturalist detail of so much allegory. In terms I have been outlining, this detail now appears not to have a journalistic function; it is more than a mere record of observed facts. It serves instead the purposes of magical containment, since the more the allegorist can circumscribe the attributes, metonymic and synecdochic, of his personae, the better he can shape their fictional destiny. Naturalist detail is "cosmic," universalizing, not accidental as it would be in straight journalism. (Pp. 198–99)

19. The associations that link slaves, women, and children are ubiquitous and operate on several levels. Besides being described in the same set of terms, these characters occupy parallel structural positions in the plot. They function chiefly as mediators between God and the unredeemed, so that, e.g., Mrs. Shelby intercedes for Mr. Shelby, Mrs. Bird for Senator Bird, Simon Legree's mother (unsuccessfully) for Simon Legree, little Eva and St. Clare's mother for St. Clare, Tom Loker's mother for Tom Loker, Eliza for George Harris (spiritually, she is the agent of his conversion) and for Harry Harris (physically, she saves him from being sold down the river), and Tom for all the slaves on the Legree plantation (spiritually, he converts them) and for all the slaves of the Shelby plantation (physically, he is the cause of their being set free).

20. For a parallel example, see Alice Crozier's analysis of the way the lock of hair that little Eva gives Tom becomes transformed into the lock of hair that Simon Legree's mother sent to Simon Legree. *The Novels of Harriet Beecher Stowe* (New York: Oxford University Press, 1969), pp. 29–31.

21. Sacvan Bercovitch, *The American Jeremiad* (Madison: University of Wisconsin Press, 1978), p. 9.

22. Ibid., p. xi.

23. Ibid., p. xiv.

24. Younger sister of Harriet Beecher Stowe. Hooker (1822–1907) was a radical feminist who was active in campaigns for women's rights and suffrage. She believed that a new millennium was coming in which the world would be ruled by a matriarchy and she would serve as one of the leaders [*Editor*].

25. For an excellent discussion of Beecher's *Treatise* and of the entire cult of domesticity, see Kathryn Kish Sklar, *Catharine Beecher: A Study in American Domesticity*

(New York: W. W. Norton, 1976). For other helpful discussions of the topic, see Barbara G. Berg, *The Remembered Gate: Origins of American Feminism, The Woman and the City, 1800–1860* (New York: Oxford University Press, 1978); Sizer, *Gospel Hymns and Social Religion;* Ronald G. Walters, *The Antislavery Appeal: American Abolitionism after 1830* (Baltimore: Johns Hopkins University Press, 1976); and Barbara Welter, "The Cult of True Womanhood, 1820–1860," *American Quarterly,* 18 (Summer 1966): 151–74.

26. Catharine Beecher and Harriet Beecher Stowe, *The American Woman's Home: or Principles of Domestic Science; Being a Guide to the Formation and Maintenance of Economical, Healthful, Beautiful, and Christian Homes* (New York: J. B. Ford, 1869), p. 18.

27. Ibid., p. 19.

28. Ibid., pp. 458–59.

29. These are Douglas's epithets; see *Feminization of American Culture,* p. 307.

30. For a detailed discussion of the changes referred to here, see Christopher Clark, "Household Economy, Market Exchange, and the Rise of Capitalism in the Connecticut Valley, 1800–1860," *Journal of Social History* 13 (Winter 1979): 169–89, and Nancy F. Cott, *The Bonds of Womanhood: "Woman's Sphere" in New England, 1780–1835* (New Haven, Conn.: Yale University Press, 1977).

31. In a recent article in *Signs,* Mary Kelley characterizes the main positions in the debate over the significance of sentimental fiction as follows: (1) the Cowie-Welter thesis, which holds that women's fiction expresses an "ethics of conformity" and accepts the stereotype of the woman as pious, pure, submissive, and dedicated to the home, and (2) the Papashvily-Garrison thesis; which sees sentimental fiction as profoundly subversive of traditional ideas of male authority and female subservience. Kelley locates herself somewhere in between, holding that sentimental novels convey a "contradictory message": "they tried to project an Edenic image," but their own tales "subverted their intentions" by showing how often women were frustrated and defeated in the performance of their heroic roles. My own position is that the sentimental novelists are both conformist and subversive, but not, as Kelley believes, in a self-contradictory way. They used the central myth of their culture, the story of Christ's death for the sins of mankind, as the basis for a new myth that reflected their own interests. They regarded their vision of the Christian home as God's kingdom on earth as the fulfillment of the Gospel, "the end . . . which Jesus Christ came into this world to secure," in exactly the same way that the Puritans believed their mission was to found the "American city of God," and that Christians believe the New Testament to be a fulfillment of the old. Revolutionary ideologies typically announce themselves as the fulfillment of old promises or as a return to a golden age. What I am suggesting here, in short, is that the argument over whether the sentimental novelists were radical or conservative is a false issue. The real problem is how we, in the light of everything that has happened since they wrote, can understand and appreciate their work. Mary Kelley, "The Sentimentalists: Promise and Betrayal in the Home," *Signs* 4 (Spring

1979): 434–46; Alexander Cowie, "The Vogue of the Domestic Novel, 1850–1870," *South Atlantic Quarterly* 41 (October 1942): 420; Welter, "Cult of True Womanhood," pp. 151–74; Helen Waite Papashvily, *All the Happy Endings: A Study of the Domestic Novel in America, the Women Who Wrote It, the Women Who Read It, in the Nineteenth Century* (New York: Harper & Bros., 1956); Dee Garrison, "Immoral Fiction in the Late Victorian Library," *American Quarterly* 28 (Spring 1976): 71–80.

Getting in the Kitchen with Dinah

Domestic Politics in Uncle Tom's Cabin

GILLIAN BROWN

◆ ◆ ◆

"MORE NOTORIOUS AND UNDENIABLE than any other abuse of the system of slavery," Harriet Beecher Stowe believed, was "its outrage upon the family."[1] Nowhere in *Uncle Tom's Cabin* is this domestic violation so marked as in the careless condition of the Southern kitchen. Dinah's kitchen in Little Eva St. Clare's New Orleans home "looked as if it had been arranged by a hurricane blowing through it."[2] In Dinah's domestic arrangements, "the rolling pin is under the bed and the nutmeg grater in her pocket with her tobacco—there are sixty-five different sugar bowls, one in every hole in the house" (I, 304); she "had about as many places for each cooking utensil as there were days in the year" (I, 297). This promiscuous housekeeping scandalizes the St. Clares' Northern cousin Ophelia, offending her domestic propriety as much as slavery disturbs her moral sense. Ophelia finds that Southerners not only neglect their "awful responsibility" for the souls of their slaves but also let their households operate "without any sort of calculation to time and place" (I, 255, 297). In Ophelia's New England home "the old kitchen floor never seems stained or spotted; the tables, chairs, and the various cooking utensils never seem deranged or disordered" (I, 227). There, "everything is once and forever rigidly in place" (I, 226).

In a vain attempt to remodel Dinah's kitchen in the New England style, Augustine St. Clare once installed "an array of cupboards, drawers, and various apparatus, to induce systematic regulation" (I, 298). Yet after discovering that "[t]he more drawers and closets there were, the more hiding-holes could Dinah make for the accommodation of old rags, hair-combs, old shoes, ribbons, cast-off artificial flowers, and other articles," St. Clare has washed his hands of kitchen affairs (I, 298–99). As long as he need not view "the hurryscurryation of the preparatory process," he can enjoy Dinah's "glorious dinners" and "superb coffee." Dinah, St. Clare advises Ophelia, should be judged "as warriors and statesmen are judged, by her success." For St. Clare, the vital point is that "Dinah gets you a capital dinner" (I, 304). Just as he represses the unsavory aspects of his domestic economy, St. Clare prefers to ignore the problems of the state Dinah represents. Worrying about the evils of slavery, he warns Ophelia, is "like looking too close into the details of Dinah's kitchen" (II, 8).

Yet Ophelia cannot disregard slavery any more than she can dismiss kitchen details. As she tells St. Clare, "You would not take it so coolly if you were housekeeper" (I, 303). Although he rhetorically asserts the correspondence between Dinah's kitchen and the slave economy, St. Clare fails to recognize the intimacy between domestic and political issues, missing the lesson of his own effort at home improvement. He could not alter Dinah's kitchen because "[n]o Puseyite, or conservative of any school, was ever more inflexibly attached to time-honored inconvenience than Dinah." The time-honored inconvenience to which Dinah is attached is not merely backward kitchen technology, but the political economy that enslaves her. Her habits manifest less her eccentricities than "the spirit of the system under which she had grown up"; Dinah simply "carried it out to its fullest extent" (I, 298). Neither redecorating Dinah's kitchen nor keeping it out of sight can satisfy good housekeeping standards, because kitchen problems cannot be remedied without reference to the system the kitchen articulates in its modes of household production. Housekeepers like Ophelia, whose business is knowing the causes and cures of domestic disorder, understand the political nature of Dinah's housekeeping and therefore recognize the political connection between Dinah's kitchen and slavery. Since kitchens both provide for families and display the systems of political economy with which domestic economy intersects, the responsible housekeeper observes the significance of kitchen things and seeks the best governing system for an orderly domesticity.[3]

What makes Dinah's imperious and "erratic" kitchen government incompatible with proper domestic economy is its reference to her desire rather than to a "systematic order" (I, 295–96). Dinah's kitchen runs by whim, its condition varying with her "irregular" moods (I, 302), which "reigned supreme" (I, 296).

Though usually "studious of ease in all her arrangements" (I, 297), "she had, at irregular periods, paroxysms of reformation." Yet even these occasional reformatory "clarin' up times" (I, 302) can achieve no better domestic order than Dinah's laziness produces; her diligent as well as her dilatory phases enact a capricious personal economy instead of the "systematic pattern" necessary to Ophelia's efficient domestic economy (I, 303). Indeed, the variable state of Dinah's kitchen exhibits the antithesis of domestic economy—the fluctuating marketplace. The reign of desires without "logic and reason" other than personal interest (I, 296), and the uncertainty it creates, characterize the market economy from which nineteenth-century domestic economy distinguished itself. Exponents of domesticity defined the home as a peaceful order in contrast to the disorder and fluctuations occasioned by competitive economic activity in the marketplace. "Our men are sufficiently money-making," Sarah Josepha Hale advised readers of the *Ladies' Magazine*. "Let us keep our women and children from the contagion as long as possible."[4] The contagion of the market has already entered the Southern home where Ophelia finds desire and disorder—the impetus and pulse of the marketplace—in the kitchen.[5]

Slavery disregards this opposition between the family at home and the exterior workplace. The distinction between work and family is eradicated in the slave, for whom there is no separation between economic and private status. When people themselves are "articles" subject to "mercantile dealings," when "the souls and bodies of men" are "equivalent to money" (II, 317), women can no longer keep houses that provide refuge from marketplace activities. Slavery, according to *Uncle Tom's Cabin*, undermines women's housework by bringing the confusion of the marketplace into the center of the family shelter, into the kitchen. The real horror that slavery holds for the "mothers of America" to whom Stowe addressed her antislavery appeal is the suggestion that the family life nurtured by women is not immune from the economic life outside it (II, 316).[6]

More than the tragedy of the slave mothers who "are constantly made childless by the American slave trade" (II, 316), the security of free white American mothers and the family institution they guard concerns Stowe. While the slave economy doesn't threaten American mothers with selling their children, it does limit their authority and efficacy when it creates households with "no time, no place, no order" (I, 304). In a home governed by Ophelia's exemplary New England domestic economy there is "nothing lost, or out of order; not a picket loose in the fence, not a particle of litter in the turfy yard." Instead of hurryscurryation, "the air of order and stillness, of perpetuity and unchanging repose" characterizes the model American home (I, 226). The Southern slave system produces what Ophelia terms "shiftlessness," haphazard "modes of procedure which had not a direct and inevitable relation to the accomplishment of some purpose." Dinah's shiftlessness, because indifferent to the carefulness and regulation necessary to the integrity of the home, appears "the sum of all evils" (I, 229).

In fashioning her abolitionist protest as a defense of nineteenth-century domestic values, Stowe designates slavery as a domestic issue for American women to adjudicate and manage. The call to the mothers of America for the abolition of slavery is a summons to fortify the home, to rescue domesticity from shiftlessness and slavery. Someone has to get in the kitchen with Dinah to eliminate hurryscurryation. The chaos in Dinah's kitchen signifies the immanence of the dissolution of domesticity's difference from the marketplace. Hence abolishing slavery means, in Stowe's politics of the kitchen, erasing the sign and reminder of the precariousness of the feminine sphere.

To read *Uncle Tom's Cabin* as Stowe's manifesto for family integrity is, of course, no twentieth-century innovation. Ever since George Sand noted in her 1852 review that "this book is essentially domestic and of the family," readers of *Uncle Tom's Cabin,* especially feminist readers, have continually noticed the novel's politicization of domesticity. In her history of literary women, Ellen Moers reinforced this reading tradition, recognizing Stowe's antislavery appeal as "proudly and openly a woman's work" on behalf of "domestic polity." "Surely no other woman writer," Moers declared, "has ever recorded the rattle and clutter of domestic life . . . with such confidence that upon these female matters rested the central moral issue before the nation: slavery."[7]

Subsequent feminist responses to *Uncle Tom's Cabin* vary in their confidence as to whether the political reform of slavery could be established upon domestic principles. Ann Douglas believes *Uncle Tom's Cabin* invokes the sentimental virtues of the home which, in her view, "provided the inevitable rationalization of the economic order." The novel therefore "in no way hinders" the system of slavery it protests. Countering Douglas's characterization of popular sentimental literature as women's "dirty work" for the advancement of industrial capitalism, Jane Tompkins emphasizes sentimental literature's feminist critique and revision of American society. According to Tompkins, "the popular domestic novel of the nineteenth century represents a monumental effort to reorganize culture from woman's point of view," and "of these efforts *Uncle Tom's Cabin* is the most dazzling exemplar."[8] The domestic values celebrated by *Uncle Tom's Cabin* and popular domestic novels represent an alternative, moral, feminine organization of life which could radically reform American society.

Tompkins's account of sentimental power offers an important reevaluation of sentimentalism, reinstating the polemical force and literary merit of the novel that Douglas dismisses. Yet Tompkins's argument for *Uncle Tom's Cabin's* literary value as a "political enterprise" overlooks the fact that Stowe's polemic for a regenerating domesticity is a critique of conventional domestic ideology as well as an attack on slavery and the marketplace.[9] What makes *Uncle Tom's Cabin* a particularly striking domestic novel is that Stowe seeks to reform American society not by employing domestic values but by reforming them. The domestic ideology from which *Uncle Tom's Cabin* derives its reformative force, is, when understood historically, a patriarchal institution. The novel addresses this relation between patriarchy and sentimental ideals by explicitly thematizing the intimacy and congress between economic and domestic endeavors, between market and kitchen systems. Therefore, the domesticity Stowe advocates must be understood as a revision and purification of popular domestic values—domestic values that Stowe regards as complicit with the patriarchal institution of slavery. Stowe's domestic solution to slavery, then, represents not the strength of sentimental values but a utopian rehabilitation of them, necessitated by their fundamental complicity with the market to which they are ostensibly opposed.

The association of *Uncle Tom's Cabin* with the cult of domesticity is thus a more complicated one than feminist interpretations have yet suggested. Stowe's critique of American society is even more radical than Tompkins realizes, precisely because it addresses the problematic status of sentimental values noted by Douglas, domestic ideology's "continuation of male hegemony in different guises."[10] In the chronology of Stowe's abolitionist argument, the alliance between domestic and market values necessitates and occasions *Uncle Tom's Cabin*'s revisionary politics. Because sentimental power is undermined by the fact that it incorporates the values it purports to supersede, Stowe calls for the reform of kitchens as a precondition to women's reform of market economy.

"A LIVING IMPERSONATION of order, method, and exactness" (I, 229), Ophelia embodies the ideal domestic economy delineated by Stowe's older sister Catharine Beecher in her popular 1841 *Treatise of Domestic Economy*.[11] Ophelia's service to "systematic regulation" (I, 304) exemplifies Beecher's dictum that "there is no one thing more necessary to a housekeeper, in performing her varied duties, than *a habit of system and order*" (*Treatise*, 144). If Ophelia is, as Stowe describes her, "the absolute bond-slave of 'ought'" (I, 230), her mistress is Beecher and her housekeeping ethics derive from Beecher's systematic domestic economy. Under the slave economy's "shiftless management," Dinah "washes dishes with a dinner napkin one day and a fragment of an old petticoat the next" (I, 304). Beecher's advice on the care of kitchens specifies what materials Dinah should use:

> Keep a supply of *nice* dishcloths hanging near the sink, hemmed and furnished with loops. There should be one for dishes that are not greasy,

one for greasy dishes, and one for pots and kettles. These should all be put in the wash every washing day.

Furthermore,

> Under the sink should be kept a slop-pail, and on a shelf, close by, should be placed two water-pails, one for hard and one for soft water. A large kettle of warm soft water should always be kept over the fire, and a hearth-broom and bellows be hung beside the fireplace. A clock, in or near the kitchen, is very important, to secure regularity in family arrangements (*Treatise*, 367).

Beecher regards women's responsibility for "regularity in family arrangements" as a patriotic and religious duty. By performing their household tasks, or, in Beecher's political terms, sustaining "a prosperous domestic state," women become agents in accomplishing "the greatest work that was ever committed to human responsibility"—"the building of a glorious temple, whose base shall be co-extensive with the bounds of the earth, whose summit shall pierce the skies, whose splendor shall beam on all lands . . ." (*Treatise*, 14). To Americans "is committed the grand, the responsible privilege, of exhibiting to the world, the beneficent influences of Christianity, when carried into every social, civil, and political institution"; and "then to American women, more than any others on earth, is committed the exalted privilege of extending over the world those blessed influences, that are to renovate degraded man, and clothe all climes with beauty" (*Treatise*, 12–13).

The manifest destiny of American women to domesticate and Christianize the world can be realized through the work they perform in their homes. Uniformity and neatness in the kitchen matter profoundly, since these habits create a standard of harmony for America. For Beecher, good housekeeping is a political practice and the home a model political province. Through maternal functions, the boundaries of the domestic province expand to encompass the nation. As mothers, women determine the characters "of the mass of people" upon whom "the success of democratic institutions" depends. "The mother writes the character of the future man; the sister bends the fibres that hereafter are the forest trees; the wife sways the heart whose energies may turn for good or evil the destinies of a nation" (*Treatise*, 13). Maternal influence travels with every individual, and in America, where individuals moved often and extensively, socially and geographically, maternal power held a limitless domain.

Stowe includes the Southern states in the limitless domain of mothers and housekeepers, for "[S]outh as well as north, there are women who have an extraordinary talent for command, and tact in educating" (I, 295). She imagines a Southern domestic order in keeping with Beecher's household economy in the Shelby Kentucky plantation. Mrs. Shelby belongs to the superior class of housekeepers Beecher envisions. Such women "are enabled with apparent ease . . . to produce a harmonious and orderly system." If such housekeepers "are not common at the South, it is because they are not common in the world" (I, 295). The Kentucky home seems a standard of domestic excellence; it becomes both the memory of home Uncle Tom cherishes and an edenic image. In front of Tom's cabin on the Shelby plantation "a neat garden patch" with "strawberries, raspberries, and a variety of fruits and vegetables, flourished under careful tending." The garden enveloped the cabin; its begonias and roses "entwisting and interlacing, left scarce a vestige of the rough logs to be seen" (I, 38).

Slavery, the snake in the garden, compromises this edenic home. Topsy, during her religious instruction from Ophelia, inquires if "dat state" our first parents "fell out of" was "Kintuck" where "we came down from" (II, 51). Topsy's ironic confusion of words and origins emphasizes the conditionality of the happy system of the Shelby housekeeping. Kentucky is lost, not just to Tom, but to domesticity, because the slave economy always subjects the home and family to market contingencies. Although Tom's wife Chloe, the Shelby plantation cook, "was a trained and methodical one, who moved in orderly domestic harness," in the best Beecher tradition, neither her "anxious interest" in kitchen preparations nor Mrs. Shelby's tactful supervision can prevent the sale of Tom (I, 296). Even the order of the best housekeeper is precarious in the slave economy; the "kindest owner" is subject to "failure, misfortune, or imprudence, or death" (I, 24). When Mr. Shelby needs to make mortgage payments, he sells Tom along with Eliza's son Harry. This failure of domestic practices to sustain both black family unity and the white mistress's authority points not only to the slave economy's disregard of domestic values but to domesticity's dependence on the whims of whatever economic practice it adjoins.

Beecher explicitly sought the conjunction of domestic economy with American economic advancement that so worries Stowe in *Uncle Tom's Cabin.* Their brother, Henry Ward Beecher, preached that "The spirit of our people, and, I think, God may say *the public spirit of the world,* is for ameliorization, and expansion and social change."[12] Catharine perceived that social change included negative as well as positive effects, noting that "Persons in poverty, are rising to opulence, and persons of wealth, are sinking to poverty" (*Treatise,* 16).

As Henry proffered a religious rationale to his upwardly mobile Brooklyn parishioners, Catharine advanced an ideology of womanhood that also matched the expanding economy and changing fortunes of individuals.[13] For her definition of women's role in America, she appropriated Tocqueville's observation that "American women support these vicissitudes with a calm and unquenchable energy" (*Treatise*, 23). In a country where "Everything is moving and changing," the virtue of women is their ability to harmonize with fluctuations; as Beecher again cites Tocqueville, "It would seem their desires contract, as easily as they expand" with the changing fortunes of their husbands (*Treatise*, 23). Because women's desires always mirror the effects of masculine desires—they expand with economic gains and contract with economic losses—women embody a model of stability achieved through complete self-denial. In Beecher's domestic economy, women's exemplary self-denial perfectly complements the economy in which their men work.[14]

Stowe's portrait of an old Kentucky home discloses the problem with this complementary alliance: the very market conditions Beecher's domestic economy supports can render domestic efforts irrelevant. If good housekeeping under slavery protects the home only so long as market circumstances permit, then domesticity's influence in Northern capitalist society is likewise limited. As long as the marketplace, of which the slave trade is the worst version, exists, the domestic sphere remains vulnerable. Stowe's worry about the dangers of capitalism to family values echoes slavery advocate George Fitzhugh's belief that "The Family is threatened, and all men North or South who love and revere it, should be up and a-doing."[15] In the minds of slavery apologists, the North failed in its parental responsibility for its wage laborers; slave labor power offered a more truly familial and stable society than the diffuse, precarious lifestyle produced by the money power of Northern capitalism. Slave power signified to abolitionists similarly chaotic, undisciplined living conditions. Slave masters like Simon Legree exemplified the extremes of capitalistic masculine self-advancement when not domesticated and regulated in a wage-labor system. Stowe, anxious about the dehumanization she discerned in both systems, originally subtitled her novel "The Man That Was a Thing."[16]

Yet *Uncle Tom's Cabin*'s critique of antebellum America also questions what the slavery debate took for granted: the character of domesticity. Nineteenth-century advocates of domestic values assumed the integrity of the family state, believing the home inviolate from the marketplace.[17] Indeed, the home was to reform the marketplace; as Beecher put it, the purpose of women's housework was "to be made effectual in the regeneration of the Earth" (*Treatise*, 14). The rhetoric of feminine difference and spiritual mission in which Beecher presented her domestic economy concealed the cooperative, accommodating function of domesticity revealed by Stowe in the insufficiency of the Shelby housekeeping. Domesticity's applicability to both slave and capitalist economies causes Stowe uneasiness about the virtues of domesticity as a replacement economy. Domesticity itself requires reformation.

The ultimate adversary to mothers and housekeepers is not slavery, not even capitalism, but the masculine sphere of the marketplace. The most effective way to save the home from the marketplace, to prevent domesticity from consorting with either slave power or money power, is to abolish the marketplace altogether. In the name of domesticity, *Uncle Tom's Cabin* attacks not only the patriarchal institution, but nineteenth-century patriarchy: not only slave traders, but the system and men that maintain "the one great market" upon which trade depends (I, 109).

While Stowe recognized the power for women in the alliance her sister forged, she also perceived the limits of women's power in a patriarchal domesticity; she sought a more radical and extensive power to be obtained through the replacement of the market economy by a matriarchal domestic economy.[18] *Uncle Tom's Cabin* revises Beecher's domesticity, disjoining it from patriarchal economic practices and severing it from service to any institution other than itself. Instead of ensuring industrial capitalism and supporting the government that passed the Fugitive Slave Law, the domestic might constitute an alternative system: an economy of abundant mother-love built on an excess of supply rather than the excess of demand and desire upon which both the slave economy and Northern capitalism operated. *Uncle Tom's Cabin* perfects and ensures domesticity in matriarchy. Mothers and mother figures initiate escapes from slavery and determine family safety. As domesticity becomes Stowe's feminist deployment of nineteenth-century femininity, housekeeping in *Uncle Tom's Cabin* becomes not merely politically significant, but a political mode: not representative of any economic order, but itself an economic order.

THE IDEAL KITCHEN in *Uncle Tom's Cabin* functions smoothly under the aegis of "motherly loving kindness" (I, 196). Rachel Halliday's kitchen in the Indiana Quaker settlement that shelters runaway slaves, is, like Ophelia's, "without a particle of dust"; but more than orderliness, its "rows of shining tins, suggestive of unmentionable good things to the appetite" indicate the value of abundance and generosity in Stowe's utopian domestic economy (I, 195). Ophelia, Stowe explains in her *Key to Uncle Tom's Cabin,* despite her "activity, zeal, unflinching conscientiousness, clear intellectual discriminations between truth and error, and great logical and doctrinal correctness," "represents one great sin": the lack of the Christian "spirit of love."[19] Rachel embodies and dispenses that spirit of love, "diffusing a sort of sunny radiance" over meal preparations

(I, 204). Making breakfast under Rachel's supervision is "like picking up the rose-leaves and trimming the bushes in Paradise," a vision of perfect, happy labor (I, 204). "There was so much motherliness and full-heartedness even in the way she passed a plate of cakes or poured a cup of coffee, that it seemed to put a spirit into the food and drink she offered" (I, 205). Rachel's domestic acts appear sacramental, her meals a communion reminiscent of edenic unity.

> Everything went on so sociably, so quietly, so harmoniously, in the great kitchen,—it seemed so pleasant to everyone to do just what they were doing, there was such an atmosphere of mutual confidence and good-fellowship everywhere,—even the knives and forks had a social clatter as they went on the table; and the chicken and ham had a cheerful and joyous fizzle in the pan, as if they enjoyed being cooked . . . (I, 205).

The spirit of mother-love creates a domesticity in the image of paradise: a world before separations, a domestic economy before markets.

Eliza, Harry, and George Harris, the runaway slaves reunited in the Halliday sentimental utopia, discover that "This, indeed, was a home,—*home*—a word that [they] had never yet known a meaning for" (I, 205). Rachel's "simple, overflowing kindness" defines the perfect home, and that kindness includes helping runaway slaves. This defiance of the Fugitive Slave Law demonstrates the Quaker community's commitment to God's love and familial feeling over man's law. In Rachel's kitchen, the boys and girls share domestic duties under their mother's guidance while their father engages in "the anti-patriarchal operation of shaving" (I, 205). Godlike mothers generate and rule this family state with their love. In Stowe's model home, domesticity is matriarchal and antinomian, a new form of government as well as a protest against patriarchy and its manifestations in slavery, capitalism, and democracy. Her domestic advice carries an addendum to the household practices Beecher assigned to women: the duty of women to oppose slavery and the law that upholds it. "It's a shameful, wicked, abominable law," Mrs. Bird, another concerned house-keeper in *Uncle Tom's Cabin,* tells her senator husband, "and I shall break it, the first time I get a chance" (I, 121). She gets her chance when Eliza collapses in the Bird kitchen after her escape from Kentucky across the frozen Ohio River. *Uncle Tom's Cabin* politicizes women's domestic role at the very moment of sentimentalizing that role, urging women to stop slavery in the name of love. Love and protest, maternal duty and political action, compose Stowe's reformulated domestic virtue.

According to domestic logic, women were naturally suited to participate in the antislavery movement. As Stowe wrote in her "Appeal to the Women

of the Free States of America on the Present Crisis in Our Country," "God has given to women a deeper and more immovable knowledge in those holier feelings which are peculiar to womanhood, and which guard the family state."[20] The public practice of this moral gift would seem to follow inevitably from Beecher's assumption of women's moral role in democracy. Yet Beecher, though opposed to slavery, could not support women's participation in political agitation. In her "Essay on Slavery and Abolition with Respect to the Duties of American Females," she argues that the abolition movement draws women away from the noncombative sphere designed for them in "the Divine Economy." Instead, women are "to win everything by peace and love . . . this is all to be accomplished in the domestic and social circle." "In this country, petitions to Congress . . . fall entirely without the sphere of female duty."[21] Women's political activism would be a fall from domestic purity, and hence from domestic power and its superior political influence through self-subordination and moral exemplification. While Beecher could never condone slavery, she also could never depart from patriarchal law in order to abolish a paternalistic institution.

Abolitionists and domestic feminists were quick to grasp the inconsistency of an ideology of feminine virtue that precluded the actual exercise of that virtue. In reply to Beecher, Quaker activist Angelina Grimké published a series of public letters in which she objected that Beecher's injunction to women to abide by the law and to stay within their own sphere meant "*Obeying man* rather than God." If women do not voice their opinions to their representatives in Congress, "they are mere slaves known only through their masters."[22] Grimké here interpreted the passivity of women in politics as slavery; in another pamphlet, "An Appeal to the Christian Women in the South," she accorded Southern women a familial responsibility for the abolition of slavery. Women "do not make the laws," but they "are the wives and mothers, sisters and daughters of those who do."[23] Angelina's older sister Sarah put the case more strongly: the Southern white woman who lives daily with the slave system suffers moral contamination by witnessing the continual violation of her black sisters. "Can any American woman look at these scenes of shocking licentiousness and cruelty, and fold her hands in apathy, and say 'I have nothing to do with slavery'? *She cannot and be guiltless.*"[24] The passive, apathetic woman was both a slave and a slave mistress, degraded and degrading. In the Grimkés' analysis, Southern domesticity not only failed to create a peaceful home environment but lowered the status of white women.[25] From this realization followed their rejection of the domestic sphere's limits and their commitment to women's rights.[26]

Contemporary activist women like Elizabeth Cady Stanton and Susan B. Anthony also discerned the bonds of patriarchal domesticity in the

patriarchal institution and thus defined abolition as a feminist cause. After the Civil War, Stanton supervised the rewriting of the Bible from women's point of view in order to counter the Christian domestic tradition of encouraging women's self-sacrifice and obedience to patriarchal authority. Stanton regularly introduced anti-Bible resolutions at suffrage conventions, prompting former slave Frederick Douglass on one occasion to defend self-sacrifice. Feminist Lucy Coleman immediately addressed the discrepancy between self-denial and the quest for freedom: "Well, Mr. Douglass, all you say may be true; but allow me to ask you why you did not remain a slave in Maryland, and sacrifice yourself like a Christian for your Master, instead or running off to Canada to secure your liberty like a man."[27]

While Stowe also propounds the feminist-abolitionist critique of domesticity and slavery, she does not reject Christian self-sacrifice as an effective reformist mode. Because Stowe regards self-denial as political, she celebrates in the deaths of Little Eva and Uncle Tom the very self-abnegation Stanton and Coleman denounce. In her own biblical commentary, *Women in Sacred History* (1874), Stowe praises "that pure ideal of a sacred woman springing from the bosom of the family, at once wife, mother, poetess, leader, inspirer, prophetess. . . ."[28] This notion of femininity as maternal, literary, political, and mystical, conjoins domestic and feminist values, incorporating both self-denial and self-assertion in the ideal woman. *Uncle Tom's Cabin* retains the Christian domestic tenet of feminine self-abnegation in order to elaborate a maternal power commensurate to the task of abolishing slavery. The novel presents Beecher's triad of maternal virtues in specifically Christian terms: self-denial as martyrdom, exemplification as typology, household unity as eternal life. Little Eva is saintlike, Uncle Tom is Christlike; homes are heavenly and family reunions are eschatological. This religious interpretation of ideal maternal practices merges motherhood with Christianity. The self-sacrifice of women, or slaves, then, signifies redemption and eternal life. *Uncle Tom's Cabin* allies this conventional feminine mode with the civil disobedience of Rachel and Mrs. Bird and the dramatic escapes from slavery, first by Eliza, and then Cassy, which comprise the activist female model Stowe proposes. For Stowe, domestic self-denial and feminist self-seeking can be complementary modes. The debate between Beecher and the Grimkés that Coleman and Douglass rehearsed is irrevelant to Stowe because maternal power manifests itself in both sacrifice and rebellion, temporality and eternity.

Domestic conventions in Stowe's abolitionism work in two directions, simultaneously pointing to the sentimental solution of the afterlife in heaven and to a radical plan of immediate action to secure better temporal conditions. Tom and Eva die in set pieces that memorialize their Christian virtues;

Eliza, Harry, George, and Cassy rebel and escape to Canada in a dramatic and often melodramatic narrative that affirms the necessity of active protest. Stowe's application of sentimental and feminist modes of belief and practice demonstrates the contradictory position in which domesticity places women by regarding them simultaneously as the embodiment of transcendent principles and as the primary support of the social fabric. She resolves this contradiction by interpreting the identification of femininity with ideal values as women's access to critical, subversive stances. Feminine virtue engenders the feminine vantage on social revision. Mrs. Bird's maternal feelings motivate and justify her critique of slavery and the laws that bolster it. The realization of the potential power of motherhood and the arrival of woman as a revisionary social critic—as "mother, poetess, leader, inspirer, prophetess"—depends upon the full exercise of what Stowe called women's faculty. Faculty, Stowe explains in her fictional portrait of Catharine Beecher in *The Minister's Wooing,* is the New England term for *savoir-faire* and refers specifically to domestic economy and household talents. "To her who has faculty, nothing shall be impossible."[29]

Stowe assumes the role her sister prescribed in order to politicize her readers. *Uncle Tom's Cabin* urges a departure from the passivity assigned women by culture, a departure that is also a return home, to the ideal matriarchal home. The book's household angel, Eva, dies and returns to heaven. Killing the Angel in the House means for Stowe the apotheosis of the angelic, domestic tradition of femininity: both the finish of patriarchal domesticity and the ascension of maternal power. Virginia Woolf's observation on the need of women writers to destroy the images and characteristics of domestic femininity foisted upon them by social tradition becomes inverted here to signify a literary act empowered by, and empowering, domesticity. Stowe's domestic feminism reconstructs the family, retaining the Angel in the House and revising history under her aegis. Abolition in *Uncle Tom's Cabin* is accordingly conveyed and understood through mothers.

Mrs. Shelby, upon learning of her husband's sale of Tom and Harry, immediately perceives the violation of her domestic values; after teaching her slaves "the duties of the family," she wonders how she can "bear to have this open acknowledgement that we care for no tie, no duty, no relation, however sacred, compared with money" (I, 57). When Mr. Shelby admonishes her for feeling "too much" about their slaves, Mrs. Shelby asserts the predominance of the emotions of the heart over the masculine economics of the mind: "Feel too much! Am I not a woman,—a mother?" (I, 110). Her sentiments echo the thought of an 1836 antislavery speech that declared abolitionism an inherent

maternal trait. "A woman not an abolitionist! No. This truth has a lodgement in the heart of every female that understands it, and deserves the name of a mother and a wife."[30] Shelby exasperatedly notes that his wife is "getting to be an abolitionist" (I, 58). He respects her "piety and benevolence," and even indulges "a shadowy expectation of getting into heaven through her superabundance of qualities" (I, 26), but insists that she doesn't "understand business;—women never do and never can" (II, 54). She cannot help him economize because "there's no trimming and squaring" his business affairs as if they were "pie crusts" (II, 54). Consistent with Shelby's disregard of domestic ideals, the state of his business is, like Dinah's kitchen, "all scamper and hurry-scurry" (II, 54).

In place of this chaotic, hurry-scurry, masculine economy in which slaves are sold to pay their master's debts, Stowe urges the "harmonious and systematic order" (I, 295) created by Mrs. Shelby's "high moral and religious sensibility and principle" (I, 26). Women offer a preserving rather than desiring version of economics, family protection rather than ventures endangering family stability. Ophelia, with the efficiency and diligence typical of her housekeeping, demands a legal deed for her possession of Topsy so that she can "save her from all the chances and reverses of slavery" (II, 137). Stowe's domesticity, then, ideally functions as an alternative to the slave-holding economy, not as a congruent, affirmative practice, but as a different ethic of possession.

Stowe's rejection of the masculine political economy finds its most explicit and emphatic expression in George Harris's renunciation of America and filial duty to its laws: "I haven't any country, any more than I have a father." When commanded by his master to forget his marriage to Eliza and to cohabit with another slave woman, George runs away to Canada "where the laws will own . . . and protect" him (I, 167). He wants the familial structure he has been denied since childhood, the company of the mother and sisters from whom he was separated. Despising the values of his white male ancestry, George chooses the feminine economy of mother-love: "My sympathies are not for my father's race, but for my mother's. To him I was no more than a fine dog or horse: to my poor heart-broken mother I was a *child*" (II, 299–300). To defend the familial relation, the rights of women as it were, George seeks another country.

George's final decision to emigrate with his reunited family to Liberia bespeaks the hope that blacks might form a republic and nationality of their own, and restates the ideals of the American family. Like women, blacks are "affectionate, magnanimous, and forgiving" (II, 302). The "mission" of the new republic of freed slaves is, like domesticity, "essentially a Christian one": "to spread over the continent of Africa" the "sublime doctrine of love and

forgiveness" (II, 302–3). While the emigration of American blacks might suggest a convenient solution to white fears about the possible retribution of freed blacks, Stowe's imagination of "this new enterprise" articulates less about fears of blacks than about fear of men (II, 301). Stowe's transplantation of heroic blacks like George and Eliza to Liberia colonizes Africa for domesticity. American men have no part in this enterprise. To feminize the world, Stowe banishes from the future all men of business such as Shelby and Legree and the slave traders. In Stowe's utopian world after slavery and markets, the men who live or who are well remembered, support domestic values.[31] The Shelby son frees his slaves to save them from "the risk of being parted from home" (II, 309); Uncle Tom preaches Christian virtues; George Harris restores his family. The removal of masculine economic desire through the disappearance of slave masters is the necessary condition for the ascendance of domestic economy.

Stowe's domestic economy interprets the Beecher tenet of self-denial as women's independence from desire and from their mirroring function for masculine desire. Domesticity imbues femininity with the "superabundance of qualities" Mrs. Shelby exhibits in her benevolence. This feminine virtue forms the foundation of a feminine economy that redefines the notion of possession. Women's plenitude obviates desire. The celebrated stillness of nineteenth-century women is thus neither a hysterical renunciation of life in order to register complaint against women's prescribed role in society, nor a historical condition summarizing the effect of women's exclusion from executive power in their society, but an annunciation of women's self-sufficiency and a claim to their immunity from desire.[32] The lack of desire reflects the imagined state of possession, that is, the condition of satiety and fulfillment, the goal of the pursuit of happiness. The nondesiring woman is therefore the embodiment of perfect ownership. In her self-sufficiency, she escapes the fluctuations attendant upon desire and achieves the ideal of the masculine economy: complete self-possession and satisfaction. In Stowe's domestic logic of possession, it becomes possible to own without having desired.

Stowe's divorce of desire from possession mitigates against conditions of insufficiency or incompletion. She perfects ownership by nullifying desire, the sign of ownership's temporality. Process and its disorders disappear in the best of New England kitchens where "nothing ever seems to be doing or going to be done." "In some silent and mysterious manner" "the family washing and ironing is there performed" and "pounds of butter and cheese there brought into existence" (I, 226–27). In the edenic order and abundance of Rachel's kitchen, "the work of getting breakfast" is so "cheerful" and harmonious that domestic labor already represents the stillness and satiety to which it is directed.

Stowe replaces the master-slave relation with the benign proprietorship of mother to child, transferring the ownership of slaves to the mothers of America. Women prefer familial ties to market relations, caring for the welfare of their dependents—children and slaves—rather than for the profits wrought from them. Slaves are synonymous with children in Stowe's matriarchal society because they lack title to themselves and need abolitionist guardianship, which is to say, maternal aid. Maternal supervision, the ideal form of owning in Stowe's reformed property relations, follows the pattern of divine care. "One good, loving woman" like Rachel can solve "difficulties spiritual and temporal" just as God's superabundant love fills the needs of humanity (I, 197). Uncle Tom wants not emancipation but this protective ownership: "the Lord's bought me and is going to take me home,—and I long to go. Heaven is better than Kintuck" (II, 280). By imitating God's parental economy, mothers approximate heaven in their homes.

Stowe's identification of maternal power with God in her model of domestic economy rejects any aspiration to ownership beyond the motherly functions of reproduction and preservation, suggesting an economy without markets and a life devoid of the problems caused by masculine desire. She fittingly situates this utopian life in heaven, the home to which Tom and Eva happily return. Tom dies uttering his longing to go home to heaven where there is "nothing *but* love!" (II, 281). The child Eva also experiences intimations of immortality as domestic bliss; she has visions of heaven's landscape and she knows she is going home to "our Saviour's home" (II, 88). Eva's father's death, entitled "Reunion," likewise brings him home; "Just before the spirit parted, he opened his eyes, with a sudden light, as of joy and recognition, and said '*Mother*' and then he was gone!" (II, 143). Eliza, just before reuniting with her husband, dreams of a heaven-like place, "a beautiful country, a land, it seemed to her, of rest, . . . and there, in a house kind voices told her was a home, she saw her boy playing, a free and happy child" (I, 203–4). She awakes in the next best place to heaven, Rachel's home. *Uncle Tom's Cabin*'s designation of heaven as home implies a return to maternal bonds; this also infers a mother God even though Stowe retains the traditional name of God the father.

Death, or some form of escape, enables homecomings and family reunions. As much as divine love and maternal care, death generates the domestic economy that maintains family unity. Eva's death epitomizes loving self-sacrifice for the family. As she tells Tom, she is "glad to die" to "stop all this misery" of slavery (II, 88). She exemplifies her father's observation that "Your child is your only true democrat" (I, 257), and the popular theme in antislavery literature that "Children are all born abolitionists."[33] Named for St. Clare's saintly

mother, Evangeline, Eva emblemizes the virtues of motherhood as well as those of childhood. Indeed, Eva is the child who is mother to the woman, Stowe's ideal of feminine potential, an angel. Ophelia realizes that Eva "might teach [her] a lesson" in loving Topsy (II, 95). Tom recognizes Eva as "one of the angels stepped out of his New Testament" (I, 213). The domestic pieties popularized by Beecher and domestic novelists culminate in Eva's redemptive death for the sins of slavery.[34]

In Stowe's abolitionist employment of sentimental motifs, death re-creates the family by sheltering it in heavenly matriarchy. Families in *Uncle Tom's Cabin* begin not in the transmission of paternal traditions but in the separation from patriarchal origin. Mothers, or God, heal the rupture; they restore and reconstitute the family away from the fallen world. Dying, therefore, becomes the ultimate domestic act in this book of many domestic activities. Such detemporalization of slavery and femininity seems to ignore or sentimentalize the problem of social injustice by opting for the rewards of the next world; however, Stowe returns from the myth of heaven to the myth of Sisyphus, to the problem of human efforts.

THE LANDSCAPE of Simon Legree's plantation, the last Southern residence Stowe describes, seems more foreign and fantastic than heaven because it is completely nondomestic, unkempt, and ungoverned.

> What was once a smooth-shaven lawn before the house, dotted here and there with ornamental shrubs, was now covered with frowsy tangled grass . . . littered with broken pails, cobs of corn, and other slovenly remains. . . . What was once a large garden was now all grown over with weeds, through which, here and there, some solitary exotic raised its forsaken head. (II, 179)

Here Tom meets Cassy, the slave woman with plans for freedom that don't involve martyrdom. Very much an actress in human affairs rather than divine or supernatural ones, Cassy confronts the issue of how to find temporal power in femininity and slavery. Cassy, kept for the pleasure of her various owners, signifies the other side of domesticity, or rather, life without the romance and virtue of domesticity. In contrast to the ideals of family unity and redemptive death characterized by Mrs. Shelby, Eliza, Rachel, and Eva, Cassy's experience dramatizes the condition of domestic violation unrelieved by Christian hope, a darker version of Eliza's plight.

Cassy's life is a textbook in domestic violation: she has lost her children to the slave trade and her sexual integrity to her various masters. She has even murdered her last child in order to prevent another separation and loss. In this act, Cassy proves the destructive maternal capability that figures alongside maternal generativity in Stowe's abolitionist deployment of femininity. The possibility for murder as well as nurture inheres in the maternal power Stowe advocates as a humane alternative to Northern money power and Southern slave power. Cassy represents outraged domesticity; violated by slavery, she protects her child from slavery by her own violence. Once called "a good angel" by her first master, Cassy now evokes from Legree the epithet "she-devil" (II, 208, 214). Yet, if a fallen angel, Cassy nonetheless recalls motherly feeling; she ministers to Tom after his beatings and she protects Emmeline, Legree's newest concubine. Stowe describes Cassy, like Eva, as always gliding in her movements and working "by magic" (II, 193). In Cassy, however, unworldliness bespeaks madness, not spirituality.

Legree interprets this insanity as deviltry, an evil force in opposition to himself, "for Cassy had an influence over him from which he could not free himself" (II, 215). Cassy's deviltry intimidates Legree because of his susceptibility to superstition; and as Stowe observes, "No one is so thoroughly superstitious as the godless man.... Life and death to him are haunted grounds, filled with goblin forms of vague and shadowy dread" (II, 256). The structure of superstition and madness in which Legree and Cassy live houses the ramifications of the lack of faith. In this house that is not a home, the prevalent feature is the absence of domesticity and maternal influence. There does not even appear to be a kitchen. Legree's superstition derives from his rejection of his mother's love. Maternal absence haunts him with a continual fear of maternal presence; "That pale, loving mother,—her dying prayers, her forgiving love,—wrought in that demoniac heart of sin only as a damning sentence, bringing with it a fearful looking for of judgment and fiery indignation" (II, 218). Legree's fear that "the form of his dead mother should suddenly appear to him" (an inversion of Tom's joyful visions of Eva in heaven) reveals the power of motherhood which without belief in goodness seems witchery (II, 220). Legree's mother had left him a lock of her hair as a dying blessing; Legree burnt the hair yet believes it rematerializes when he discovers in Tom's belongings Eva's farewell token—a golden curl.[35] Legree's immersion in such Gothic phenomena signifies life without motherly influence, which is equivalent to life without God. This absolute bastardy marks the homelessness of both the slave and slave master.

Cassy's alienation and insanity, "the strange, weird, unsettled cast to all her words and language," articulate the suppression of maternal feeling rather than the absence and replacement of mother with devil Legree experiences (II, 257). Cassy finally asserts her motherliness in her flight with Emmeline to the North where she reunites with her daughter Eliza. She plays ghost to effect this escape, posing as the ghost of Legree's mother and thus symbolically dying for freedom. A strategic and pragmatic imitation of Little Eva occurs: the death of a woman which is not a death but a return of the mother, the mother of Legree and the mother in Cassy. Cassy's theatrics explore women's subversive possibilities, illustrating "that the most brutal man cannot live in constant association with a strong female influence, and not be greatly controlled by it" (II, 257). Cassy and the memory of Mrs. Legree so radically control Legree that Cassy's ghostly impersonation of his mother scares him into a fatal drinking bout. The redemptive, generous motherhood of ideal domesticity is here transformed to a murderous maternity in service to Stowe's activist feminine program for abolition.

Through Cassy's stratagem, Stowe instructs women to exploit their idealized status: to domesticate and literalize their spirituality, to enact Eva's saintly mission by taking immediate abolitionist action. Stowe certainly did not expect her readers to perform either Eva's martyrdom or Cassy's murder. In her letter to Gamaliel Bailey, editor of the *National Era,* announcing the plan for the serial *Uncle Tom's Cabin,* Stowe wrote, "the time is come when even a woman or child who can speak a word for freedom and humanity is bound to speak." She hoped in particular that "every woman who can write will not be silent." The situation of America in 1851 reminded Stowe of the Carthagenian women who "in the last peril of their state cut off their hair for bowstrings to give to the defenders of their country."[36] Simon Legree's mother bestowed her hair to the reformation of her son; this maternal cord of sustenance enslaves him to his superstitions and chains him to drink, the nineteenth-century sign of the homeless, finally destroying him. *Uncle Tom's Cabin* urges that women, like Cassy, pull their strings.

Emancipation waited another decade after *Uncle Tom's Cabin,* and Stowe's great-niece Charlotte Perkins Gilman was still designing matriarchal utopias in the early twentieth century.[37] Yet these facts, instead of qualifying the influence of the novel, attest to the scope and ambitiousness of Stowe's domestic project. *Uncle Tom's Cabin* reinterprets domesticity as a double agentry in which women simultaneously act within society as its exemplars (Mrs. Shelby, Eva) and at the boundaries of society as its critics and revolutionaries (Rachel, Mrs. Bird, Cassy). Stowe envisions the revolt of the mother: the imaginative emergence of repressed feminine potential, what we might call the "gothicization" of the sentimental mode, the transformation of Eva into Cassy. Domestic traditions culminate in Cassy as well as in Eva; homemakers and housekeepers evolve into activists when their sustaining convention, the integrity of women and their homes, is threatened. In immediate political terms this means the enlistment of mothers in the abolitionist movement. Once enforced by powerful institutions—the Presidency, Congress, the Army, and domesticity—abolition takes effect. Stowe's larger goal, the advent of mother-rule, requires a feminized world and domestic economy, the post-patriarchy of Liberia or a reformed America. The consolidation of domestic hegemony relies on the acceptance of Stowe's proposition that patriarchy be replaced with matriarchy for the good of the family.

Stowe's utopia of family unity awaits, then, not an afterlife at the end of conventions, but its own conventionality. The institutionalization of Stowe's domesticity is obviously a more problematic matter than abolition because it involves the erasure of masculinity. For familial peace, a peace of maternal love, of heavenly property, men as we know them cannot exist. Men must become like women, dedicated to the family and detached from the desire that constitutes marketplaces. In the Quaker community that exhibits Stowe's domestic economy of mother-love, the men, in an "antipatriarchal" gesture, shave their beards and subordinate the laws of men to the laws of God and mothers.[38] *Uncle Tom's Cabin* sacrifices the beards of the fathers, the slave masters, and the unregenerate sons to the history of a matriarchal family. Stowe seeks to weave a new civilization with the female hair that can alternately protect and terrify.

Yet the fact that Stowe retains the name of the male God throughout her matriarchal design suggests that her imagination of a feminized world still requires the sanction of male authority, or at least the modes associated with masculine power. Her utopian female dominion seems uncannily familiar, not only because it invokes popular domestic ideals, but because it resembles masculine practices of power. Stowe borrows from patriarchal authority the prerogative to dispatch human destinies, the very same prerogative exercised by men and slave masters. Finally, violence in *Uncle Tom's Cabin* not only is executed by the slave economy and masculine desire that endanger the family and home, but is embedded in the very foundation of home. For Stowe, only a house divided, a house divested of men, markets, and desire, can be a home.

Notes

1. Harriet Beecher Stowe, *The Key to Uncle Tom's Cabin* (1853: rpt. New York: Arno Press, 1969), 257.

2. Harriet Beecher Stowe, *Uncle Tom's Cabin: or, Life Among the Lowly* (1852: rpt. Columbus, Oh.: Charles E. Merrill, 1969), 1, 297. This edition is a reprint of the first edition published in 1852 by John P. Jewett and Co. The long serial appearing in *The*

National Era from 1851 to 1852 became a two-volume book. All future references will be to this edition; volume and page numbers are given in parentheses in the text.

3. I am here following Elizabeth Fox-Genovese's definition of domestic economy as "an integral component" of the ideology of "any system of political economy" that it "intersects, reinforces, and counters." Fox-Genovese provides an excellent description and analysis of the role of domestic economy as the "handmaiden of emerging capitalism" in nineteenth-century France. See "The Ideological Basis of Domestic Economy: The Representation of Women and Family in the Age of Expansion," in Elizabeth Fox-Genovese and Eugene Genovese, *Fruits of Merchant Capital: Slavery and Bourgeois Property in the Rise and Expansion of Capital* (New York: Oxford Univ. Press, 1983), 299–336.

4. *Godey's Ladies Magazine,* 3 Jan. 1830. Quoted in Nancy F. Cott, *The Bonds of Womanhood* (New Haven: Yale Univ. Press, 1977), 68. For another informative account of the domestic cult's distinction between the home and marketplace, see Mary Ryan, *Womanhood in America* (New York: New Viewpoints, 1979), 75–117.

5. Abolitionists often associated slavery with the contagious marketplace "spirit of gain." Their plan "to plant the self-sacrifice of a rigid Anti-Slavery" in America was frustrated by a "money-loving country, intensely devoted to the love of material gain." See Ronald C. Walters, *The Antislavery Appeal: American Abolition After 1830* (Baltimore: Johns Hopkins Univ. Press, 1976), 112–28.

6. For an exposition of Stowe's fear of slavery "as an emblem of market economy," see Walter Benn Michaels, "Romance and Real Estate," *Raritan.* 2 (Winter 1983), 66–87. Michaels elaborates the constitutive role of desire in market economy in "*Sister Carrie's* Popular Economy," *Critical Inquiry* 7 (1980), 376. My own interest is Stowe's presentation of the fear of both market economy and the desire that characterizes it in domestic terms. For an interesting discussion of the transposition of public issues to the private familial realm in the English industrial novels contemporaneous with *Uncle Tom's Cabin,* see Catherine Gallagher, *The Industrial Reformation of English Fiction: Social Discourse and Narrative Form, 1832–1867* (Chicago: Univ. of Chicago Press, 1985). Family life in the industrial novels, Gallagher argues, is "presented as society's primary reforming institution" and therefore must "be separated and purged of the ills infecting the public realm." I would like to take this opportunity to thank Howard Horwitz, Michael Paul Rogin, and Eric J. Sundquist for discussions of the issues treated in this essay.

7. Quoted in Stowe, "Introduction to the 1881 Edition," *Uncle Tom's Cabin* (1881; rpt. New York: Collier, 1978), 33–37; Ellen Moers, *Literary Women* (Garden City, N.Y.: Doubleday, 1976), 37. Moers also points out that for Stowe "the true horror was not the inhumanity of slavery but its very human, easygoing alignment with the normal procedures of the marketplace" (86).

8. Ann Douglas, *The Feminization of American Culture* (New York: Avon, 1977), 11–12; Jane P. Tompkins, "Sentimental Power: *Uncle Tom's Cabin* and the Politics of Literary History," *Glyph,* 8 (1981), 81–82.

My own exploration of Stowe's political domesticity is indebted to Douglas's landmark study of sentimental values and American Victorian culture, to Tompkins's valuable reassessment of sentimentalism's revisionary force, and to Elizabeth Ammons's insightful observations of Stowe's critique of capitalism and masculine practices of power. Ammons notes Stowe's advocacy of "cooperation" and "love" "as possible foundations for social organization." Elizabeth Ammons, "Heroines in *Uncle Tom's Cabin,*" *American Literature,* 49 (1977), 16–79.

9. Tompkins, "Sentimental Power," 83.

10. Douglas, *Feminization of American Culture,* 13.

11. Catharine Beecher, *A Treatise on Domestic Economy* (1841; rpt. New York: Schocken, 1977). All subsequent references are noted in parentheses in the text.

12. Sermon by Henry Ward Beecher, Oct. 1849. Quoted in Martin Rugoff, *The Beechers: An American Family in the Nineteenth Century* (New York: Harper and Row, 1981), 371.

13. On the Beechers and their role in nineteenth-century America, see Rugoff, *The Beechers;* William G. McLaughlin, *The Meaning of Henry Ward Beecher; An Essay on the Shifting Values of Mid-Victorian America* (New York: Knopf, 1970); Kathryn Kish Sklar, *Catharine Beecher: A Study in American Domesticity* (New York: Norton, 1976).

14. For detailed treatment of the social changes domesticity accompanied, see Nancy F. Cott, *The Bonds of Womanhood;* Thomas Dublin, *Woman at Work: The Tranformation of Work and Community in Lowell, Massachusetts, 1826–1860* (New York: Columbia Univ. Press, 1979); Julie Matthaei, *An Economic History of Women in America: Women's Work, The Sexual Division of Labor, and the Development of Capitalism* (New York: Schocken, 1982).

15. George Fitzhugh, *Cannibals All! or, Slaves without Masters* (1857; rpt. Cambridge: Belknap Press/Harvard Univ. Press, 1973), 198. Eugene Genovese explicates the slaveholders' critique of capitalism in "The Logical Outcome of the Slaveholders' Philosophy: An Exposition, Interpretation, and Critique of the Social Thought of George Fitzhugh of Port Royal, Virginia," in *The World the Slaveholders Made* (New York: Vintage, 1971), 118–244.

16. Rugoff, *The Beechers,* 321.

17. Barbara Welter describes in detail the rhetoric of domestic sanctity in "The Cult of True Womanhood," in *Dimity Convictions* (Athens: Ohio Univ. Press, 1976), 21–41.

18. It is interesting that once slavery was abolished, Stowe could fully endorse Beecher's domestic economy. After the Civil War, Stowe collaborated with her sister in revising the *Treatise* and republishing it as *The American Woman's Home* in 1869. They now shared a utopian matriarchal project: the establishment of "the model Christian Neighborhood." The Beecher sisters' contributions to feminist architectural designs are discussed in Dolores Hayden, *The Grand Domestic Revolution: A History of Feminist Designs for American Homes, Neighborhoods, and Cities* (Cambridge: MIT Press, 1981).

19. Stowe, *The Key to Uncle Tom's Cabin,* 257. For similar observations on Rachel's ministerial function in a redemptive matriarchal order, see Ammons, "Heroines in *Uncle Tom's Cabin,*" and Tompkins, "Sentimental Power."

20. Harriet Beecher Stowe, "Appeal to the Women of the Free States of America on the Present Crisis in Our Country," *Liberator*, 3 March 1854.

21. Catharine Beecher, *Essay on Slavery and Abolition with Respect to the Duties of American Females* (Philadelphia: Anti-Slavery Society, 1837).

22. Angelina Grimké, "Letter XI," in *Letters to Catharine Beecher* (Boston: Isaac Knapp, 1836), 103–4.

23. Angelina Grimké, "Appeal to the Christian Women of the South" (New York, 1836); reprinted in Gail Parker, *The Oven Birds: American Women on Womanhood 1820–1920* (New York: Anchor, 1972), 124.

24. Sarah Grimké, "Letter VIII," *Letters on the Equality of the Sexes* (Boston, 1838); reprinted in Alice Rossi, ed. *The Feminist Papers* (New York: Bantam, 1974), 315.

25. Southern diarist Mary Boykin Chesnut saw slavery's humiliation of white women in terms of the adultery and miscegenation practiced by their husbands: "Mrs. Stowe did not hit the sorest spot. She makes Legree a bachelor." *A Confederate Lady's Diary*, excerpted in *The Root of Bitterness: Documents of the Social History of American Women*, ed. Nancy F. Cott (New York: E.P. Dutton, 1972), 210.

26. Gerda Lerner, *The Grimké Sisters from South Carolina: Pioneers of Women's Rights and Abolition* (New York: Schocken, 1975). On the abolitionist roots of the women's rights movement, see Barbara Berg, *The Remembered Gate: Origins of American Feminism* (New York: Oxford Univ. Press, 1980); Ellen Carol Dubois, *Feminism and Suffrage: The Emergence of an Independent Women's Movement in America 1848–1869* (Ithaca: Cornell Univ. Press, 1980).

27. Quoted in Barbara Welter, Introd., *The Woman's Bible*, by Elizabeth Cady Stanton (1895; rpt. New York: Arno Press, 1974), xxii–xxiii.

28. Harriet Beecher Stowe, *Women in Sacred History* (New York: J. B. Ford, 1874), 1.

29. Harriet Beecher Stowe, *The Minister's Wooing* (1859; rpt. New York: AMS Press, 1967), 2.

30. Quoted in Walters, *The Antislavery Appeal*, 103.

31. Kenneth Lynn also remarks on the primacy of domestic values in the novel in his "Introduction" to *Uncle Tom's Cabin* (Cambridge: Belknap Press/Harvard Univ. Press, 1962). On the theological force of *Uncle Tom's Cabin*'s domesticity, see Alice Crozier, *The Novels of Harriet Beecher Stowe* (New York: Oxford Univ. Press, 1969).

32. Interesting discussions of the sexual manifestations of the ideology of nondesire are: Nancy F. Cott, "Passionlessness: An Interpretation of Victorian Sexual Ideology, 1790–1850," in Cott and Elizabeth H. Pleck, eds., *A Heritage of Her Own* (New York: Simon and Schuster, 1979), 162–81; Carroll Smith-Rosenberg, "Sex as Symbol in Victorian Purity: An Ethnohistorical Analysis of Jacksonian America" in John Demos and Sarane Spence Boocock, eds., *Turning Points: Historical and Sociological Essays on the Family* (Chicago: Univ. of Chicago Press, 1978), 212–47.

33. Quoted in Walters, *The Antislavery Appeal*, 98.

34. On the cult of Little Eva and the sentimental novelists' domestication of death, see Douglas, *Feminization of American Culture,* 1–13, 240–72.

35. For an interesting discussion of the transformation of Eva's token of hair into the lock of hair Simon Legree received from his mother, see Crozier, *Novels of Harriet Beecher Stowe,* 29–31.

36. Harriet Beecher Stowe, Letter to Gamaliel Bailey, 9 March 1851, Garrison Collection, Boston Public Library, Boston, Mass.

37. Charlotte Perkins Gilman, *Moving the Mountain* (1911); *Herland* (1915); *With Her in Ourland* (1916). All appeared in Gilman's monthly magazine, *The Forerunner,* which she wrote and published from 1909 to 1919.

38. For a similar account of Stowe's elimination of men from positions of power, see Tompkins, "Sentimental Power," 98.

Sharing the Thunder

The Literary Exchanges of Harriet Beecher Stowe, Henry Bibb, and Frederick Douglass

ROBERT B. STEPTO

◆　◆　◆

IN AN OCTOBER 1852 number of *Frederick Douglass's Paper* appears a book notice entitled "Stolen Thunder." Briefly described therein is W. L. G. Smith's *Life at the South; or Uncle Tom's Cabin as It Is,* one of the many books that followed close upon Harriet Beecher Stowe's novel in an attempt to gain a corner of the market *Uncle Tom's Cabin* had singlehandedly created. In regard to Smith's book, "stolen thunder" has a double meaning, for, according to the reviewer, Smith is not just attempting to "make money out of the popularity of 'Uncle Tom's Cabin,'" but also seeking "withal a little capital for the 'patriarchal institution.'"[1]

"Stolen thunder" aptly describes most of these publishing ventures, particularly those that were shamelessly entrepreneurial and those pursued by white Americans, even when, like Stowe, they vilified slavery. But the phrase falls short of the complex relationship between Stowe's novel and the many Afro-American antislavery texts published in the late 1840s and early 1850s. Some of these appear to have followed the stolen thunder pattern: Solomon Northup's *Twelve Years a Slave* (1853), for example, was dedicated, with great flourish, to Stowe ("whose name, throughout the world, is identified with the GREAT REFORM") and was generally promoted—and received—as "another key to Uncle Tom's Cabin," or, as one newspaper put it, "Uncle Tom's

Cabin—No. 2."[2] On the other hand, the relationship between *Uncle Tom's Cabin* and *Twelve Years a Slave* is not a simple one of promotion and sales or of two products vying for the same finite market. The two narratives share internal features that bind them together in literary history: When Northup divulges the existence of a thriving slave market in the nation's capital city, exposes the brutal forms of slave life in the Red River region of Louisiana, or rehearses the figure of Stowe's George Shelby in his own "saviors" from the North (Henry B. Northup of New York, but also the Canadian Samuel Bass), he is not so much stealing Stowe's thunder as substantiating the anti-slavery literary conventions established (if not exactly invented) by her—all the while telling his own story, of course. *Uncle Tom's Cabin* did not provide Northup with his tale or his stance against the "peculiar institution," but it may well have affected his autobiographical acts of remembering. In this re-gard especially, the relationship between Stowe's and Northup's works is both complex and literary; the textual conversation between the two narratives prompts the idea that Stowe and Northup shared the antislavery thunder of the 1850s: Despite the activities of his white editor and amanuensis, David Wilson, Northup cannot be said to have poached upon Stowe's success.

The relationship between *Uncle Tom's Cabin* and Frederick Douglass's novella, "The Heroic Slave" (1853), provides an even more interesting study of antislav-ery textual conversation, partly because Douglass, unlike Northup, was easily Stowe's equal as a prominent antislavery activist and partly because Douglass and Stowe knew each other and corresponded repeatedly during the period in which their antislavery fictions were being composed. Although dedicated alike to the task of eradicating slavery and to other causes such as the pro-motion of temperance, Stowe and Douglass differed profoundly on certain related issues—for instance, African colonization and the extent to which the American church community had succored slaveholders and hence abetted slaveholding. Although they debated these matters directly in their corre-spondence, and indirectly in public pronouncements, it can also be said that they conversed further in the pages of their antislavery fictions. The features of this exchange—of this sharing of the antislavery thunder—are explored in the rest of this essay.

IN JULY 1851, a scant month after the Washington, D.C., *National Era* had begun its serialization of *Uncle Tom's Cabin*, Harriet Beecher Stowe wrote Frederick Douglass a rather spirited letter. She began politely with a request for Douglass's assistance in acquiring accurate information about the details of life and work on a southern cotton plantation, but soon thereafter shifted her subject and tone, taking Douglass to task for what she understood to be his critical view of the church and of African colonization. Both parts of this letter tell us something about the composition of *Uncle Tom's Cabin* and are suggestive as well about what may be termed the countercomposition of "The Heroic Slave." Stowe's request of Douglass is expressed in this way:

> You may perhaps have noticed in your editorial readings a series of articles that I am furnishing for the Era under the title of "Uncle Tom's Cabin or Life among the lowly"—In the course of my story, the scene will fall upon a cotton plantation—I am very desirous to gain information from one who has been an actual labourer on one—&. it occurs to me that in the circle of your acquaintance there might be one who would be able to communicate to me some such information as I desire—I have before me an able paper written by a southern planter in which the details &. modus operandi are given from *his* point of sight—I am anxious to have some more from another standpoint—I wish to be able to make a picture that shall be graphic &. true to nature in its details—Such a person as *Henry Bibb,* if in this country might give me just the kind of information I desire you may possible know of some other person—I will subjoin to this letter a list of questions which in that case, you will do me a favor by enclosing to the individual—with a request that he will at earliest convenience answer them—[3]

Above and beyond what I sense to be a remarkable admixture of civility and imperiousness, two features of this statement warrant mention. One is that, although Stowe was undeniably an armchair sociologist of the South, here she appears to be rather assiduous in gathering southern testimony and in seeking the forms of black testimony that could both counter and corroborate the white testimony she already had in hand. The idea of weighing white and black testimony alike in order to gain a "picture" of plantation life that is "true to nature" was probably anathema to most white southerners of the late 1850s. But Stowe's practice here shows clearly that, contrary to the opinion of many southern whites (including Mary Boykin Chesnut), she did assay southern views, white and black, while composing *Uncle Tom's Cabin.*

The other signal feature is Stowe's reference to Henry Bibb. Bibb was a Kentucky slave, born probably in 1815, who escaped from bondage only to return repeatedly to Kentucky to rescue his family as well. None of his efforts met with success; indeed, at one point, Bibb was recaptured and sold "down river" with his family to slaveholders in the Red River region. Further attempts to escape as a family were also thwarted. Eventually, Bibb once again escaped on his own, arriving in Detroit, but only after additional trials of bondage, including a time in which he was the property of an Indian slaveholder, and after another brave effort to save Malinda, his wife, which ended when he discovered she had become her master's favorite concubine. Bibb's account of his story was published in 1849 under the title *Narrative of the Life and Adventures of Henry Bibb, an American Slave, Written by Himself;* it was undoubtedly one of the principal slave narratives discussed in antislavery circles during the period in which *Uncle Tom's Cabin* was being composed and first serialized.

Interest in Bibb's narrative continues today. Gilbert Osofsky included it among the narratives collected in *Puttin' On Ole Massa* (an anthology that, along with Arna Bontemps's *Great Slave Narratives,* introduced a generation of fledgling Afro-Americanists to slave narratives other than Douglass's of 1845), and I have elsewhere discussed its particular narrative strategies.[4] Among its enduring features is Bibb's story of his Indian captivity, an account that places the narrative in the popular tradition of captivity narratives and that, however obliquely, touches upon a key issue of Bibb's day—whether the practice of slaveholding should be allowed to expand into the Indian Territories, especially once they had become states of the Union. Another key feature is Bibb's love for and dedication to his still enslaved family, particularly as repeatedly expressed in his willingness to venture back across the Ohio River, deep into the bowels of danger, in order to attempt their rescue and release. His portrait of family unity against the odds (unity up to a point—since, as we know, Bibb was eventually compelled to abandon them) unquestionably struck a chord with the abolitionists of the 1850s, who brought it forth as further proof of slavery's sinful assault upon the slave's effort to maintain a semblance of Christian home life. Moreover, it is one of the accounts that has encouraged historians of our time, including Herbert Gutman and John Blassingame, to insist that the slave family could and did, in Gutman's words, "develop and sustain meaningful domestic and kin arrangements."[5]

A third feature, as central to Bibb's narrative as the portrait of family life, is his caustic view of the complicity between the church and the institution of slaveholding. Although Bibb is presented by his guarantors—abolitionists in Detroit—possibly out of necessity as a member of a Sabbath school and a man of "Christian course," it is clear in the body of *his* text that he has been variously wounded by the conduct of American Christians, and that as a result he is suspicious of them and "their" church. Fairly early in the *Narrative,* for example, Bibb makes his way back south in quest of his family, but is captured by a mob of slaveholders and soon imprisoned in Louisville. Of the mob, he says:

> In searching my pockets, they found my certificate from the Methodist E. Church . . . testifying to my worthiness as a member of that church.

And what made the matter look more disgraceful to me, many of this mob were members of the M. E. Church, and they were the persons who took away my church ticket, and then robbed me also of fourteen dollars in cash, a silver watch for which I paid ten dollars, a pocket knife for which I paid seventy-five cents, and a Bible for which I paid sixty-two and one half cents. All this they tyranically robbed me of, and yet my owner, Wm. Gatewood, was a regular member of the same church to which I belonged.[6]

Much later in the narrative, after Bibb and his family have been sold into an abominable state of bondage in Louisiana, he records the following about his new master, a church deacon:

And while I was offering up my prayers to that God who never forsakes those in the hour of danger who trust in him, I thought of Deacon Whitfield; I thought of his profession, and doubted his piety. I thought of his handcuffs, of his whips, of his chains, of his stocks, of his thumb-screws, of his slave driver and overseer, and of his religion; I also thought of his opposition to prayer meetings, and of his five hundred lashes promised me for attending a prayer meeting. I thought of God, I thought of the devil, I thought of hell; and I thought of heaven, and wondered whether I should ever see the Deacon there. And I calculated that if heaven was made up of such Deacons, or such persons, it could not be filled with love to all mankind . . . as we know it is from the truth of the Bible.[7]

In light of these pronouncements, grounded as they were in the most bitter of experiences, it is not surprising that Bibb claims elsewhere in his story that "I never had religion enough to keep me from running away from slavery in my life."[8]

Finally, Bibb's *Narrative* endures as much for its figurative language as for its rhetoric and ideology. I refer here to Bibb's descriptions of the Ohio River (which separated freedom in Ohio from bondage in Kentucky) as a road to freedom and, for the bonded black, a river Jordan. The most remarkable passage in this vein begins:

Sometimes standing on the Ohio River bluff, looking over on a free State, and as far north as my eyes could see, I have eagerly gazed upon the blue sky of the free North, which at times constrained me to cry out from the depths of my soul, Oh! Canada, sweet land of rest—Oh! when shall I get there?[9]

As the passage concludes, Bibb's language reminds us first of Frederick Doug-lass's earlier description of the images of freedom offered by Maryland's Chesapeake Bay, and then of more contemporary imaginings, such as those moments in John Edgar Wideman's *Brothers and Keepers* (1984) when he explores the irony of his brother's incarceration in a prison (called "Western") along the banks of the Ohio:

> I have stood upon the lofty banks of the river Ohio, gazing upon the splendid steamboats, wafted with all their magnificence up and down the river, and I thought of the fishes of the water, the fowls of the air, the wild beasts of the forest, all appeared to be free, to go just where they pleased, and I was an unhappy slave![10]

I have quoted at some length from Bibb's narrative principally to suggest that Mrs. Stowe's interest in it may not have been limited to Bibb's account of life on Red River cotton plantations (for which, see his chapters X–XII). At the very least, I would argue that her portrayal of Eliza Harris's escape to freedom across the ice patches of the Ohio River was prompted in part by Bibb's high symbolism of the Ohio as a pathway of freedom. It also seems clear that Bibb's allegiance to his family gave impetus to Stowe's portraits of the Harris fam-ily and of Tom's family as well. It also seems altogether possible that Stowe's George Harris is a fictive Bibb—in his light skin, which would have abetted his escape, and in his vociferous allegiance to family, his vivid dreams of freedom in Canada, and his occasional grave doubts about the social and moral efficacy of Christian practice.

In short, Stowe's story of George and Eliza Harris is roughly that of Henry and Malinda Bibb, once a happy outcome to the Bibbs's plight has been, as some nineteenth-century pundits liked to say, "bestowed." Altogether, Stowe's debt to Bibb's *Narrative* is as great as that she incurred while reading another 1849 narrative, *The Life of Josiah Henson, Formerly a Slave, Now an Inhabitant of Canada, as Narrated by Himself.* Much has been made over the decades, some by Stowe her-self, of Tom's resemblance to Henson, and of how Henson's escape to Canada may have inspired Stowe's presentation of the Harrises' settlement there. But when we study the texts alone, it is clear that the parallels between George Harris and Bibb are as pronounced and that Bibb's experiences on a Red River cotton plantation probably had as much to do with the composition of *Uncle Tom's Cabin* as did Henson's escape to Canada. Indeed, Harris in Canada is some-thing of a Henson and a Bibb, much as Tom in Louisiana is both a Bibb and a Henson.

If Stowe's novel favors Henson's text, the evidence is in her treatment of the two subjects that take up the balance of her 1851 letter to Douglass. Having made her request of him and referring to Bibb in the process, Stowe writes:

—I have noticed with regret, your sentiments on two subjects,—the church—&. African Colonization—&. with the more regret, because I think you have a considerable share of reason for your feelings on both these subjects—but I would willingly if I could modify your views on both points.[11]

Nothing comes of her intention to debate Douglass's criticisms of African colonization. But in what remains of the letter, she is thoroughly impassioned in defending the church: She is, as she says, a minister's daughter, a minister's wife, the sister of six ministers, and she thereby chooses to take questions of the church's stand on slavery as in some measure charges against her own and her family's conduct. Having defended herself and her kin ("it has been the influence that we found *in the church* & by the altar that has made us do all this"), Stowe ends her letter in this way:

After all my brother, the strength &. hope of your oppressed race does lie in the *church*—In hearts united to Him.... Every thing is against you—but *Jesus Christ* is for you—&. He has not forgotten his church misguided &. erring though it be.... This movement must &. will become a purely religious one ... christians north &. south will give up all connection with [slavery] &. later up their testimony against it—&. thus the work will be done—[12]

Given these views, it is not surprising that in *Uncle Tom's Cabin* Stowe created both Tom and George Harris, and chose to present them, albeit in rough, nearly unrealized fashion, as a kind of bifurcated, black antislavery hero—one almost white, the other very black; one hot-tempered, the other stoic to the point of meekness; one impelled by circumstances farther and farther north, the other farther and farther south; one central to her narrative ideologically, as an emblem of African colonization, the other central spiritually, and hence the "better half" of Stowe's hero, since he is emblematic of exalted Christian faith. The curiosity of this construction is that, although Tom is the "better" and true hero of Stowe's novel, whose character and presence create strong ties between her own and Henson's text—ties that would endure well into the remainder of the century through the other publishing activities of Stowe and Henson alike—it is in George Harris, not Tom, that Stowe confronts what were for her and other white Americans the most troubling issues in the antislavery debate, and confronts as well the tone and argument of the more problematic (though doubtless inspiring) slave narratives of the late 1840s: those of Bibb, Douglass, and a few other miscegenated hotheads. In Tom, Stowe expresses her consuming respect for Henson. In George Harris, she creates a composite portrait of Bibb, Douglass, and the rest of their type; and although she honors them throughout the bulk of her long novel, judiciously imagining how they, had they been Harris, would have responded to a given crisis or turn of events, she also sends them packing, first to Canada and then to Liberia. In short, the paragraphs on African colonization missing from Stowe's letter to Douglass are to be found in the chapters of *Uncle Tom's Cabin* that she would write soon after. She revises the close of Bibb's *Narrative,* where it is evident that he resides not in Canada but (still) in the United States, and replies as well to Douglass's many criticisms of the church and colonization alike, suggesting that he might just consider, in light of his views, removing not merely from Boston to Rochester, as he had just done, but from the Afro-American's New World to his Old.

Much as Stowe completed her letter in the pages of *Uncle Tom's Cabin,* so Douglass responded in his written account of the slave revolt hero, Madison Washington, whose story he had offered many times in the 1840s, here and abroad, in oral tellings. Known as "The Heroic Slave," the novella shares certain features with Stowe's novel but also challenges her text, especially in its presentation of a black hero as dark-skinned as her Tom (apparently magnificently so) and yet as rebelliously violent and skeptical of the American church as her George Harris. In this regard, and in its hero's "self-extrication" from the United States to the Bahamas, Douglass's novella of 1853 converses with Stowe's novel and replies to her 1851 letter, written during the composition of *Uncle Tom's Cabin.*

"The heroic slave" was written as Douglass's contribution to *Autographs for Freedom,* a publication created by the Rochester (New York) Ladies' Anti-Slavery Society to subsidize *Frederick Douglass's Paper* (known prior to 1853 as *The North Star*). Stowe herself was a contributor: She submitted an "autograph" and also took part in certain editorial activities, as the following 1852 announcement of the society suggests:

> We intend to publish an anti-slavery annual. . . . It was first designed to name the book, *"The Anti-Slavery Autograph,"* but the gifted authoress of *"Uncle Tom's Cabin"* has christened it *"Autographs for Freedom;"* and *we willingly accept her baptism for the forthcoming volume.*[13]

Douglass shared the society's regard for Stowe and her novel. In a March 1853 account of a visit to the Reverend and Mrs. Stowe at their Andover, Massachusetts, home, Douglass remarks upon what he perceives to be her modest demeanor and then writes:

> It is only when in conversation with the authoress of *"Uncle Tom's Cabin"* that she would be suspected of possessing that deep insight into human character, that melting pathos, keen and quiet wit, powers of argumentation, exalted sense of justice, and enlightened and comprehensive philosophy, so eminently exemplified in the *master book* of the nineteenth century.[14]

Soon thereafter, Douglass developed a set piece of praise for *Uncle Tom's Cabin* and its commanding international influence, which he worked into many speeches, no matter what the occasion or topic. In one version of the piece, Douglass implores that a fugitive slave act be passed every day of the week, so that "fresh feelings and new editions of *Uncle Tom*" may be created.[15] In most other versions (of 1853 and 1854), he argues that the American abolitionist movement cannot be thwarted, either by silencing its speakers or by burning its books, including Stowe's novel:

> They might cut out my tongue, and the tongue of every abolitionist in the States north of Mason &. Dixon's line; they might disband every anti-slavery organization in the land; they might gather together all the tracts, pamphlets, and periodicals ever published against slavery; they might take "Uncle Tom's Cabin" out of the ten thousand dwellings of this country, and bring them all into their splendid capitol—in their magnificent metropolis, Washington—and there set fire to them, and send their flame against the sky, and scatter their ashes to the four winds of heaven; but still the slaveholder would have no peace.[16]

Douglass's praise of Stowe was, I think, variously motivated. For one thing, he truly respected her gift and accomplishment, perhaps especially so in 1852 and 1853, when he was wrestling with the written version of Madison Washington's story, a story he had told orally, but usually quite sketchily, many times. (The doubts of a beginning fiction writer are surely expressed when Douglass says of Stowe in 1853, "We are all looking for examples, and we look for them among the great ones; if we cannot imitate them in their great works we can, at least, imitate them in their manners and bearing."[17]) On the other hand, we should acknowledge that Douglass praised Stowe partly because he wanted something from her—her support, including that of a monetary nature, for one of his pet projects of the 1850s, an industrial college for black youth, preferably to be located in his newly adopted city of Rochester. Douglass never realized the project, as we know, though the dream was fulfilled decades later when Samuel C. Armstrong created Hampton Institute and Booker T. Washington later founded Tuskegee. But while the school was still a possibility, Douglass praised Stowe publicly and for the most part chose to debate their differences "in conference," or, if publicly, often circuitously. His most ingenious act of circuity was, as I have been suggesting, "The Heroic Slave."

In comparing *Uncle Tom's Cabin* and "The Heroic Slave," one sees immediately which antislavery literary conventions the works share. Unlike most novels of the 1850s, but clearly in anticipation of the work to come from Mark Twain and the local colorists, both works offer an almost formidable display of American vernaculars and dialects, issuing from white and black characters alike. Stowe and Douglass differ in their pursuit of this convention in the range of vernaculars attributed to blacks. In *Uncle Tom's Cabin,* the gamut runs from the standard English of George Harris (hardly the vernacular of a racial character) to the folksy, if not exactly broken, speech of, say, Aunt Chloe: "Missis let Sally try to make some cake, t'other day, jes to *larn* her, she said. 'O, go way, Missis,' said I; 'it really hurts my feelin's, now, to see good vittles spilt dat ar way! Cake ris all to one side—no shape at all; no more than my shoe; go way!'"[18] In Stowe, the various black vernaculars reinforce what she suggests in other ways about black stratification according to color, ambition, employment, geographical location, possibly gender, and, quite often, given name: The most degraded slaves in the novel, such as Simon Legree's black accomplices, Sambo and Quimbo, are in name, speech, and sensibility "African residuals," whereas Tom, Emmeline, and others are, by contrast, to be received as Afro-Europeans of some order, their names functioning as indicators of the plausibility of their high feelings, unswerving religiosity, and fierce moral convictions.

Douglass proceeds in another fashion, preferring the voice of a single slave hero to an exhibit of the sociolinguistic range of a race. On the other hand, his strategy is similar to Stowe's in that his black hero's name—Madison Washington—is as much a sign of his literacy as it is of his state of origin (Virginia), his credentials as a revolutionary, and his quintessential Americanness. One result is that Madison's speeches, not unlike some of George Harris's, are overwrought and hence not "true to nature," except perhaps in being much like some of Douglass's addresses and those of Virginia's other famous sons. Another result, much in keeping with Douglass's predilections and activist strategies, is that every serious discussion of slavery in the novella is conducted on a dignified level, each speech exhibiting grammatical correctness as well as social courtesy, especially when the exchanges are between blacks and whites. We turn to other, presumably lower, levels of American conversation only when whites discuss slavery amongst themselves. Here Douglass employs diacritical simulations of American speech, not to suggest the condition of the lowest blacks but to characterize the lowest whites—those who are, in effect, confreres of Stowe's Simon Legree and who speak his language, or worse.

Stowe and Douglass also shared an interest in American symbolic geography as seen from the slave's point of view. This leads, in both fictions, to a meticulous presentation of the geography of freedom, which focuses on Ohio as well as Canada. As suggested before, Stowe picks up where Bibb leaves off in depicting the significance and risk of a slave's managing to cross the Ohio River—recall here Eliza Harris's leaping from river ice patch to ice patch while grasping her child, in flight from her would-be captors. But whereas Bibb is altogether scant in portraying his north-of-the-Ohio benefactors, including Mr. D_____, perhaps because he fears compromising their service to other escaping slaves, Stowe works up an elaborate study of Senator and Mrs. Bird, who assist Eliza Harris, and of the many Quakers who eventually help the Harris family as a whole.

Unlike Stowe and Bibb, Douglass does not pause in "The Heroic Slave" to sketch the northern banks of the Ohio as freedom's green shore; eloquence of that sort and for that subject is reserved instead for the prospect of safety on British soil, in Canada and later the Bahamas. However, the state of Ohio is, for Douglass, unquestionably a portion of freedom's realm, less because of its famous southern river than because of the brave souls residing there who choose to aid fugitive slaves. In this regard, he proceeds quite differently than he does in his 1845 *Narrative,* where he is most circumspect about how he escaped and about who, if anyone, assisted him: He joins Stowe in offering what are probably thinly veiled portraits of active abolitionists and their families. Douglass's Ohio abolitionists, the Listwells, turn out to be an economical creation as well: They constitute a composite portrait of helpfulness, understanding, and antislavery zeal, not only because they probably represent many actual abolitionists but also because they perform all the tasks and express all the feelings that Stowe distributes among at least three groups—the Birds, the Shelbys, and the Quakers.

In their presentation of social spaces, Stowe and Douglass proceed rather uniformly. For both, the striking contrast between model domestic settings and the seamy affairs of tavern life, repeatedly and variously elaborated, is a principal means of clarifying phenomenologically the distinctions between good and evil, heaven and hell, family life and other coarser, possibly "unnatural," arrangements, and the right and wrong sides of the slavery issue. In "The Heroic Slave," Douglass's strategy is as simple as it is effective. At the heart of the novella, much is made of the contrast between the Listwells' Ohio home, where Madison Washington found comfort and aid, and the appointments inside and out of a Virginia tavern frequented by loafers and slave drivers. Quite to the point, the tavern had once been a house, complete with outbuildings and other physical features suggesting the honorable pursuit of animal husbandry and agriculture. But now the property bears the "ineffaceable marks" of "time and dissipation": "The gloomy mantle of ruin is, already, outspread to envelop it, and its remains . . . remind one of a human skull, after the flesh has mingled with the earth."[19] The fact that the tavern had been a home before it became a setting for knavery and intemperance allows Douglass to build his comparison in relentless detail. Barn is compared with barn, hearth with hearth, good housekeeping with its absence, nourishing food with debilitating drink. Even the dogs are made use of, Listwell's faithful Old Monte being an obviously better companion than the listless hounds that lie about the tavern. Douglass varies his strategy in the final section of the novella, where two Virginia sailors discuss the *Creole* revolt and the slavery question in general in a tavernlike setting. Although the scene rehearses to a degree the conversation between Listwell and the loafer in the earlier Virginia tavern—and is indebted particularly to the singular exchange between George Harris and his former employer, Mr. Wilson, in what is perhaps Stowe's most important tavern episode (Chap. 11)—it takes on its own ideological character in Douglass's insistence that the place is not a tavern but a coffee house. Possibly because of his temperance movement activities, Douglass refused to join Stowe in suggesting, even in fiction, that serious discussion could take place in the presence of alcohol.[20]

Stowe's tavern episodes—recall that she begins the novel with one—are as numerous as those of model domestic life, and the two settings pair up accordingly. We are thus led to compare the elder Mr. Shelby, in a "dining parlor" with the brandy-drinking Haley, with Shelby at home in the company of his virtuous wife. Likewise, the tavern scene depicting Haley and his henchmen is answered in the activities and serious, moral talk of the Bird household, and the tavern discussion of George Harris and Mr. Wilson is followed by the sequestering of the Harrises in the Quaker settlement, a place so domestically harmonious, according to Stowe, that "even the knives and forks had a social clatter as they went on to the table" (Chap. 13).

Stowe's most ingenious and ideological handling of these contrasts appears in the Simon Legree chapters—for example, Chapter 32, "Dark Places." The description makes clear that Legree's shabby house was once a handsome home, sheltering a family as opposed to the motley assembly of miscegenated women who variously and sullenly serve him. So, too, we are to understand that its rooms were once used for much loftier domestic purposes than the drinking bouts Legree now conducts in them. In short, a once proud home is now something of a brothel and much of a tavern; in this regard, it is fair to say that Legree's degraded domicile is the model for Douglass's Virginia tavern. Stowe's great touch involves not her descriptions of dissipation but her resolution of these affairs by the captive women. Weakness for drink delivers Legree into Cassy's hands and softens him for the stratagems she works against him. Although Cassy's success does not fully restore domesticity to the Legree household, it does allow her and Emmeline to have a "home of their own" in the upper rooms that Legree dares not enter.

Despite such sharings, Stowe and Douglass created quite different fictions, the differences reflecting contrasting views on the church and colonization as well as the portrayal of black heroism. On the latter score, one may observe that the primary features of Bibb's *Narrative* that Stowe chose not to rehearse are, in fact, reproduced in Douglass's novella. For example, the heroic return from safety to danger in quest of captive kin is undertaken in *Uncle Tom's Cabin* only by white near kin, like young George Shelby, seeking Tom's release. In contrast, Douglass's hero, like Bibb's persona, undertakes this task himself, traveling south from Canada to a slave state, undergoing recapture and reenslavement, and suffering as well the loss of a wife when he regains his personal freedom. Tom is not reunited with Aunt Chloe any more than Bibb and Washington are reunited with their wives, but at least in their versions of the common tale of slave families torn apart, it is the black male family co-head, and not a white surrogate, who seeks reunification.

Moreover, whereas Stowe acknowledges black skepticism about the church's role in the fight against slavery but relegates all such concern to her secondary black hero, George Harris, Douglass, like Bibb, locates this skepticism in the character of his primary hero. That skepticism even touches Listwell, Douglass's primary white hero, who remarks of Washington:

> To him those distant church bells have no grateful music. He shuns the church, the altar, and the great congregation of Christian worshippers, and wanders away to the gloomy forest, to utter in the vacant air complaints and griefs, which the religion of his times and his country can neither console nor relieve.[21]

Listwell obviously is an abolitionist of a different stripe than the Beechers and the Stowes. He is, in brief, a western abolitionist, not a New England one; at the very least, he completes Douglass's vision of such a figure.

Regarding African colonization, Stowe's views appear in the Harrises' successful escape to Canada, their removal thence to France—where George gains the university training he probably cannot receive elsewhere—and their eventual emigration to West Africa to help found a new black society. This is pure Stowe; neither Bibb nor Henson was interested in any such final solution. Nor was Douglass, although in his fiction if not in fact he was keener on forsaking the United States than was Bibb. In "The Heroic Slave," Madison Washington escapes finally to the British Bahamas—that is, to a New World territory free of slavery with a large black population. Washington's presence there, rather than in Africa or Canada, is much in keeping with Douglass's view that, far from submitting to any removal schemes, American blacks should stick together in the New World. As he put it elsewhere, "Individuals emigrate—nations never."[22]

Although Stowe's and Douglass's differing portrayals of black heroism may be seen to arise from their differences about the church and colonization, their handling of the issue of color is also significant here. In *Uncle Tom's Cabin,* Tom is dark and George is fair, a time-hallowed arrangement supporting all the myths of black meekness and white aggression, myths that dictate the heroic qualities of each man. In "The Heroic Slave," Douglass squarely challenges such myths, refusing to bifurcate his hero as well as emphasizing his blackness and valor alike. In this respect, Douglass specifically revises Stowe's characterization of Tom. A comparison of the physical descriptions of Stowe's Tom and Douglass's Washington makes this clear. Here is Stowe's first "daguerrotype" of Tom:

> He was a large, broadchested, powerfully-made man, of a full glossy black, and a face whose truly African features were characterized by an expression of grave and steady good sense, united with much kindliness and benevolence. There was something about his whole air self-respecting and dignified, yet united with a confiding and humble simplicity. (Chap. 4)

Douglass revises this in his portrait of Washington:

> Madison was of manly form. Tall, symmetrical, round, and strong. In his movements he seemed to combine, with the strength of the lion, a lion's elasticity. His torn sleeves disclosed arms like polished iron. His face was "black but comely." His eye, lit with emotion, kept guard, under a brow as dark and as glossy as the raven's wing. His whole appearance betokened Herculean strength; yet there was nothing savage or forbidding

in his aspect. A child might play in his arms, or dance on his shoulder. A giant's strength, but not a giant's heart was in him. His broad mouth and nose spoke only of good nature and kindness. But his voice, that unfailing index of the soul, though full and melodious, had that in it which could terrify as well as charm. He was just the man you would choose when hardships were to be endured, or danger to be encountered—intelligent and brave. He had the head to conceive, and the hand to execute. In a word, he was one to be sought as a friend, but to be dreaded as an enemy.[23]

Tom and Madison are both kind, benevolent, good-natured, and steady, as well as big, handsome, and black. But Madison is also intelligent, brave, possessed of a body promising action and a voice promising speech. Obviously, Madison revises Tom, but the point is that the revision occurs by way of addition to Tom, or rather, to Stowe's portrait of him. Since it can be said that Tom is in his way brave, intelligent, and so forth, the issue is not that he lacks these qualities but that Stowe chooses not to see or remark upon them. It may be argued that Stowe in this way creates space for her other, "brighter" hero, George Harris. It may also be argued that Stowe had no such strategy and simply portrayed Tom in the truncated form she wished him to assume. From this latter point of view, she seems, like Garrison and other New Englanders Douglass grew to distrust, the very sort of "blind" abolitionist he sought to enlighten in "The Heroic Slave." Douglass's revision of Tom in Madison Washington not only renders Tom fully visible, it forces abolitionists of a certain, Yankee stripe to see him.

In his essay "Everybody's Protest Novel," James Baldwin argues that Afro-American protest fiction began with *Uncle Tom's Cabin,* and further, that protest fiction has never quite worked its way out of the "cage" Stowe created for it. One feature of that cage is the notion, among black and white protest writers alike, that when God created blacks, He did not do so in His image.[24] Baldwin's argument produces an impassioned assessment of Stowe and Richard Wright, but it does little justice to Douglass's "The Heroic Slave." Madison Washington suffers doubts, but not about his blackness: He never sees himself as one of God's lesser children. And it may be that Baldwin did not fully take in the complexity of Stowe either. Tom may conform to Baldwin's views, but Nat Turner does not, and it was Nat Turner and his insurrection that she took up in her next novel. In a sense, Douglass won his debate with Stowe, for he could claim some role in inducing her to write about a black revolutionary. But she won, too: When she wrote about a rebel, she wrote about one—from Virginia—who failed.

Notes

1. "Stolen Thunder," *Frederick Douglass's Paper.* October 22, 1852, p. 2.

2. Sue Eakin and Joseph Logsdon, Introduction to Solomon Northup, *Twelve Years a Slave* (1853; rpt. Baton Rouge: Louisiana State University Press, 1968), p. xiv.

3. Harriet Beecher Stowe, Letter to Frederick Douglass, July 9, 1851, in Charles Edward Stowe, ed., *Life of Harriet Beecher Stowe* (Boston: Houghton Mifflin, 1890), pp. 149–53.

4. Gilbert Osofsky, ed., *Puttin' On Ole Massa* (New York: Harper & Row, 1969); Arna Bontemps, ed., *Great Slave Narratives* (Boston: Beacon, 1969); Robert B. Stepto, *From Behind the Veil: A Study of Afro-American Narrative* (Urbana: University of Illinois Press, 1979), pp. 6–11.

5. Herbert B. Gutman, *The Black Family in Slavery and Freedom, 1750–1925* (New York: Vintage, 1977), p. xxi.

6. Henry Bibb, *Narrative of the Life and Adventures of Henry Bibb, an American Slave, Written by Himself,* in Osofsky, ed., *Puttin' On Ole Massa,* p. 105.

7. Ibid., p. 127.

8. Ibid., p. 114.

9. Ibid., p. 72.

10. Ibid.

11. Stowe, Letter to Douglass, July 9, 1851; see note 3.

12. Ibid.

13. *Frederick Douglass's Paper,* November 19, 1852, p. 3. The announcement appears at least once again, on November 26, 1852.

14. Frederick Douglass, "A Day and Night in 'Uncle Tom's Cabin,'" in Philip S. Foner, ed., *The Life and Writings of Frederick Douglass,* vol. 2 (New York: International, 1950), p. 227.

15. Frederick Douglass, "Slavery the Life Issue: Addresses Delivered in Cincinnati, Ohio, on 11–13 April 1854," in John W. Blassingame, ed., *The Frederick Douglass Papers, Series One: Speeches, Debates, and Interviews,* vol. 2 (New Haven, Conn.: Yale University Press, 1982), p. 468.

16. Frederick Douglass, "Bound Together in a Grand League of Freedom: An Address Delivered in Toronto, Canada West, on 21 June 1854," in Blassingame, ed., *The Frederick Douglass Papers, Series One,* vol. 1, p. 495.

17. Douglass, "A Day and Night in 'Uncle Tom's Cabin,'" p. 227.

18. Harriet Beecher Stowe, *Uncle Tom's Cabin,* ed. Kenneth Lynn (Cambridge, Mass.: Harvard University Press, 1962), Chap. 4.

19. Frederick Douglass, "The Heroic Slave," in Abraham Chapman, ed., *Steal Away: Stories of the Runaway Slaves* (New York: Praeger, 1971), p. 169.

Topsy and the End Man

Blackface in Uncle Tom's Cabin

SARAH MEER

◆ ◆ ◆

[It has] scenes of Negro humour that will send our wits digging in a new vein, and drive the exhibitors of nigger melodists to despair.

—"Uncle Tom's Cabin," *Nonconformist* (London),
8 September 1852

THE FIRST REVIEWS OF *Uncle Tom's Cabin* lingered not only over the weepy deathbeds of Eva and Uncle Tom but also over comic aspects of the novel. Unlike later critics, nineteenth-century observers were particularly struck by the humor in the book, which was attested to by reviewers from both the North and the South in the United States as well as in Britain. The *National Era*, a Washington antislavery paper, noted *Uncle Tom's* "drollery," while a letter to the *New York Independent* from New Orleans reported that readers had been both "moved to tears" and "convulsed with laughter."[1] An article in New York's *Putnam's Monthly* implied that the novel inevitably produced these two extremes, relating the story of a man sleeping in a strange house: "Being annoyed by hearing somebody in the adjoining chamber alternately groaning and laughing, he knocked upon the wall and said, 'Hallo, there! What's the matter? Are you sick, or reading Uncle Tom's Cabin?'"[2]

This conjunction of comedy and sentiment was not unusual in the 1850s: a year after *Uncle Tom* came out, the narrator of Herman Melville's "Bartleby the Scrivener" would boast of his knowledge of "divers histories, at which good-natured gentlemen might smile, and sentimental souls might weep."[3] And as Robert Weisbuch points out, this particular set of reactions would have been recognized by contemporary readers as a "Dickensian effect."[4] Yet

Stowe's comedy was constructed out of materials new both to Dickens and to his many American imitators.

The reviews implicitly recognized as much: their appreciations of *Uncle Tom's* comedy were accompanied by special praise for the novel's black characters. In London the *Times* declared that "a little black imp, by name Topsy . . . [is] one of the best sketches in the book" and picked out "scenes in which the negroes are represented at their domestic labors or conversing with each other." Another review declaimed, "One Topsy is worth a dozen little Evas."[5] The *New Englander* characterized "the dramatic interest which so enlivens Uncle Tom's Cabin" in a list of aspects missing from another text: It rarely takes the form of a dialogue; it gives no specimens of negro-English dialect; it is almost wholly destitute of humor."[6] These, by implication, were the strengths of Stowe's novel.

The emphases on comedy, on black life, and on dialogue and "negro-English" and the fascination with Topsy's "impishness" single out aspects of *Uncle Tom's Cabin* that were also the attributes audiences claimed to enjoy in blackface entertainment. More pointedly, many reviews explicitly invoked the minstrel show as a comparison. The *Literary World* remarked that "the element of the popular performances on the stage and elsewhere, the Jim Crow oddities, the Ethiopian serenaders, the Christy minstrels . . . will be found also to be the essence of the humor in Uncle Tom's Cabin."[7] Even when readers argued that Stowe's work was a new departure, it was blackface that provided the contrast. In the passage from the *Nonconformist* quoted in the epigraph to this chapter, *Uncle Tom's Cabin* is declared to contain "scenes of negro humour" that will drive minstrel show promoters to "despair." The *Times* announced that Stowe avoided "the slang of 'Ethiopian Serenaders'" and remarked "how refreshing it is to be separated for a season from the conventional Sambo of the modern stage."[8] Unusually for a pronouncement by the *Times,* this was echoed by a correspondent for *Frederick Douglass' Paper.* William Wilson also described the novel as an antidote to images derived from the theater: "Shopkeepers that heretofore . . . exhibited in their windows Zip Coon, or Jim Crow, with his naked toes kicking out the panes, for general amusement, profit and loyalty to the Southern God; . . . are now proud to illume those very windows through the windows of my *Uncle Tom's Cabin,* while good Old Aunt Cloe [*sic*] peeps out just to see what the matter is."[9]

Wilson's description of Uncle Tom figures replacing Jim Crows in a shop window suggests how the commercialization and duplication of Stowe's images would come to rival those of the 1840s blackface clown. Tom and Topsy would become images as ubiquitous as Jim Crow or Zip Coon and possibly even more long-lived. *Uncle Tom's* characters would occupy some of the same structural positions in American and European culture as those of the minstrel stage: Uncle Tom and Chloe would take over not only literal shop windows but also figurative ones.

Far from signaling a break with blackface representation, the interchangeability of Stowe's characters with stage ones is an indication of their kinship. Wilson's efforts to disassociate Stowe's imagery from that of the minstrel show testify to the power of blackface, ironically indicating the necessity of measuring Stowe's characters against blackface ones like Jim Crow or Zip Coon, just as the *Times* forged the connection it sought to repudiate between the novel and the minstrel troupe the Ethiopian Serenaders. They illustrate the inescapable cultural authority blackface held in the 1850s and that it was the benchmark against which portraits of African Americans had to be tested. Even though *Uncle Tom's Cabin* would break blackface's monopoly, these quotations suggest how much Stowe's depictions both were and would remain entwined with earlier ones.

Stowe herself almost certainly never saw a minstrel show. She famously disapproved of the theater and cautioned against even the sympathetic dramatization of *Uncle Tom's Cabin,* as it might give the form an unwarranted imprimatur of gentility.[10] It would seem all the more unlikely that she would countenance minstrelsy's rowdier style of performance. Lott admits to "equivocation" in his connection of the two cultural forms, "*Uncle Tom's Cabin* as a break from but also a continuation of blackface minstrelsy," locating these contradictions in the "unavoidable . . . ambiguity of the revolutionary 1850s."[11] Yet the conjunction of blackface and the sentimental antislavery text seems less surprising when we acknowledge the cultural power of minstrelsy in the 1850s.

By the time Stowe began her book blackface had permeated U.S. culture, and both its icons and versions of its acts could be found everywhere. As Wilson's article for *Frederick Douglass' Paper* suggests, shopkeepers used images of blackface characters for advertising in their shopwindows, and in Nathaniel Hawthorne's *The House of the Seven Gables* (published in the year *Uncle Tom* was serialized) they featured as confectionery—Hepzibah Pyncheon sells gingerbread Jim Crows.[12] Moreover, minstrel show songs were available as sheet music, its jokes and sketches were published in books, and devotees admiringly repeated its material on the streets. Many years later, Stowe's Hartford neighbor Mark Twain would try out blackface turns for guests in the parlor: it is likely that the audiences of the 1840s and 1850s also carried their enthusiasms out of the shows and into their homes.[13] Minstrelsy was as pervasive in popular culture and as readily adapted to nontheatrical purposes as *Uncle Tom* would come to be. In fact, *Uncle Tom's Cabin* was a symptom of the extent to which blackface imagery and humor were available to Americans outside the minstrel hall, and it would demonstrate how the ambiguities and ironies minstrelsy applied to racial politics could be equally useful off the stage. And in its turn, of course, *Uncle Tom* mania would extend blackface's reach into a wider culture.

It has been assumed that it was the experience of living in Cincinnati between 1832 and 1851 that eventually made slavery such a compelling topic for Stowe. The often intense racial tensions in the city during this period resulted in riots and a bitter controversy at Lane Seminary, where Stowe's father, Lyman Beecher, was president and her soon-to-be husband, Calvin, taught.[14] In addition, Cincinnati's location just north of a slave state made it both a hub of trade with the South and a prominent stop on the Underground Railroad. It was also a place where planters took black mistresses and educated their illegitimate children.[15]

But it should also be noted that the city played an important part in the history of minstrelsy. Many blackface troupes visited Cincinnati in the 1840s: Christy's Minstrels in 1846 and 1847; the Sable Harmonists three times in 1847, once in 1848, and again in 1849; and also the Sable Troubadours, Kneass's Great Original Sable Harmonists, T. D. Rice, and Campbell's Minstrels.[16] Not only that, but one version of the legend of T. D. Rice's invention of Jim Crow, the routine that earned him his reputation as the "father of blackface," stipulated that Rice had borrowed his song from a black stage driver of that city.[17] As I discuss in chapter 2, Cincinnati was also home to minstrelsy's most famous composer, Stephen Foster, between 1846 and 1850. Commentators on both Stowe and Foster have surmised that Cincinnati could have provided experience both of black people and of racial issues that later contributed to their writing; it also offered a chance to hear minstrel songs.[18]

Blackface is usually identified with a very different audience from that of the sentimental novel: male not female, working class not bourgeois, rowdy not genteel.[19] The blackface elements in *Uncle Tom* suggest the novel's links with a very different aspect of 1850s culture and imply that the book may have had a much broader class and gender appeal even than those of its fellow sentimental novels. The moments when Stowe's book evokes the minstrel show could indicate some ambivalence about the middle-class femininity it at other times celebrates. Blackface aspects of *Uncle Tom* could also work to cushion the impact of its politics by dissolving them in irony and contradictions.

Uncle Tom's ties to minstrelsy are more comprehensible when we acknowledge the shifts in performance style in the 1850s that were bringing blackface more into line with sentimental aesthetics. By the 1850s there was plenty in blackface that would have chimed with Stowe's sensibilities. *Uncle Tom's Cabin* was only one of many antislavery productions to capitalize on the popularity of blackface, and Stowe's book also coincided with a change in the content and the projected audience of minstrel entertainments, which were coming to be pitched at more respectable bourgeois patrons and to be larded with sentimental ideals of home and family very like her own.

What Robert Winans calls the "earthy[,] . . . comic and antisentimental" tone of early minstrel show music began to change in the mid-1840s. From the start, many minstrel songs were republished for the home market with more genteel lyrics and without the dialect of stage versions.[20] But whatever real gap existed between blackface and parlor music began to narrow with the mid-1840s development of the plantation song, which had musical and lyrical ties to the sentimental ballad.[21] This form was often used for songs that affected to have some sympathy for the slave, such as Sam Sanford's 1844 song "Lucy Neal," which describes her tragic separation from her lover, but even in this there was room for equivocation, as there were several versions of the lyrics whose implications for slavery varied, and the tune itself suggested a humorous tone.[22]

As minstrel tunes became more like parlor songs, the middle classes began to come more to minstrel shows, and they in turn increasingly took on the shape of concerts.[23] Gentlemen and even sometimes ladies were appearing in minstrel hall audiences, especially the larger, more respectable ones in the cities, by the 1850s, and some showmen arranged promotions especially directed at women and children.[24] Eventually, minstrelsy would become so respectable that bourgeois men began to learn the banjo, and even the British Prince of Wales would take lessons from one of the blackface Bohee Brothers.[25] *Uncle Tom's Cabin* thus emerged as the minstrel show itself was being adopted by the very classes for whom Stowe's novel was designed.

Moreover, blackface's musical history was closely bound up with avowedly antislavery music throughout the 1840s. The four-part harmonies of the singing Austrian family, the Rainers, inspired troupes like the Virginia Minstrels and Christy's Minstrels as well as the antislavery Hutchinson Family Singers, who campaigned as they performed but whose use of humor and rhythm signaled their musical proximity to minstrelsy.[26] The English singer Henry Russell, who also toured extensively in the United States, sang both antislavery songs and "negro melodies," though he did not wear blackface; many minstrels in turn sang Russell's songs.[27] Moreover, throughout the 1840s and 1850s abolitionists themselves frequently put antislavery lyrics to minstrel show tunes. "Lucy Neal," "Old Dan Tucker," "Dandy Jim," "Dixie's Land," and "Lucy Long" were all adapted in this way, and antislavery collections appeared with what Sam Dennison calls "parodies, copies, and flagrant borrowings from the minstrel repertoire."[28]

Such attempts to package earnest arguments in an entertaining format failed entirely to draw on the provocativeness and irony that were partly responsible for blackface's mass appeal. The fast fiddle-dance tune of "Old Dan Tucker," for instance, must have sat oddly with the elevated sentiment of the lyrics sung to it at an antislavery picnic in 1845:

> Our fathers fought on Bunker's Hill
> For liberty and independence,
> And freedom fires are glowing still,
> Deep in the souls of their descendants.
> Rouse up the flame—rouse up the flame—
> Rouse up the flame, throughout the nation,
> Death to slavery and oppression![29]

Stowe's achievement in *Uncle Tom's Cabin* was to harness the tone as well as the trappings of blackface, but she necessarily also borrowed the racial portraiture along with them. Whereas antislavery songs dealt with abstract principles, Stowe would try to infuse the slaves' plight with dramatic interest, which is why *Uncle Tom's Cabin* imported all minstrelsy's ambivalent attitudes to African Americans along with its theatrical power.

The minstrel stage, meanwhile, adeptly turned the abolitionists' weapons back at them. The Hutchinson Family Singers, who were famous for Jesse Hutchinson's 1844 emancipation song "Get off the Track" (itself set to "Old Dan Tucker"), were often parodied there.[30] "Get off the Track" also shared blackface's fascination with the railroad: while in the Hutchinsons' lyrics the "Car Emancipation / [Rode] majestic thro' our nation," blackface troupes played the "Railroad Overture," an instrumental imitation of the "slocomotive bullgine, dat at de fust ob de beginning is very moderate, den as de steam rises, de power of de circumvolution exaggerates itself into a can'tstopmization, and runs clar ob de track."[31]

As W. T. Lhamon has pointed out, the blackface trick of imitating a locomotive's whistle is duplicated by both Harry and Topsy in *Uncle Tom's Cabin,* but the most famous juxtaposition of abolitionism with this midcentury fascination with locomotive technology lies, of course, in the idea of the Underground Railroad.[32] The term inspired both George Allen's antislavery parlor song "The Underground Rail Car, or Song of the Fugitive" and Dan Rice's blackface jokes about "De Railroad dat's *underground.*"[33]

In exploiting each other's success abolitionists and blackface artists increasingly blurred their respective positioning in class and cultural niches.

While the showmen mocked the Hutchinsons as a sign of the genteel taste to which the family troupe appealed (along with many other such signs), and while abolitionist songwriters in the 1840s had attempted to take over the cultural territory of blackface by adapting its songs, by the 1850s the two kinds of performance and of racial representation had an increasing tendency to merge.

If minstrelsy's co-option by abolitionist forces in the 1840s may have suggested Stowe's adoption of blackface in *Uncle Tom's Cabin,* it was also already offering a fictional version of the plantation that was readily adapted for the novel. The fantasy plantations of the minstrel show purported to offer audiences an ethnographic glimpse of real slave life. Parts of the show in 1840s programs were explicitly labeled "as Southern Darkies" or "as Plantation Darkies," while the Virginia Minstrels advertised themselves as an insight into slave life in America, promising "sports and pastimes of the Virginia Colored Race, through the medium of Songs, Refrains, and Ditties as sung by the Southern slaves."[34]

That Stowe's idea of plantation life closely resembled such representations is suggested by a facetious article about minstrelsy in an 1845 *Knickerbocker Magazine* that sketched out a plot mingling blackface with domestic sentiment. This could also have described, almost exactly, that of *Uncle Tom's Cabin.* James Kennard's article "Who Are Our National Poets?" was self-consciously ludicrous, but it would take only a small shift in tone to render it into a crude outline of Stowe's novel.

Kennard's tongue-in-cheek argument was that our national poets were blackface ones and that minstrel songs were the first American poetry. He built a little scene of slave life around two current tunes of the minstrel stage whose plot and characterization bear striking similarities to the book Stowe later wrote. Kennard imagines a character, "poor Sambo," hoeing while he sings about a master and mistress who promised him his freedom but died, leaving him still "hillin'-up corn!" Kennard sympathizes: "Poor fellow! it seems a hard case. His 'massa and misse' are freed from *their* bonds, but Sambo still wears his." But Kennard's creation is uncomplaining and grateful for small mercies: "He might here very properly stop and water the corn with his tears. But no; Sambo is too much of a philosopher for *that.* Having uttered his plaint, he instantly consoles himself with the thought that he has many blessings yet to be thankful for." Kennard's Sambo thus prefigures Uncle Tom not only in his disappointment at not being manumitted (in Tom's case St. Clare promises him his freedom but then dies before he can effect it) but in his possession of the kind of "grateful joyous" heart that makes him bear his trials stoically.[35]

Both Sambo and Tom live in happy domestic comfort and in log cabins overgrown with flowers: Tom's is "covered by a large scarlet bignonia and a native multiflora rose" and has "flourishing" flower and vegetable beds, and Sambo's "is embowered in Catalpa and Pride-of-India trees."[36] They also have capable wives: Aunt Chloe cooks "corn-cake, in all its varieties of hoe-cake, dodgers, muffins, and other species too numerous to mention," and scolds the children, while Sambo's Jenny "gives the hommony another stir, looks at the hoe-cake, and [gives] the young ones a tight cuff or two on the side of the head, to make them 'hush.'"[37] Even the fate Stowe envisages for her hero is foreshadowed in Kennard's imaginary scene setting for his minstrel songs, for, like Tom, Sambo is subject to the financial situation of his master, who squanders his fortune on the horses, "and poor Sambo and his family may be sold, separated, and sent just where their new masters please; possibly to labor on a sugar plantation—the hell of the blacks."[38] In *Uncle Tom's Cabin* Tom's master, Shelby, makes similar "speculations" that of course result in Tom being sold away from his family, and he too ends up doing back-breaking work in a plantation "hell" (*UTC,* 16–17).

What was different was the tone. Kennard's is a fake sympathy in the parodic tradition of early minstrelsy's mockery of genteel and sentimental culture. His apparent praise for black creativity is a staple of blackface humor, drawing attention to the travesty by pretending to take it for reality.[39] Sambo's predicament afflicts real people, but Kennard derives amusement from imagining blackface as also subject to it, confusing slaves with blackface characters. Although he calls on his audience to sympathize with his slave in the same way as Stowe does for Tom, Sambo is actually a mechanism to celebrate the artifice of blackface.

Despite Kennard's use of it, however, blackface sometimes allied itself more sincerely with sympathy for the slave. Some early minstrel songs, for instance, dealt with the cruelty of white people to black ones, including among the charges sexual exploitation, the separation of families, underfeeding, overworking, and brutality. However, shows were inconsistent, and such songs would be freely mingled with cheerful or comic ones. As Robert Toll asserts, "contradictory feelings about slavery" could be fostered by the structure of the minstrel show, in which the same evening's entertainment could feature both complacency and disquiet.[40]

In this way, watching a minstrel show worked very differently from reading a sentimental novel: rather than directing emotion inward, the show generated contradictory feeling and then diffused it, dispelling by laughter not internalization. The minstrel show could offer complex devices for winning over the public, mechanisms in which slave characters were endeared to audiences even as they were apparently demeaned. *Uncle Tom's* neutralizing effect on the disturbing question of slavery may well be the reason mid-nineteenth-century readers found it so compelling, but that effect could be due not only to sentimental tears but to blackface comedy.

The mystery of *Uncle Tom's Cabin's* extraordinary success at a time when publishers believed that books about slavery did not sell has been explained by the antirevolutionary reassurance that the novel's sentimentality offered readers. Eric Sundquist argues that "sentiment, not antislavery made the book popular" and that the popular appropriation of *Uncle Tom* "gave conventional expression to subversion and thereby contained and controlled it."[41] Sundquist's analysis builds on a succession of critics' emphasis on the "sentimental power" of the novel—its direct appeal to readers' emotions, its idealization of motherhood and domesticity. These qualities have been assumed to explain its sales figures, aligning it with the other sentimental novels produced in the 1850s, many of which were also written by women, featured female heroines, and were commercially successful. These novels also helped produce what Ann Douglas called the "feminization of American culture" in the mid-nineteenth century.[42] Clearly, part of the answer does lie here in the way Stowe privileges passive martyrdom and feminine "influence" over more direct or aggressive approaches to political change. But perhaps *Uncle Tom's* popularity bears more than a coincidental relationship to the equally remarkable craze for minstrelsy in the 1850s.

Certainly, if one is conscious of the contemporary prevalence of blackface performance, it is immediately apparent that a number of characters in Stowe's novel are minstrel show types.[43] Both little Harry and Topsy are explicitly called "Jim Crow" and perform for white audiences: Harry dances and does imitations, while Topsy combines her dance with acrobatics and her startling whistle. It has even been ingeniously suggested that George Harris's disguise during his escape is a kind of blacking-up.[44] Tom is the novel's only black character without close blackface cousins, though, as I have suggested, he may have an ancestor in Kennard's Sambo, and on the stage he was later conflated with the old "uncle" figures of sentimental songs like Foster's.

However, *Uncle Tom's Cabin* draws not only on minstrel conventions of characterization but also on comic routines from the blackface tradition. Patterns of dialogue, the structure of the double act—these are transported from the stage and converted into some of the novel's most distinctive moments. Stowe's borrowing was creative not derivative, and her transformations of theatrical material contributed to the realignment of the traditional gender and class positions of much early blackface performance.[45] But *Uncle Tom's* version of blackface also complicated the sentimental identifications with domestic femininity that are often assumed to be the crux of the novel. Blackface moments in the book sometimes encapsulate sentimental values and sometimes convey ambivalence about them, and at one point the two are explicitly contrasted. Recent criticism has emphasized the way the text celebrates bourgeois femininity, but the novel also cracks jokes at its expense. The feminized heroism of Uncle Tom is shadowed, sometimes supportively, sometimes subversively, by Stowe's recasting of Jim Crow.

Minstrel show set pieces, which themselves contained a number of possible ways of relating to the characters on the stage, were converted in Stowe's novel into powerful devices for reallocating sympathy. One tradition Stowe reworked with particular subtlety, the dialogues between the end man and the interlocutor, worked in the minstrel show both to dramatize class tension and to supplant conflict with the ludicrous and nonsensical. Class is crucial in Stowe's writing—her sentimental vision of matriarchal power is implicitly middle class. However, the end man–interlocutor scenes in the minstrel show are highly ambivalent about precisely the social world *Uncle Tom* valorizes, approaching it with a fine balance of mockery and aspiration. By incorporating such scenes into her novel, even in an adapted form, Stowe complicated its class appeal, positing an ironic distance from bourgeois values as well as an identification with them. Like the members of minstrel show audiences, *Uncle Tom*'s readers inhabit several positions at once.

In the minstrel show the debates between the end man and the interlocutor took place in the first act, between performers sitting in a semicircle on the stage. The end men, who wore rags and spoke with "black" accents, bantered with the immaculately suited interlocutor, whose diction was not only middle class but prone to exaggeratedly complex and Latinate phrasing. As they traded remarks, the end men frequently misunderstood and vulgarized the interlocutor's point, while the interlocutor struggled vainly to assert the respectable, or standard English, interpretation of his utterance. Often he took on specific roles, imitating reformers, preachers, or academics, all those "who from the vantage point of superior class, education, or morality, presumed to lecture the mob."[46] As with most blackface, the weight of the comedy varied in different performances, but often the jibes were not only directed at "black" misuse of language but also worked to undercut the genteel airs of the interlocutor. What appeared to be and sometimes was also a racist attack on black speakers was also a dig at the standardizing and ornate language of the upper echelons.

These exchanges are echoed a number of times in *Uncle Tom's Cabin,* and Stowe not only reproduced the double-edged quality of the stage satire but

also extended and complicated its possibilities. In an early scene that dramatizes the way positions can be simultaneously censored and celebrated in the
novel, Mrs. Shelby is instructing Sam to help the slave catcher go after Eliza
and her child. She is also signaling, less overtly, that she would rather be helping them get away. In the midst of her doublespeak, Mrs. Shelby herself is distracted by Sam's propensity for taking his Maker's name in vain. What ensues
could be an end man–interlocutor exchange, during which Mrs. Shelby takes
on the interlocutor role, ordering, teaching, and reforming, and Sam becomes
the end man, disrupting, mocking, and blaspheming:

> "Why have you been loitering so, Sam? I sent Andy to tell you to
> hurry."
>
> "Lord bless you, Missis!" said Sam, "horses won't be cotched all in a
> mimit; they'd done clared out way down to the south pasture, and the
> Lord knows whar!"
>
> "Sam, how often must I tell you not to say 'Lord bless you, and the
> Lord knows,' and such things? It's wicked."
>
> "O, Lord bless my soul! I done forgot, Missis! I won't say nothing of
> the sort no more."
>
> "Why, Sam, you just *have* said it again."
>
> "Did I? O, Lord! I mean—I didn't go fur to say it."
>
> "You must be *careful* Sam."
>
> "Just let me get my breath, Missis, and I'll start fair. I'll be berry
> careful."
>
> "Well, Sam, you are to go with Mr. Haley, to show him the road,
> and help him. Be careful of the horses, Sam; you know Jerry was a little
> lame last week; *don't ride them too fast.*" (*UTC*, 39–40)[47]

Mrs. Shelby, as interlocutor, instructs Sam in correct linguistic practice and
demands reverent comportment. Persistently transgressing, Sam achieves the
end man's dance between ignorance and mockery in his counterproductive
attempts to stop blaspheming. He conceals a hint of cheek in a hopeless attempt to conform. Yet in the larger context of the slave-catching chapters,
this scene's class configurations are more subtle and more surprising than the
minstrel duality would suggest.

Sam has been tipped off that Mrs. Shelby privately hopes that the fugitives
will get away. His blasphemies, which necessitate Mrs. Shelby's reprimands
and instruction, cause delay, which buys time for Eliza and Harry. Although
Sam's language appears to challenge Mrs. Shelby and to set up confrontation,
its time-consuming provocation also works in her interest, increasing the

chances that the runaways will escape. Thus, the interval produced by this end man–interlocutor role play represents both class conflict and also a cross-class alliance. The end man and the interlocutor's combat is also a conspiracy. To mix matters up still further, Haley, the white slave catcher, has been established in the opening scenes of the novel as deeply uncouth, in speech as in all else. While Sam's slips and errors work in alignment with Mrs. Shelby's prim disapproval, their opponent is "coarse," "low," and "over-dressed." White gentility is in league with black vulgarity against white "coarseness": Sam's exclamations, however sacrilegious themselves, are arraigned against the "profane" slave trader (*UTC,* 1).

This alliance is still in operation when Sam induces Haley's horse to unseat his owner, "accidentally" waves his palm leaf in its eyes, and unleashes "a miscellaneous scene of confusion" while horses bolt, dogs bark, and Mike, Mose, Mandy, and Fanny "raced, clapped hands, whooped, and shouted, with outrageous officiousness and untiring zeal" (*UTC,* 41). This could be minstrel show slapstick; as on the stage, it could also represent a disruption of the industrial work ethic, enabling first-generation urban audiences to laugh with as much as at black characters who would rather dance and go hunting than put in long hours of labor.[48] Yet if this scene similarly enshrines both an apparent critique of black shiftlessness and a delight in it, it differs from the minstrel show in suggesting the genteel sanction of Mrs. Shelby. Stowe includes her middle-class forces of discipline and order in the novel; unlike those of the stage interlocutors, they are often explicitly feminine, and here they are also in league with blackface chaos.

Uncle Tom's Cabin thus adapts the minstrel show's capacity, in Dale Cockrell's words, "to ridicule both up and down the social ladder simultaneously," reapplying it with significant adjustments to class and gender.[49] It is not just ridicule that moves in this scene but also sympathy, and it is not a straight forward journey. Whether the reader identifies most with Sam's linguistic license or with Mrs. Shelby's corrective impulse, procrastination brings the two into collusion. Social position here cannot be marked out simply as rungs on a ladder, and sympathy must chart a path complicated enough to encompass both mistress and slave without visiting the lower-class white.

The oscillating satire and sympathy of the end man–interlocutor dialogues demonstrate the way in which comically uneducated, self-serving, or cowardly characters can also serve to make digs at white slave-owning society. If the novel is inspected for blackface dualities, some of its most demeaning portraits can be found at points where sentiment has the greatest force. The sentimental also amplifies the comedy, adding another layer of meaning to blackface wordplay that is often an antislavery point. On the stage, parodies of sermons, lectures, and stump speeches evinced the same pattern of overt mockery of (and discreet pleasure in) linguistic anarchy as the end man dialogues, and the novel also adapted this blackface convention.

After his triumph over the slave catcher Sam shows off his "speechifying" (*UTC,* 64). Like blackface oratory, this is a self-aggrandizing affair that evinces errors of logic, narcissism, and overinflated and inaccurate use of language. He asserts that his afternoon's work is an example of his determination to "stand up fer [his people's] rights," explaining that his wavering intentions were a sign of his "*conscience,*" one of a series of terms he glosses in contradiction to conventional usage: "[W]hen I thought of gwine arter Lizy, I railly spected Mas'r was sot dat way. When I found Missis was sot de contrar, dat ar was conscience *more yet,*—cause fellers allers gets more by stickin' to Missis's side,—so yer see I's persistent either way, and sticks up to conscience, and holds on to principles" (*UTC,* 66).

Sam's "black" accent and his novel definitions—of "persistence," "conscience," and "principles"—were all staples of the blackface form. He also produces other common aspects of such performances—muddled terms of address ("ladies of de other sex"), self-serving and circular arguments (it is a matter of conscience both to go after Eliza and not to go after her; he is principled because he acts in the belief that "fellers allers gets more by stickin' to Missis's side"), and malapropisms and neologisms ("they's perquisite to dese yer times, and ter *all* times") (*UTC,* 66).[50]

This speech could appear to work merely as unpleasant ridicule, painting Sam as ignorant and conceited and his listeners as gullible. When Andy questions Sam's account, he receives a reply in the same nonsensical vein: "[B]oys like you, Andy, means well, but they can't be spected to collusitate the great principles of action." Nevertheless, the protest is quelled, "rebuked, particularly by the hard word collusitate, which most of the youngerly members of the company seemed to consider as a settler in the case" (*UTC,* 66). If all the mockery in this scene were directed at Sam and his listeners, the reader would function here like those minstrel show spectators who may have felt superior and witty in contrast to the speaker. But the stump speech did not always or not only work to mark off the punters' abilities from those of the characters on the stage. Parts of the speech could poke fun at the audience, parts at black speakers, parts at the middle-class aficionados of its many "highbrow" targets: Shakespeare, opera, phrenology, politics, religion, and science. Lhamon argues that the language of the stump speech actually identified the speaker as a trickster, highlighting and partly endorsing his assaults on taboo. Adroitness with language in the form of puns was part of the pleasure of such pieces, especially when embedded in examples of apparent clumsiness.[51] Holmberg and Schneider suggest further subtleties. Stump speakers, particularly in sermons, addressed the audience as if it were a black one, making it participate in their disarranging of language and logic. The audience could thus participate in the joke or else was mocked itself in quips masked by the momentary confusion over who was being addressed.[52]

Not all of these ambiguities are possible in the novel, where the narration mediates between Sam and the reader, partly cutting off the possibility of our identification with his listeners. The page cannot encompass all the shades of identification of minstrel performances, but even here the stump speech offers some complications. Sam's perorations, like the ones in minstrel shows, are also sometimes double-edged. Sam accompanies Shelby to political meetings,

> where, roosted on some rail fence, or perched aloft in some tree, he would sit watching the orators, with the greatest apparent gusto, and then, descending among the various brethren of his own color, assembled on the same errand, he would edify and delight them with the most ludicrous burlesques and imitations, all delivered with the most imperturbable earnestness and solemnity; and though the auditors immediately about him were generally of his own color, it not unfrequently happened that they were fringed pretty deeply with those of a fairer complexion, who listened, laughing and winking, to Sam's great self-congratulation. (*UTC*, 64)

Like those aspects of blackface that may have been derived from black parodies of white dancing, speech, or style, Sam's oratory is sometimes a lampoon of white performances at political events. He is as liable to expose the weaknesses and self-aggrandizements of white speakers as to demonstrate the fallibilities of black ones. His audiences are complicit with him in this (not the butts of the joke but themselves enjoying it), and his white spectators occupy the fringes, not the prime seats. It is claimed that black dancing for mixed audiences may have contributed to the origins of blackface; this scene stages a white enjoyment of black performative skills alongside a black commentary on white ones.[53] Sam's discussion of the slave-catching exhibits a number of the racially derogatory characteristics of minstrel show speeches—the non sequiturs, mispronunciations, and digressions. However, his antics at political meetings offer the "clever sallies at local personalities and public affairs" that undercut the effects of his minstrel speech traits, again finding targets across the social spectrum.[54]

One of the most typical elements of the set-piece speech in the minstrel show, the malapropism, itself demonstrates some of the complexities of Sam's language. Linguists have described the way the malapropism can itself be in fact a sophisticated play on words, both in minstrel show versions and in the black linguistic practices to which they allude.[55] Sam thoroughly misleads Haley about the road they should take, achieving the paradox of convincing him that Eliza has taken the dirt track while truthfully explaining that it would be impossible. In the course of this elaborate deception he uses a malapropism with a sting. Haley believes that Sam is trying to trick him to take the turnpike, but it is in fact a sophisticated double bluff. Sam wants Haley to use the other road, so when he says, "Now, when I study 'pon it, I think de straight road do best, *deridedly*," it is not so much a mistake as it appears (*UTC*, 50). While the straight road would "decidedly" be the best one, his word coinage reveals another truth: he is in fact deriding the slave trader.

The reader's sympathy in this instance helps convert the apparent malapropism into something entirely apropos, and it makes both Sam's hidden meaning and the joke itself accessible. Sympathy is not just linked with the comedy in this case, it is an integral part of it, and together they conspire to transform Sam's language from a sign of ignorance into a hint of his power.

Chloe's idiosyncratic pronunciation in the novel also embeds multiple significances in blackface malapropism, but where the comedy of Sam's vocabulary conceals sentiment, Chloe's openly directs the reader to empathize with her. As with Sam's speech, Chloe's can be read against conventional usage, but the effect is more poignant than comic. Chloe, we are told, "had a particular fancy for calling poultry poetry," and she also persists in calling the confectioner (to whom she hires herself out in an attempt to buy back her husband) a "perfectioner." These transpositions take place in a scene where Mr. Shelby has callously suggested that she forget Tom and "marry" someone else. Chloe is at this point pitiable but also heroic, because when Mrs. Shelby offers to raise the money to redeem Tom, Chloe volunteers to earn it herself. Chloe is not a risible figure at this point, and, given her enthusiasm for cooking fowl, calling poultry "poetry" is not in her case inappropriate. Considering the urgent reason for her stint at the confectioner's, even "perfectioner's" may not be incorrect. Here the blackface convention is conscripted to assist the sentiment in the novel, where the laughter and the tears demanded by the genre were evoked almost in the same moment and by the same device.

But the novel allocates sympathies in more complex ways than these. In some blackface performance comedy was only apparently disparaging, often cloaking a guilty fascination. Outrageous inclinations, at least for its genteel readers, were also at work in *Uncle Tom's Cabin*, despite the exemplary role models it also provided in the forms of Eva and Tom. As well as offering official aspirations to follow these paragons, the book takes a secret pleasure in behavior that provides a systematic contrast. Its unofficial celebrations of a blackface style form one of the most remembered aspects of the novel, and they also provide one of its most concentrated antislavery hits. These moments in the text derive from blackface at its most subtle and paradoxical, and they are extraordinarily effective.

The scenes in which Miss Ophelia is pitted against Topsy could be interpreted as symbolic of a clash of values, in which immaculate New England housekeeping wars with domestic chaos. As several critics have shown, Stowe uses good housekeeping as a marker of decent society. Gillian Brown has argued that the disarray of Dinah's kitchen, with its onions and hair grease and damask tablecloths jumbled together in drawers, can serve as an explanation of the novel's critique of slavery.[56]

In her relation to Dinah's kitchen, though, as in her relation to Topsy, Miss Ophelia is a difficult figure to identify with. There is an element in the text that secretly condones Dinah's style, and she is, after all, "a native and essential cook, as much as Aunt Chloe" (*UTC,* 179). In Dinah's case, as in Topsy's, the novel pulls in two different directions, overtly lamenting chaos and quietly allowing, even encouraging, readers to enjoy it. Both Dinah and Topsy simultaneously reinforce and suggest an escape from the middle-class domestic ideal. This tension between identification and denial clearly echoes a central feature of blackface performance, during which audiences were able both to enjoy the attributes and antics of the men on stage and to use the burnt cork mask to distance themselves from it.

Topsy's encounters with Miss Ophelia replicate this tension, in contrast to the unalloyed sentimental instruction of her scenes with Eva. Topsy's appearance suggests the exaggerated makeup and impoverished attire of Jim Crow, but a feminized one. Jim Crow was, in fact, played by the seven-year-old Miss Wray in 1835, though women performers were otherwise rare.[57] There were female characters in blackface, usually played in drag (in the 1830s there was a stage "Mrs. Crow," and the minstrel show later developed a female "wench" figure), but they were adult roles and often highly sexualized. For these transvestite "wenches," the incongruity of white men dressed as black women was often the focus of the joke.[58] In what were often vicious blackface songs, such as the extremely popular "Lucy Long," the singers lusted after women described not only as unattractive but specifically as unattractive because of racial characteristics. Their skin was dark and their mouths were wide, as their blackface makeup confirmed, and their feet or heels were long, as their oversized floppy shoes implied. Though the wench danced, it was probably another ("male") performer who sang about her.[59] Topsy, on the other hand, does her own singing, as well as dancing, somersaults, and whistling. Unlike

Lucy Long, Topsy is a child, her hair still "braided in sundry little tails, which stuck out in every direction," and never in the novel is she associated with sexual innuendo (*UTC,* 206). Whereas songs like "Lucy Long" presume that the signs of blackness are physically repulsive, Topsy's function is to demonstrate the irrationality and inhumanity of such a feeling: her need for love teaches Miss Ophelia to overcome her fear of black bodies.

Topsy's most memorable lines in the novel occur in duets with Ophelia, mimicking the classic minstrel double act. Like Mrs. Shelby, Miss Ophelia is a feminine interlocutor, representing the forces of decency and respectability, which Topsy, like a good end man, disrupts.[60] As with the earlier invocations of end man and interlocutor in the novel, the exchanges between Topsy and Miss Ophelia work on a number of levels, enabling virtually contradictory interpretations. Topsy's perversion of the catechism is a good example. The scene echoes Pearl's failure to repeat hers in Hawthorne's *The Scarlet Letter,* scandalizing the Puritan elders, but Pearl's behavior is purely mischievous—she is withholding what she knows.[61] Topsy's error is a product of the ignorance engendered by slavery. In the course of her enforced call-and-response, Topsy is expected to respond, "Our first parents, being left to the freedom of their own will, fell from the state wherein they were created." She interrupts the recitation with a question, "Was dat ar state Kintuck?" (*UTC,* 218). Topsy's willful misparroting of the formula personalizes and even domesticates it, echoing the end man's reinterpretation of educated or sentimental culture in prosaic and ludicrous terms.

An undated minstrel show sketch called "Blackberrying" illustrates this process, showing how much Stowe's famous scene resembles the structure of such blackface humor. In "Blackberrying" the interlocutor is called "Tambo":

BONES: Den she axed me if I would go to the 'pothecary shop for some medicine. I said yes; so I went down to Dr. Night Bell—
TAMBO: No, not to Dr. Night Bell; that's the name of the bell on the door, the night bell.
BONES: Well, I called him Dr. Night Bell, anyhow.
TAMBO: I presume he was a pretty good physician?
BONES: No, he wasn't fishin', he was home.
TAMBO: Oh no, I mean he was a doctor of some note.
BONES: Yes, he was counting out his notes when I went in.
TAMBO: No, Bones, you do not understand. I mean he was a doctor of some standing.
BONES: No, he wasn't standin', he was sittin' on a three-legged stool.[62]

Bones's interpretation of the sign on the doctor's door works both to illustrate his capacity to misunderstand and to undermine the conventions of polite speakers like Tambo and the doctor himself. Bones's misapprehensions and mishearings interrupt the flow of Tambo's questions, so that every line of inquiry is arrested by the necessity to rephrase or reexplain. Topsy's interjections serve the same purpose, distracting Miss Ophelia from the solemn progression of the catechism. With his anarchic imagery, Bones simultaneously reveals and undermines Tambo's value system, as Tambo's status-conscious inquiries about the doctor's professional standing serve paradoxically to evoke the ludicrous and venal picture of the physician counting his money on a three-legged stool. Topsy's transformation of the phrase from the catechism into the irreverent image of Adam and Eve "falling" out of Kentucky works the same way, perfecting an alteration from the sublime to the ridiculous.

Topsy's jokes involve the same kind of seditious literalism or faux naïveté that the end man used to undermine his opponent. Her false confessions of theft also echo this kind of play: "'Why, Missis said I must 'fess; and I couldn't think of nothin' else to 'fess'" (*UTC*, 213). Like Bones's, Topsy's interpretation is ostensibly wrong, but it allows her to best Miss Ophelia, just as Bones's error in the sketch reduces the doctor to the sign of his nighttime summons. Topsy's apparent illogic and ignorance take on Miss Ophelia's (and the reader's) worldview and refute it. The end man in the minstrel show could license the audience's identification with the forces of disorder; in the same way Topsy's function here is to provide enjoyable pokes at authority. One of Topsy's roles in the novel is to demonstrate the destructiveness of slavery and the redeeming power of its antithesis, Little Eva. Topsy lies and steals and knows no better because slavery has deprived her both of family and a moral order. One drift of the narrative confirms this, as Eva teaches her to love and Ophelia makes a missionary of her. But the novel also pulls in another direction, fostering the secret desire to revel in Topsy's upsets and oddities, to challenge the constraint and self-discipline represented by Miss Ophelia.

Some of Topsy's most profound challenges to convention are also attacks on the domestic and the feminine. In these episodes too the text provokes conflicting responses. The scene in which she disperses a bed instead of making it, scattering sheets and spreads and feathers, dressing "the bolster up in Miss Ophelia's night-clothes, and enact[ing] various scenic performances with that," brings her style of theatrical disorder to housekeeping, and she mounts a similar assault on the delicate pursuit of needlework: "[S]he broke her needles, threw them slyly out of windows, or down in chinks of the walls; she tangled, broke, and dirtied her thread, or, with a sly movement, would throw away a spool altogether.... [T]hough Miss Ophelia could not help feeling that so many accidents could not possibly happen in succession, yet she could not, without a watchfulness which would leave her no time for anything else, detect her" (*UTC*, 216, 215).

These vignettes are reminiscent of minstrelsy's fantasies of revolt against the middle-class work ethic, but Topsy's recalcitrance is directed at *domestic* work, at the insistence that she sew fine stitches and help keep a spotless house. Topsy's rebellion is against the feminine version of the factory ideal, the well-ordered home. Richard Beale Davis calls Topsy "a bundle of perversities reflecting the guilty consciences of her owners."[63] Her mischief is obviously a reflection as well as a product of the moral disarray Stowe believes is occasioned by slavery, but it would also appeal to anyone who has secretly chafed at the domestic yoke: it is blackface subversion for girls.

Topsy's catchphrase, "I'se so wicked," was later turned into two songs, singling out her defiance of conventional piety as her most marketable characteristic.[64] In this as in her exchanges with Ophelia Topsy's resistance is enjoyable: comic, punishable, ultimately to be corrected, but also potentially delicious. Given what we know of Stowe's own scatty and impatient approach to housework and her extended flight from domestic responsibility to the Brattleboro Water Cure, the writer herself may have taken some pleasure in Topsy's assault on the home.[65]

Yet just as Stowe invoked blackface comedy to solicit forbidden sympathy for Topsy the imp, so she also used it to press home the plight of Topsy the slave. In this, the sketch "Blackberrying" again elucidates Stowe's method:

> BONES: Ah! Tambo, she's gone dead.
> TAMBO: Is she dead, Bones?
> BONES: Yes, Tambo. She sent for me three days after she died.
> TAMBO: No, Bones, you mean three days previous to her decease.
> BONES: No; she had no niece; she was an orphan.[66]

Topsy's assertion, upon well-meaning interrogation, that she "never was born" exactly parallels Bones's assertion that his girl sent for him "three days after she died": it is an affront both to reason and to the interrogator. Topsy's illogical outburst, "I 'spect I grow'd," is closely related to Bones's, and both work by challenging our common assumptions about life, death, and family structures. Like Bones's denial of the finality of death, Topsy's rejection of the necessity of birth is, at one level, a comic display of ignorance and, at another level, oddly disturbing.[67] Topsy's statement upsets Ophelia's attempts to establish origins and order, and it is amusing as much because it nonplusses the interlocutor as because it makes no sense. Yet despite the reader's strong temptation to enjoy them, Topsy's rejections of order and logic also unsettle the reader, and the text's invocation of such contradictory feelings is especially powerful here. In Topsy's case the comedy is intensified by pathos: she has been "raised by a speculator," and so her ignorance of her birth reflects the slave owner's indifference to her humanity. Stowe is both playing with a comic convention in Topsy's line and giving it a moral resonance. Topsy's "never was born" can be compared not only with the blackface sketch but with the opening of slave narratives, in which the absence of the usual biographical details makes the same point.[68]

Topsy's famous comment used a minstrel device to extraordinary political effect. However, although blackface assisted in the novel's complex marshaling of readerly emotion, and although some of the most potentially derogatory scenes in the novel also encourage readerly identification with slaves, it should not be forgotten that Stowe's antislavery weapon here is a minstrel figure. Blackface, so politically elusive, always so close to mockery, would ever be a mischievous servant. Despite the power Stowe invested in the ambiguities of Topsy's characterization, it was not difficult for later readers to convert Stowe's character into a sign of irrepressible black childishness, especially for proslavery propaganda. Like many blackface figures, Topsy was a fantasy projection for those afflicted by bourgeois repressions, but although this role complicated her relation to race, it did not negate it.

Worse, just as the minstrel show itself could harbor violently degrading images alongside invitations to imagine oneself with the characters on the stage, so does *Uncle Tom's Cabin.* Some of the most highly charged scenes of black-white encounter in the novel seem to owe more to the fear or disgust expressed in some minstrel performance than to those acts that encoded fascination or a sense of shared conspiracy. These episodes lack the fine balance of empathy and amusement that make earlier scenes both powerful and open to multiple readings, and they demonstrate the dangers of conscripting blackface to do antislavery work. Where Stowe's racial portraiture is least equivocal, there is most indication of how it might also be damaging.

A certain unease is manifested first in the characterization of St. Clare's household. The valet, Adolph, is very like the blackface dandy, typified by Zip Coon, in his dress, manner, and speech (*UTC,* 142–43). However, Adolph, unlike Chloe, is not a sentimentalized version of a blackface tradition, nor does his role, unlike Sam's, involve a complex antislavery play across its conventions. Adolph's activities in the novel are unsavory: he pilfers from his master, flirts with Jane and Rosa, and despises Ophelia for working: "[S]he was no lady" (*UTC,* 206). Jane and Rosa, who are similarly overdressed and inclined to "airs," scoff at Dinah, who is too dark to go to the "light-colored" ball, and at Topsy too. Unlike the scenes with Sam or Topsy, these instances of dandyism are not complicated by any reversals of sentiment in the novel, and there are no secret devices to endear these characters to the reader. In fact, they are partly punished in the narrative, for when St. Clare dies his wife takes the opportunity to have Rosa whipped and Adolph sold.

In the minstrel show figures like Adolph could satirize both working-class dandies and the upper-class style they aspired to, as well as expressing anxiety about wealthy free blacks, but in the novel, which so frequently makes a white middle-class lifestyle normative, the satire is not so broadly shared.[69] Whereas Topsy's sallies against bourgeois femininity may offer the reader the pleasures of vicarious rebellion, it is Adolph, Jane, and Rosa who are ridiculed, not "airs" per se. Black dandies in the novel indicate a narrower set of transgressions than those on the stage, as Stowe's characters get above their station, rather than lampooning their self-styled betters. In these moments Stowe's characterization is far less generous to her fictional slaves even than her blackface model; it presages more the vicious slurs typical of later pro-slavery novels.

Those novels would have even more use for Sambo and Quimbo.[70] Legree's black adjuncts are, like Topsy, illustrative of the effects of cruel and irresponsible enslavement, but they have none of her redeeming hilarity. Stowe paints a grotesque and frightening portrait of these two, who are positively menacing in appearance: "coarse, dark, heavy features; their great eyes, rolling enviously on each other." Their language reinforces this impression: "barbarous, guttural, half-brute intonation" (*UTC,* 299–300). As with Topsy, the contrast between Sambo's and Quimbo's dark features and their eyes imitates blackface makeup, and "their dilapidated garments fluttering in the wind" mimic minstrel costume, but the "barbarous" accents are a far cry from Sam's acute malapropisms (*UTC,* 300). As we see Quimbo "viciously [driving] two or three tired women" from the corn mill, or Sambo kicking Lucy to fainting point, there is none of the oscillation of sympathy that Stowe motivates for Sam or for Topsy (*UTC,* 301, 305–6). Like those characters, however, they are immeasurably more powerful when hell raising than when heaven-bent, as when Cassy hears "the sound of wild shrieking, whooping, halloing, and singing . . . mingled with the barking of dogs, and other symptoms of general uproar" (*UTC,* 325). This passage is reminiscent of the "rough noise" that Cockrell identifies as one of the folk practices behind early blackface or the raising Cain that Lhamon argues remained one of its primary impulses. It is also not far off from the uproar produced when the Shelby slaves delay the slave hunt or from the commotion Topsy tends to engender. But in Legree's house rowdiness is sinister; it is not a festival of misrule. Legree and his overseers are "in a state of furious intoxication," and their "making all manner of ludicrous and horrid grimaces at each other" is not rebellious role play but a possible precursor of real violence (*UTC,* 325).

Blackface in the final section of the novel is thus the source of sinister images, not, as earlier, of comic pleasures or a dose of antislavery sentiment. There is no longer the sense, as in many of the scenes set on the Shelby and St. Clare plantations, that blackface is designed to snare readerly sympathy for the forces of riot; rather, gentility and order are endorsed more completely. The signal for this comes when Legree demands a song from the "dispirited" slaves he is carrying home. When Tom strikes up a "Methodist hymn" Legree silences him and demands a song that could easily belong to the blackface repertoire: "Mas'r See'd Me Cotch a Coon."[71] Stowe calls the song "one of those unmeaning songs, common among the slaves," a judgment she almost immediately contradicts, observing that "there was a prayer in it, which Simon could not hear" (*UTC,* 297).[72]

This snatch of blackface signals a deep rift between white and black signification, in stark contrast to the earlier alliances between Mrs. Shelby and Sam or Topsy and the reader. The secreting of a "prayer" in a song, which partly parallels Stowe's blackface envelopes for antislavery messages, is also a desperate measure. Tom's fellows are not exploiting the distance between genteel and blackface culture in the way that the novel itself does in earlier episodes. At this point the reader is not encouraged to enjoy the "rowdy" entertainment, even unofficially. The song is pitted against piety, but, where the text winked at Topsy's and Sam's irreverence, here sanctity prevails. Legree believes that when his slaves sing they are neither expressing despondent feelings nor experiencing them, which is easier on his conscience and useful in his efforts to subdue his workforce. The song's rowdiness links it with Legree's degenerative rejection of middle-class values and makes it incompatible with Uncle Tom's godly tunes.

In her later defense of the novel, *A Key to Uncle Tom's Cabin,* Stowe's collection of documents to "prove" the central tenets of *Uncle Tom's Cabin* reveals what she believes to be crucial to the novel's argument. Tom's piety and domesticity are emphasized. A whole chapter is devoted to historical examples of black people with Tom's qualities, as is one to those of George Harris. Stowe does not accord her borrowings from blackface the same importance. It is striking that the *Key* does not produce authenticating examples of blackface behavior. There are no sources cited for Sam and Andy, and although there is a chapter devoted to the issues raised by Topsy, this is restricted to the possibility of educating slaves: "[T]he appeal to the more generous part of the negro character is seldom made in vain."[73] Although Stowe used minstrel characterization and set pieces in her novel, she did not spell out any ideological implications for them in the way she did for Uncle Tom's piety or the state of Chloe's cabin. Yet the association of minstrel songs with Legree in the novel does suggest some unease about blackface.

Whereas Topsy's Jim Crow act could coexist with a susceptibility to Eva's instruction, Tom is only ever a moral beacon. In Tom Stowe signaled most clearly where readers' sympathies should be directed: his personification of Christian strength works without the ambiguities of other figures in the text. Tom's religion protects him from the dismissive readings Topsy's black-face act leaves open, and whenever Uncle Tom is the novel's focus of sympa-thy, blackface is once more the antithesis of feminine sentimental culture: impious and uncouth. All through the novel multiple, conflicting, and even contrary identifications are opened up for the reader, and its quiet encour-agement to cheer for Topsy's chaos or Sam's insurrections could also call out other more oblique readings. Minstrel show devices could help *Uncle Tom's Cabin* inspire antislavery feeling in stealthy, unconfrontational ways, but they could not guarantee it. *Uncle Tom*'s readers, like blackface audiences, could take from the novel what they wished, and that included less benign interpretations.

The blackface in *Uncle Tom* suggests that many of the ambiguities and unpredictabilities of performance could be incorporated into fiction. Lott has suggested that audience responses at the minstrel show blended apparent contradictions: "mordant irony and suspension of disbelief" and "disavowal or ridicule of the Other and interracial identification with it." Lott compares this with theories of the contemporary cinema, at which spectators "succes-sively identify, across gender lines, with logical screen representatives of our-selves (heroes, victims), then with seeming adversaries (villains, killers)."[74] In the same way the viewer of blackface could serially imagine solidarity with or his own superiority to the racialized figure on the stage. Yet many of the same paradoxes of audience identification are apparent in the process of reading fiction. Even with a novel readers can interpolate themselves into narratives in peculiar ways.

Some of the possibilities are suggested by Frances Hodgson Burnett's rec-ollection of the impact of *Uncle Tom's Cabin* on her as a child in England in the 1850s. Burnett's imaginative appropriation of Stowe's novel suggests that its readers could harbor sympathies as multiple and perverse as those of any blackface audience. She describes acting out the novel in solitary play, recast-ing *Uncle Tom* with herself, at different times, in almost every role. In the fol-lowing passage, in which Burnett coyly refers to her younger self as the "Small

Person," she suggests how the plot was advanced with the characters shared among the child and a couple of dolls:

> [A] cheerful black doll was procured immediately and called Topsy; her "best doll," which fortunately had brown hair in its wig, was Eva, and was kept actively employed slowly fading away and dying, while she talked about the New Jerusalem, with a hectic flush on her cheeks. She converted Topsy, and totally changed her gutta-percha nature, though it was impossible to alter her gutta-percha grin. She conversed with Uncle Tom (then the Small Person was Uncle Tom), she cut off "her long golden-brown curls" . . . and presented them to the weeping slaves. (Then the Small Person was all the weeping slaves at once.)[75]

The confusion of pronouns in this passage (who exactly converts Topsy?) suggests the rapid shifting of identities under way, and the writer seems to be as absorbed in Eva's conversion as in Topsy's resistance. But the most surprising identification the girl makes is manifested in a scene her mother accidentally stumbles upon, starring the doll who had hitherto played Topsy. The child is discovered, "apparently furious with insensate rage, muttering to herself as she brutally lashed with one of her brother's toy whips, a cheerfully hideous black gutta-percha doll who was tied to the candelabra stand and appeared to be enjoying the situation."[76]

Here the Small Person, formerly Uncle Tom and "all the weeping slaves at once," has been transformed into Legree, while the doll, formerly Topsy, has become Uncle Tom. The doll, because of the fixed grin on its inanimate face, seems in its unchanged expression to retain the irrepressible good humor of its earlier role, and this impression helps to convert Burnett's version of Stowe's antislavery image into something more like masochistic fantasy. The young girl and Stowe's villain have been fused together into a "little fury with the flying hair," while Uncle Tom and Topsy have together coalesced into a rubber doll who is taking Tom's fatal punishment with every sign of enjoyment.[77]

This scenario, which the child's mother finds "alarming" and "distressing," surely denotes an unexpected allocation of empathy in Stowe's young reader. Critical readings of slave narratives have revealed the pornographic function of the accounts of whippings such texts produced as evidence of the victimization of women slaves. Deborah McDowell's analysis of such scenes highlights the aptness of Frederick Douglass's comment that he was not only a "witness" of such events but thereby also a "participant."[78] Burnett's anecdote illustrates the way identification with the injured can also be disturbingly inflected by a fascination with the violence of the scene. Jenny Franchot suggests that Douglass's description of his Aunt Esther's whipping disrupts the narrative path of his autobiographies, its "aesthetic power" arresting their trajectory of self-liberation.[79] Franchot's argument offers the possibility that Douglass's whipping scene resonates beyond its antislavery function and that it spills out from its illustrative role in the narrative. Burnett's story indicates that the whipping of Uncle Tom could similarly escape its primary role in Stowe's novel. Legree is an intense object of interest even for a reader who sympathizes with "all the weeping slaves." Not simply evoking "feeling" or "sympathy," Legree's physical assault on Tom could itself attract a guilty identification, even from a child who at other moments was imagining herself as the abused martyr. As well as the sentimental heroine and the comic, tragic, and incidental slave characters, Burnett's "feeling" could also take in the villain.

Burnett manages in the course of her games to identify across gulfs of age, class, gender, and race. Not only does her play illustrate the "movement of sympathy in all its anxious appeals" across such grounds of difference, which Shirley Samuels describes as the work of sentimental literature, it turns the crossing of those lines into a multidirectional roller-coaster ride. Samuels argues that "the sentimental complex . . . situates the reader or viewer: that is, the act of emotional response the work evokes also produces the sentimental subject who consumes the work."[80] Stowe bears this out in the declaration in her preface that her "object" has been "to awaken sympathy and feeling for the African race, as they exist among us," and her plea in the conclusion that readers "see to it that *they feel right*" (*UTC*, xiii, 385). The parting of Tom from his family, Eliza's flight across the ice, the deaths of Tom and Little Eva are all clearly designed to inspire empathy of this kind. Yet Burnett's example indicates that this process may be only partially successful: her acting out of the novel does make her the kind of sentimental subject who "feels right," but it also involves a much more experimental kind of readerly subjectivity.

Burnett's staging of *Uncle Tom's Cabin* in the nursery points to the intricacies of the play of sympathy in the novel, echoing a complexity that was not confined to the imagination of her childhood reenactments. Even at the most apparent structural levels of the text, it is not only the virtuous who monopolize the reader's emotions or who inspire a sense of kinship. There are scenes in the novel that demand sympathy without pity or pathos or that even play with readerly sympathy, shuttling it between antagonistic characters and surreptitiously attracting it to unlikely recipients. Sympathy takes circuitous, evanescent, and sometimes multiple simultaneous routes through the text, creating a slipperiness and paradoxicality that is more typical of the minstrel show. Burnett's rapid imaginative movements across identity boundaries are anticipated in the book when Stowe complicates even the crossings and blurrings characteristic of blackface, sometimes radically redistributing minstrelsy's most typical class and gender loyalties.

Most commentators overlooked what Burnett unconsciously recognizes, the way Stowe's book borrowed some of the performative ambiguities of minstrelsy. Blackness in the shows was theatrical, and its staginess licensed readers to make silent identifications with characters' prankish assaults on gentility. Minstrel audiences could at once laugh at "black" characters on the stage and simultaneously delight in their affronts to decent society and respectable manners. Richard Butsch asserts that minstrelsy offered "a dual message of racism and anti-intellectualism"; it could also be described as hiding class conflict in apparent (and often offensive) racial parody.[81] *Uncle Tom's Cabin* captured for the novel some of the multiple meanings blackface embedded in performance, offering readers a comedy of secret sympathy in which black characters could be at once ludicrous, seductively subversive, and aligned with moral rectitude. Blackface structures in the novel opened conduits for cross-class and cross-racial empathy, both overt and antislavery in purpose and also more covert and rebellious in their effects.

But if, like a blackface show, *Uncle Tom's Cabin* could be read with multiple and even competing sympathies, it could also be read as straightforward racial portraiture. The reviews of Stowe's novel also cast light on a long-standing controversy amongst commentators on blackface—was it really taken to represent black people? By assuming that the portrayal of African Americans was blackface's preserve, *Uncle Tom's* readers suggest it was. Most recently, critics have been fascinated by the complexities and ambiguities of blackface performance, Cockrell and Lhamon arguing that in its earliest forms it mingled interracial cultural exchange and social subversiveness.[82] In these accounts blackface was neither entirely white in culture nor only inspired by racism. Yet nineteenth-century celebrations of minstrelsy often claimed it was derived from specific black musicians and dancers.[83] Constance Rourke was arguing as late as 1931 that many of the rhythms in minstrel music, its dances, and the content of many of its songs showed unmistakable "negro" origins.[84] Such assertions distracted from the facts that historians have since emphasized: that many early minstrels and their music had white and Northern origins, that minstrelsy was "shaped by white expectations and desires and not by black realities," and that white working-class rivalry lay behind blackface, making stage blacks the objects both of envy and of contempt.[85] The insistence on blackface's verisimilitude, while it may not have been entirely specious, obscured the racist purposes minstrelsy could serve. The naturalization of blackface imagery in *Uncle Tom's Cabin* may have reinforced this effect: most commentators ignored white culture's investment in Stowe's images, just as they did with blackface. Like the minstrel show spectators who turned Jim Crow into a "representative of the negro," some contemporaries took Stowe's characters to be the definitive *literary* representations.

As *Uncle Tom's Cabin* increasingly supplied the reference points for transatlantic discussions of slavery in the United States, many of these reviewers, like Burnett, were British. The *Times* review of the novel declared, "We know of no book in which the negro character finds such successful interpretation, and appears so life-like and so fresh. The scenes in which the negroes are represented at their domestic labours or conversing with each other reveal a familiar acquaintance with negro life, and a capacity for displaying it that cannot be mistaken."[86]

George Eliot shared this confidence in the fidelity of Stowe's representation of the "negro character" and "negro life," asserting in an 1856 review of Stowe's second novel, *Dred,* that "Mrs Stowe has *invented* the Negro novel."[87] *Uncle Tom's Cabin*'s many imitators—the pro- and antislavery novels, the slave narratives, the parodies, dramatizations, and rewritings—are testimony enough to its hold on representations of slavery in the 1850s and beyond. As Richard Yarborough has asserted, Stowe "helped to establish a range of character types that served to bind and restrict black authors for decades."[88] For the rest of the century and beyond, *Uncle Tom* tended to determine and delimit the scope for putting African Americans in fiction, just as minstrelsy dominated their portrayal on the stage.

Moreover, *Uncle Tom*'s hegemony extended farther than fiction. After reading the novel, Stowe's former colleague, the teacher Mary Dutton, remembered a trip they had taken in 1833 to visit the family of a pupil on their farm in Kentucky: "Harriet did not seem to notice anything that happened, but sat much of the time abstracted in thought. When the negroes did funny things and cut up capers, she did not seem to pay the slightest attention to them. Afterwards however, in reading 'Uncle Tom,' I recognised scene after scene of that visit portrayed with the most minute fidelity."[89] What is striking about this passage is Dutton's conflation of "the negroes," Stowe's novel, and minstrel-type theatricality. It seems merely a matter of course that they should do "funny things and cut up capers" and for Dutton to describe her memories with the dramatic term "scenes." Blackface plays through Dutton's recollections, and it is used to align them with her impressions of *Uncle Tom's Cabin.*

Uncle Tom and blackface between them helped structure Dutton's memories of slaves after the event, but they also exerted an influence over interpretations of Southern encounters as they were experienced. In 1857 a newly married British couple took a wedding trip through North America. The wife— feminist, reformer, and painter Barbara Bodichon—had strong antislavery sympathies.[90] While they traveled in Louisiana, Bodichon's views were in part fueled by *Uncle Tom,* to which she referred several times in letters.[91]

Stowe's novel becomes in Bodichon's writings a touchstone on the slavery question. She reads its absence from Southern homes as a sign of pervasive misinformation: "The lies I have read! here in newspapers and *Cabins* (answers to *Uncle Tom* which deluge the South, where the original is not to be found on any table)," and when Bodichon meets a Southern woman claiming to hate Mrs. Beecher, she observes that "every trace of humanity disappeared, under the influence of this feeling."[92] By the time of Bodichon's journey Stowe had become an obvious guide for a British traveler attempting to interpret the South. Bodichon was also filtering her impressions through her reading of Stowe, ironically so, since the novelist had herself only ever made the one trip South, and that no deeper than Kentucky. Yet the traveler's encounters were shaped by her reading, and Bodichon was seeing as well as writing after *Uncle Tom's Cabin.* Encountering a group of black children in Carrolton, Bodichon turns the event into a weak comic dialogue about her unusual sketching dress—blue-tinted spectacles, large hat, and Balmoral boots: "Six negro children who were playing stopped, stared and then began to run away, frightened by my appearance. 'I do not eat niggers,' I said—so they came up to me and one said, 'why it's a woman!' 'Why do you wear boots?' 'Because it is wet!' 'Why do you wear spectacles?' 'Because I can't see without.' 'Why do you wear a hat?' 'Because I can't carry a parasol!' So we became good friends."[93]

This exchange falls far short of the end man–interlocutor acts it faintly resembles, though, interestingly it is the black children who take up the interlocutor position in this case, questioning Bodichon's deviation from conventional dress for a woman of her race and class. Sadly, Bodichon's assertions of the practicality of her getup don't make for much of a joke, and it is not as obvious as she implies why the children make friends, especially given the epithet she applies to them. But Bodichon does more than borrow the comic device Stowe had adapted from the minstrel show. Stowe's novel provides the model for Bodichon's understanding of these "jolly children, half naked," and a real child is transformed in the Englishwoman's account into a fictional character: "One was a real little Topsy who sang and danced, and then seized the youngest and screamed to me, 'I'll sell you this child for two dollars.' The poor little thing howled and cried and I gave Topsy a scolding for such a wicked joke."[94]

A naughty little girl becomes, for Bodichon, Stowe's creation, and the image in the novel absorbs the identity of the young slave. Disturbingly, of course, Bodichon's "Topsy" is herself mimicking slave society, satirizing the commodification of human life. Bodichon could have seen her as a Louisiana trickster with a vital point to make about slavery. Instead she reads her—and writes her—as *Uncle Tom*'s blackface slave girl. The fluidity of identification that Frances Hodgson Burnett had discovered in her Manchester nursery has gone. Whereas the English girl could slip in and out of a range of imaginative roles derived from Stowe's novel, the black child's role is determined by it.

Uncle Tom's Cabin harnessed the minstrel show's potential for ambiguity and developed it to an extraordinary extent. Minstrelsy relied on performative conventions to sidestep the contentious, and it used theatrical unreality to allay anxieties about race and slavery. *Uncle Tom* reorganized stage material precisely to mine those anxieties, exploring even under an innocuous and irreverent surface the desperate human circumstances that occasioned them. But the flexibility, the paradoxicality, and the multiplication of sympathies in the text, which partly lent it its power, also laid it open to endless reappropriation and helped impress its images on the likes of Bodichon's "Topsy." Blackface was valued for its ability to make whiteness merge into blackness. Bodichon's story suggests how Stowe's novel could, for some readers, allow blackness to disappear into blackface.

Notes

1. "The White Slave: or, Memoirs of a Fugitive," *National Era*, 5 August 1852, 126; quoted from the *New York Independent* in "Uncle Tom's Cabin As It Is," *Liberator*, 8 October 1852, 163.

2. Charles Briggs, "Uncle Tomitudes," *Putnam's Monthly* (January 1853): 101.

3. Herman Melville, "Bartleby the Scrivener," 1853, in *Billy Budd and Other Stories*, ed. Harold Beaver (Harmondsworth: Penguin, 1985), 59.

4. Robert Weisbuch, *Atlantic Double-Cross: American Literature and British Influence in the Age of Emerson* (Chicago: University of Chicago Press, 1986), 45.

5. "American Slavery," *Times* (London), 3 September 1852. Reprinted in *New York Daily Times*, 18 September 1852, 5; Briggs, 101.

6. "Literature of Slavery," *New Englander* (November 1852): 607.

7. "The Uncle Tom Epidemic," *Literary World*, 4 December 1852: 355–58, 357. See also the review "*Uncle Tom's Cabin*, by Harriet Beecher Stowe," *Literary World*, 24 April 1852: 291–92.

8. "American Slavery."

9. William J. Wilson, "From Our Brooklyn Correspondent," *Frederick Douglass' Paper*, 17 June 1852: 3.

10. Harry Birdoff, *The World's Greatest Hits: Uncle Tom's Cabin* (New York: S. F. Vanni, 1947), 23.

11. Eric Lott, *Love and Theft: Blackface Minstrelsy and the American Working Class* (New York: Oxford University Press, 1993), 212.

12. Nathaniel Hawthorne, *The House of the Seven Gables*, 1851 (Harmondsworth: Penguin American Classics, 1986), 36, 50–51.

13. Shelley Fisher Fishkin discusses this episode in some detail in *Was Huck Black? Mark Twain and African American Voices* (New York: Oxford University Press, 1993), 112–13.

14. Raymond Walters, *Stephen Foster: Youth's Golden Gleam* (Princeton: Princeton University Press, 1936), 51. See Forrest Wilson on the Lane Scandal, on the originals of George and Eliza, and on the Underground Railroad (*Crusader in Crinoline: The Life of Harriet Beecher Stowe* [London: Hutchinson, 1942], 79–81, 86–87, 107); see Joan Hedrick on Lane and abolition in Cincinnati (*Harriet Beecher Stowe: A Life* [New York: Oxford University Press, 1994], 102–109.

15. Ken Emerson, *Doo-Dah! Stephen Foster and the Rise of Popular Culture* (New York: Da Capo Press, 1988), 116–20; Hedrick, 67.

16. Walters, 60–61. For a detailed account of this period in Stowe's life, see Hedrick, 67–217.

17. Robert P. Nevin, "Stephen C. Foster and Negro Minstrelsy," *Atlantic Monthly* (November 1867): 608.

18. For accounts of this period in Foster's life see Walters, and also Emerson, 116–48.

19. In fact, minstrel audiences varied significantly over time and according to venue and location. Always largely white and predominantly male, they did include women and children at the larger, more respectable minstrel halls in big cities. Minstrelsy may have been largely working class, but gentlemen also attended. See Richard Butsch, *The Making of American Audiences from Stage to Television, 1750–1990* (Cambridge: Cambridge University Press, 2000), 87–93.

20. See Robert B. Winans, "Early Minstrel Show Music, 1843–1852," in *Musical Theatre in America: Papers and Proceedings of the Conference on the Musical Theatre in America*, ed. Glenn Laney (Westport, CT: Greenwood, 1984), 83; Nicholas E. Tawa, *Sweet Songs for Gentle Americans: The Parlor Song in America, 1790–1860* (Bowling Green, OH: Bowling Green University Popular Press, 1980), 91.

21. Charles Hamm, *Yesterdays: Popular Song in America* (New York: Norton, 1979), 137.

22. See Sam Dennison, *Scandalize My Name: Black Imagery in American Popular Music* (New York: Garland, 1982), 114–15; Hamm, *Yesterdays*, 137.

23. See Winans, 83, 91, 93; Tawa, 89, 97. Jon Finson suggests that the frequency with which the press attacked genteel amateurs for singing minstrel songs indicates that middle-class interest in blackface predated the more "respectable" forms (*The Voices That Are Gone: Themes in Nineteenth-Century American Popular Song* [New York: Oxford University Press, 1994], 222).

24. See Butsch, 89–93.

25. Derek B. Scott, *The Singing Bourgeois: Songs of the Victorian Drawing Room and Parlour* (Milton Keynes: Open University Press, 1989), 92.

26. Scott, 85; Winans, 80; Emerson, 75. On the Hutchinsons see Hamm, *Yesterdays,* 141–61, and Hamm's comments on this in chapter 4 of *Putting Popular Music in Its Place* (Cambridge: Cambridge University Press, 1995), 98–100. See also Philip D. Jordan, *Singin' Yankees* (Minneapolis: University of Minnesota Press, 1947) and Caroline Mosely, "The Hutchinson Family: The Function of Their Song in Ante-Bellum America," *Journal of American Culture* (1978): 713–23.

27. Scott, 83–84.

28. A number of these may be found in Vicki L. Eaklor, *American Antislavery Songs: A Collection and Analysis* (New York: Greenwood, 1988). See, for instance, the adaptation of "Old Dan Tucker" written for an antislavery picnic in Danvers from 1845 (163–64) or Justitia's 1858 rendition of "Lucy Neal" (221–22). See also Dennison, 159.

29. Printed in the *Liberator,* 8 August 1845, reprinted in Eaklor, 163–64, 163.

30. Jesse Hutchinson, "Get off the Track," reprinted in Eaklor, 254–55. In one of a number of stage references, the Hutchinsons' 1844 number "The Old Granite State" was parodied by the Ethiopian Serenaders as "The Old Virginny State" (George C. Odell, *Annals of the New York Stage* [New York: Columbia University Press, 1928], 5: 56).

31. Jesse Hutchingson, "Get off the Track," quoted in Dennison, 168; program note, "Georgia Champions," 1845, quoted in Winans, 90.

32. W. T. Lhamon, *Raising Cain: Blackface Performance from Jim Crow to Hip Hop* (Cambridge, MA: Harvard University Press, 1998), 90–98; on Stowe see 97–98.

33. Dennison, 170–71.

34. Robert Toll, *Blacking Up: The Minstrel Show in Nineteenth-Century America* (New York: Oxford University Press, 1974), 68; "Virginia Minstrels," program, Dublin, 1844, quoted in Toll, 34.

35. J. Kennard, Jr., "Who Are Our National Poets?" *Knickerbocker; or, New York Monthly Magazine* (October 1845): 333–34. Both the songs are from minstrel shows; "Jenny Get Your Hoe-cake Done" was a popular hit dating from at least 1840 and was sung by Sweeney and Whitlock. See the playbills in Charles C. Moreau, ed. *Negro Minstrelsy in New York,* 2 vols. (New York: N.p., 1891), 717–18, and in Dennison. The other, ironically, was later widely adapted and sung by blacks well into the twentieth century. See also Lawrence W. Levine, *Black Culture and Black Consciousness: Afro-American Folk Thought from Slavery to Freedom* (New York: Oxford University Press, 1977), 192–93.

36. Kennard.

37. Harriet Beecher Stowe, *Uncle Tom's Cabin,* 1852, ed. Elizabeth Ammons (New York: Norton, 1994), 17, 19 (hereafter cited in the text as *UTC*).

38. Kennard.

39. In a different version of the same joke, Mark Twain claimed to have convinced his mother and Aunt Betsey Smith that the Christy Minstrel Troupe were African missionaries (Twain, *Autobiography of Mark Twain* [London: Chatto and Windus, 1960], 62).

40. Toll, 80–82, 86.

41. Eric J. Sundquist, "Slavery, Revolution, and the American Renaissance," in *The American Renaissance Reconsidered,* eds. Walter Benn Michaels and Donald E. Pease (Baltimore: Johns Hopkins University Press, 1985), 18.

42. On Stowe and sentimental or domestic literature see Herbert Ross Brown, *The Sentimental Novel in America 1789–1860* (Durham, NC: Duke University Press, 1940), Helen Waite Papashvily, *All the Happy Endings: A Study of the Domestic Novel in America, the Women Who Wrote It, and the Women Who Read It, in the Nineteenth Century* ((Port Washington, NY: Kennikat Press, 1972), Nina Baym, *Woman's Fiction: A Guide to Novels by and about Women in America, 1820–1870* (Ithaca, NY: Cornell University Press, 1978), Mary P. Ryan, *The Empire and the Mother: American Writing about Domesticity, 1830–1860* (New York: Haworth Press, 1982), Mary Kelley, *Private Woman, Public Stage: Literary Domesticity in Nineteenth-Century America* (New York: Oxford University Press, 1984). On Stowe and heroines see Elizabeth Ammons, "Stowe's Dream of the Mother-Savior: *Uncle Tom's Cabin* and American Women Writers before the 1920s," in *New Essays on* Uncle Tom's Cabin, ed. Eric J. Sundquist (Cambridge,: Cambridge University Press, 1986), 155–95. Ann Douglas attacks Stowe, along with other sentimentalists, in *The Feminization of American Culture* (New York: Alfred A. Knopf, 1977). Jane Tompkins champions them in *Sensational Designs: The Cultural Work of American Fiction 1790–1860* (New York: Oxford University Press, 1985). There are more critical readings of Stowe's sentimental politics in Rachel Bowlby, "Breakfast in America—*Uncle Tom's* Cultural Histories," in *Nation and Narration,* ed. Homi K. Bhabha (London: Routledge, 1990), 197–212, Gillian Brown, *Domestic Individualism: Imagining Self in Nineteenth-Century America* (Berkeley: University of California Press, 1990) and Shirley Samuels, ed., *The Culture of Sentiment: Race, Gender and Sentimentality in Nineteenth-Century America* (New York: Oxford University Press, 1992).

43. Several critics have noted that some of Stowe's characters fit blackface types. I argue that minstrelsy provided Stowe with much more than techniques of characterization. Richard Beale Davis argued that "many of Stowe's people of color owe something of their comic characters to the minstrel show" ("Mrs. Stowe's Characters-in-Situations and a Southern Literary Tradition," in *Essays on American Literature in Honor of Jay B. Hubbell,* ed. Clarence Gohdes [Durham, NC: Duke University Press, 1967], 114). Leslie Fiedler asserted that there were "standard minstrel-show types among the astonishing array of Afro-American characters . . . comic darkies brought on for comic relief" (*What Was Literature? Class Culture and Mass Society* [New York: Simon and Schuster, 1982], 167). Lott surmises that Uncle Tom, Topsy, and Adolph "are surely inheritances from the minstrel show" (222). Lhamon argues that Stowe "sluiced into abolitionist tableaus some of the power of minstrel conventions" (96, 140–45).

44. Lhamon, 96–97.

45. See Dale Cockrell, *Demons of Disorder: Early Blackface Minstrels and Their World* (Cambridge: Cambridge University Press, 1997), 85, and Lhamon, 19, on the early blackface milieu.

46. Jules Zanger, "The Minstrel Show as Theater of Misrule," *Quarterly Journal of Speech* 60 (1988): 34. On the structure of the minstrel show and on this part of the act see Toll, 52–57.

47. I would not dispute Davis's argument that Sam's "hilarious fun-loving semi-roguery" here is "kin" to that of servant figures in Walter Scott and his disciples James Fenimore Cooper and William Gilmore Simms, but the dialectical structure of this dialogue is more specifically derived from the stage (114).

48. See David Roediger, *The Wages of Whiteness: Race and the Meaning of the American Working Class* (London: Verso, 1991), 61–81; also Alexander Saxton, *The Rise and Fall of the White Republic: Class Politics and Mass Culture in Nineteenth Century America* (London: Verso, 1990), 165–82. Lhamon also comments on the blackface aspects of Topsy's "raising Cain" (144).

49. Cockrell, 94.

50. For examples of blackface stump speeches see Toll, 55; Carl Bryan Holmberg and Gilbert D. Schneider, "Daniel Decatur Emmett's Stump Sermons: Genuine Afro-American Culture, Language and Rhetoric in the Negro Minstrel Show," *Journal of Popular Culture* 19 (Spring 1986): 27–38.

51. Lhamon, 190.

52. Holmberg and Schneider, 34.

53. See Lhamon, 190.

54. Zanger, 35.

55. See Holmberg and Schneider, 32. J. L. Dillard, discussing the attribution of this phenomenon primarily to black speakers, points out that to speakers of black varieties of English apparent malapropisms may actually be the correct usage for that variety and may only seem to be mistakes to the standard English listener (*Black English: Its History and Usage in the United States* [New York: Random House, 1972], 107).

56. Brown, 45.

57. Cockrell, 180 n. 97.

58. Cockrell, 147. On this point I differ from Lhamon, who does connect Topsy with the wench (142).

59. Lott discusses the wench role in general (160–68) and "Lucy Long" in particular (160–61).

60. Lhamon also identifies this scene as an end man-interlocutor exchange (145).

61. Nathaniel Hawthorne, *The Scarlet Letter,* 1850; ed. Nina Baym (Harmondsworth: Penguin, 1986), 134.

62. "Blackberrying," in *Dramas from the American Theatre, 1762–1909,* ed. Richard Moody (Boston: Houghton Mifflin, 1970), 486–87.

63. Davis, 114.

64. In 1855 the Howard family announced a new song for their *Uncle Tom* at the National Theatre, "Oh! I'se So Wicked," while in the Moore and Burgess minstrel version the other slaves sang "She's the Wickedest Critter in the World." See "Testimonial to Manager A. H. Purdy," Playbill, Purdy's National Theatre, New York, 1855; Harvard Theatre Collection; and Moore and Burgess Minstrels, *Uncle Tom's Cabin Told in Musical Tableaux Vivants by George R. Sims,* Music by Ivan Caryll (London: J. Miles & Co., n.d.).

65. See Hedrick, esp. 125, 173–85.

66. "Blackberrying," 486.

67. These jokes resemble what one commentator called "the insoluble conundrum and the indigestible jest" blackface had borrowed from the circus ("American Popular Ballads," *Round Table,* 6 February 1864, quoted in Emerson, 92). See also the lyrics to Stephen Foster's 1847 hit "Oh! Susanna": "It rained all night de day I left,/De wedder it was dry;/The sun so hot I froze to def," and so on (quoted in Emerson, 127).

68. The classic example is the opening of Frederick Douglass's *Narrative of the Life of Frederick Douglass, an American Slave,* 1845, ed. Houston A. Baker (London: Penguin, 1986).

69. On the blackface dandy see Cockrell, 92–109; Lott, 131–35; Rosemarie K. Bank, *Theatre Culture in America, 1825–1860* (Cambridge: Cambridge University Press, 1997), 160–62.

70. Sambo and Quimbo may in their names have brought to mind grotesque and degrading portraits, and their appearances in the novel would have reinforced them. "Sambo" was, at the time Stowe wrote, a cliched generic name for a black male; although it was probably derived from West African names, it would have brought to mind hostile representations of blacks (Dillard, 131, 130).

71. On songs in the novel see William W. Austin, *"Susanna," "Jeannie," and "The Old Folks at Home": The Songs of Stephen C. Foster from His Time to Ours* (New York: Macmillan, 1975), 229–32.

72. As Austin points out, Stowe seems by this to echo Frederick Douglass's famous description of slave songs, which contain a coded desperation only the initiated can hear: the song is not only not "unmeaning," it has two meanings for its listeners (231; Douglass, 58).

73. Harriet Beecher Stowe, *A Key to Uncle Tom's Cabin* (Boston: Clarke, Beeton, 1853), 95.

74. Lott, 124.

75. Frances Hodgson Burnett, *The One I Knew the Best of All* (London: Frederick Warne, 1893), 51.

76. Burnett, 49.

77. Burnett, 51.

78. Deborah E. McDowell, "In the First Place: Making Frederick Douglass and the Afro-American Tradition," in *Critical Essays on Frederick Douglass,* ed. William L. Andrews (Boston: G. K. Hall, 1991), 203.

79. Jenny Franchot, "The Punishment of Esther: Frederick Douglass and the Construction of the Feminine," in *Frederick Douglass: New Literary and Historical Essays*, ed. Eric J. Sundquist (Cambridge: Cambridge University Press, 1990), 143.

80. Samuels, "Introduction," in Samuels, 6.

81. Butsch, 85. For different interpretations of this paradox see Lott, Cockrell, Lhamon, and Zanger, 33–38.

82. Cockrell traces the absorption of European folk rituals into black traditions in the New World and the reappearance of both in early blackface. Lhamon . . . shows that in the financially impoverished and racially mixed district of New York's Catherine Market black "charisma" and performative traditions were prominent in the interplay of cultures that produced blackface. Both these writers stress the differences between early minstrelsy and its incarnations after the 1840s: as middle-class audiences took to blackface, it lost its satirical bite and ambiguities and became more clearly derogatory. The minstrelsy with which *Uncle Tom* was associated, in other words, was more likely than earlier forms to be read explicitly as racial portraiture and tended in its content to be more hostile to African Americans (Cockrell 147, Lhamon 45).

83. "Jim Crow" was attributed variously to a Kentucky stable boy, a Cincinnati stage driver, and a porter from Pittsburgh; other writers provided more fanciful ideas about supposed black authors. See C. L., "An Old Actor's Memories: What Mr. Edmon S. Conner Recalls about His Career," *New York Times*, 5 June 1881, 10; Nevin, 608–609; Kennard, 334–41; Y. S. Nathanson, "Negro Minstrelsy, Ancient and Modern," *Putnam's Monthly Magazine* (January 1855): 72–79.

84. Constance Rourke, "Traditions for a Negro Literature," in Constance Rourke, *The Roots of American Culture and Other Essays* (New York: Harcourt Brace, 1942), 262–74, 265–66. The insensitivity of this claim has sometimes blinded readers to the subtlety of Rourke's commentary, however, which was alert to blackface's cultural fusions and qualities of travesty.

85. Alan W. C. Green, "'Jim Crow,' 'Zip Coon,': The Northern Origins of Negro Minstrelsy," *Massachusetts Review* 11 (1970): 385–97; Toll; Saxton; Roediger; Lott. Other accounts of minstrelsy include Joseph Boskin, *Sambo: The Rise and Demise of an American Jester* (New York: Oxford University Press, 1986); Laurence Hutton, "The Negro on Stage," *Harper's New Monthly Magazine* 79 (1889): 131–45; Blyden Jackson, "The Minstrel Mode," in *The Comic Imagination in American Literature*, ed. Louis D. Rubin, Jr., (New Brunswick, NJ: Rutgers University Press, 1973), 149–56; Brander Matthews, "The Rise and Fall of Minstrelsy," *Scribner's Magazine* 57 (1915): 754–59; Meade Minnigerode, *The Fabulous Forties: 1840–1850* (New York: Putnam, 1924); Hans Nathan, *Dan Emmett and the Rise of Negro Minstrelsy* (Norman: University of Oklahoma Press, 1962); Constance Rourke, *American Humor: A Study of the National Character*, 1931 (Garden City, NY: Doubleday Anchor Books, 1953), 3–28; Carl Wittke, *Tambo and Bones: A History of the American Minstrel Stage* (Durham:, NC: Duke University Press, 1930).

86. "American Slavery."

87. George Eliot, "Review of *Dred: A Tale of the Great Dismal Swamp* by Harriet Beecher Stowe, in *Critical Essays on Harriet Beecher Stowe,* ed. Elizabeth Ammons (Boston: G. K. Hall, 1980), 43; emphasis in original.

88. Richard Yarborough, "Strategies of Black Characterization in *Uncle Tom's Cabin* and the Early Afro-American Novel," in *New Essays on Uncle Tom's Cabin,* ed. Eric J. Sundquist (Cambridge: Cambridge University Press, 1986), 72.

89. Quoted in Wilson, 70.

90. On Bodichon see Pam Hirsch, *Barbara Leigh Smith Bodichon: Feminist, Artist and Rebel* (London: Pimlico, 199); Sheila R. Herstein, *A Mid-Victorian Feminist, Barbara Leigh Smith Bodichon* (New Haven, CT: Yale University Press, 1985).

91. See Barbara Leigh Smith Bodichon, *An American Diary 1857–1858,* ed. Joseph Reed, Jr. (London: Routledge and Kegan Paul, 1972).

92. Bodichon, 130, 62.

93. Bodichon, 77. On Bodichon's dress see Hirsch, 154. Bodichon also scandalously eschewed corsets (Herstein, 57).

94. Bodichon, 77.

"This Promiscuous Housekeeping"

Death, Transgression, and Homoeroticism
in Uncle Tom's Cabin

P. GABRIELLE FOREMAN

◆ ◆ ◆

Oh, grave, where is thy victory?
Oh, death, where is thy sting?
—1 Corinthians 15.55

I

M ARY BOYKIN CHESNUT'S QUIP, "Stowe did not hit the sorest spot. She made Legree a bachelor," is to this day one of the most famous one-line responses to *Uncle Tom's Cabin.*[1] Yet it may have been Chesnut who missed the spot, so to speak, for although Harriet Beecher Stowe reserves her discussion of explicit sexual abuse for the gothic plantation of Tom's third master Legree, illicit relations are evident throughout the novel. The focus of this essay will be the fissures created by the coded and repressed moments of illicit sexuality in the household of a married couple, the Shelbys (Tom and his wife Chloe and the mulatta Eliza's masters), and the homoerotics displayed at the estate of Tom's second master, the father of little Eva, Augustine St. Clare.[2]

I argue that death in *Uncle Tom's Cabin* acts as an insistent sign not of redemption but of the consequence of sexual transgression. The "meanings" of death and sex in sentimental literature are informed by several cultural and literary traditions. In addition to its biblical legacy as purification and redemption in innocence, death is a received literary convention of earlier seduction tales;[3] it often figures as the result of a woman's "fall" from the status of "true woman."[4] Death, then, does not only symbolize an extension of the political act of self-denial; it is not simply the "self-abnegation" some critics find it to be in *Uncle Tom's Cabin*.[5] It is also the punishment for indulging in sex and self, despite or in opposition to dominant cultural and particularly racial mores. One can argue, then, that in *Uncle Tom's Cabin* death marks the sexual transgression of the two major protagonists, Tom and Eva. As self-sacrificial figures central to Stowe's matrifocal revision of American society, Tom and Eva can be read as transgressors of the first order who die not for others' sins but for their own. As Hortense Spillers demonstrates, neither's death occurs because they are too pure, too good, to live in this world—as so many critics assume they are—but because theirs is a relationship where race, status, and desire intersect.[6]

When we extend our examination to two of Tom's masters, Mr. Shelby and St. Clare (the only principal characters who die besides Tom and Eva), we see death as the consequence of sexual transgression marking *Uncle Tom's Cabin* in even more complicated ways. Interdicted interracial sexual relations pervade domestic settings Stowe seems at first to figure as sacred. Stowe's text turns out to be a sexual minefield of illicit desires that she struggles to keep safely outside of Christian and domestic settings.[7] Further, prohibited sex coincides with what is, in Stowe's feminized domestic economy, the inconceivable realm of male homosocial desire.

In *Uncle Tom's Cabin* the mapping of power relations alongside desire on the Shelby plantation sets the stage for a more explosive unveiling at the St. Clare estate. The sexual abuse repressed at the idealized Kentucky setting also calls into question the white mistress's, Mrs. Shelby's, position in the calculus of race, domesticity, and capital production. As Karen Sanchez-Eppler notes, "The less easily race can be read from [a light-skinned slave's] flesh, the more clearly the white man's repeated penetrations of the Black body are imprinted there."[8] I would argue further that within the implicit logic of nineteenth-century gender ideologies, the failure of the *white* woman to perform her duty as a "true woman," to purify white men through her domestic union with them, and to purify Black women by her example, is inscribed on these light bodies. Stowe avoids involving the reader in *explicit* situations where the sexual dynamics inscribed on the bodies of Stowe's mulatta characters could explode. We do not see rape or interracial concubinage within a white domestic setting. Indeed, the mere presence of white women relegates the interdicted desire of married men, the sorest spot, to the subtext.

II

Stowe seems to signal that the Shelby household is in most ways a model one, for its mistress is a model lady. Emily Shelby is a

> woman of a high class, both intellectually and morally. To that natural magnanimity and generosity of mind which one often marks as characteristic of women of Kentucky, she added high moral and religious sensibility and principle, carried out with great energy and ability to practical results.[9]

Though Mrs. Shelby is the intelligent true woman's "true woman," on every occasion until her husband's demise she cedes ability to womanly submissiveness (even though she is practical as well as pious, able, and energetic, rather than purely submissive). Benefiting from her companionship, we are told, Mr. Shelby is "good natured and kindly, and disposed to easy indulgence. . . . There had never been a lack of anything which might contribute to the physical comfort of the negro on his estate" (63). He sells Tom and Eliza's son, despite his close relationship with Tom and his wife's attachment to her mulatta maid-in-waiting, only, he maintains, because he has fallen into debt. He assures his wife that there is no choice "between selling these two and selling everything" (88). Eliza, overhearing this, takes her son and runs, stopping on the way to warn Tom. Yet they do not talk about escape, passing routes, or wisdom; instead she repeats the master's rhetoric:

> Master don't want to sell; and Missis—she's always good. I heard her plead and beg for us; but he told her 'twas no use; that he was in the man's debt, and that this man had got the power over him; and that if he didn't pay him off clear, it would end in his having to sell the place and all the people and moving off. Yes, I heard him say there was no choice between selling these two and selling all, the man was driving him so hard. Master said he was sorry. (93)

Eliza's language calls attention to itself so verging on the absurd is her repetitive defense of the master who has just sold her son; who, we must ask, is Eliza, is Stowe, trying to convince? Or is this the text's project at all?

Despite Mr. Shelby's professions and Eliza's belief in them, the text constantly undermines his disclaimers. His own language suggests that far from paining him, he can casually dismiss this sale. He ponders that the slave trader, Dan Haley,

> knows how much he has me at advantage. If anybody had ever said to me that I should sell Tom down south to one of those rascally trad- ers, I should have said, "Is thy servant a dog, that he should do this thing?" . . . And Eliza's child, too! (62)

Here Shelby is at his most introspective. Yet his very next thought—"so much for being in debt—heigh-ho. The fellow sees his advantage, and means to push it" (62)—slips into another register. Shelby frames the passage with his oft-repeated "I was in his power and *had* to do it"; more than just deflecting responsibility, he posits himself as a helpless victim, in the position that his slaves sold south should occupy. Despite the myth he seeks to maintain, his own language moves from stern regret to casual dismissal and suggests that his justifications are to be treated skeptically.

Mrs. Shelby knows that the break-up of slave families is "a curse to the mas- ter and a curse to the slave" (88), just as she must know that what "obliges" her husband to sell off two favorite slaves is not destitution and that he does not effectively invoke the "horrible system of slavery" to legitimize his selling.[10] Instead, Shelby's choice actualizes the "curse" to the slave family and symbol- izes the potential disruption of the master's family as well. Mrs. Shelby's order- ing is telling; she first articulates the curse to the *master*. Economic desire does not by itself obstruct her own realization of true womanhood, of the peace and power of domesticity safe from the intrusions of the market place. Specific, if muted, sexual desire disrupts her domestic ideal as well.

Outside of the sphere of her mistress's protecting presence, Eliza is sexual- ized. Indeed, Stowe's language signals that Eliza's sexual status is a constant one, only temporarily held in abeyance. She is introduced as Haley admires her child:

> There needed only a glance from the child to her, to identify her as its mother. There was the same rich, full, dark eye, with its long lashes; the same ripples of silky black hair. The brown of her complexion gave way on the cheek to a perceptible flush, which deepened as she saw the gaze of the strange man fixed upon her in bold and undisguised admiration. Her dress . . . set off to an advantage her finely moulded shape; a deli- cately formed hand and a trim foot and ankle were items of appearance that did not escape the quick eye of the trader, well used to run up at a glance the points of a fine female article. (58)

Haley's defining eyes, the framing "glances" turned "undisguised" gaze, set the terms of Eliza's presentation. In the introductory description of Mrs. Shelby already noted, Stowe stresses the mistress's interior qualities; not one physical characteristic is offered. In contrast, Eliza is a flushing double, an "attractive" reification of the sullied physical body. *Mother,* the epitome of womanhood in Stowe's lexicon, signals a distinct signifying chain when Eliza is its immediate referent. In the realm of the physical, *mother* is decapitalized; the words *slave mother* are cleaved from each other; the latter is deprived of subjectivity as it is eclipsed by *slave* and replaced with the more accurate referent *breeder*. Eliza's privileged status, her protected place, is decentered in this introduction before it is even described.

Eliza becomes a purely sexual commodity, an object of "speculation" on which an illegal and illicit fortune can be made. The "female artifice" (111) Mrs. Shelby uses to contain Haley's power while in her home does not extend outside its parameters. Once in the male sphere of a tavern, Haley meets with other traders who agree to help him only if they get Eliza as a bounty, though she should be returned to the Shelbys. Eliza escapes, however, by leaping across blocks of ice on the Ohio river:

> With wild cries and desperate energy she leaped to another and still another cake;—stumbling,—leaping,—slipping,—springing upwards again! Her shoes are gone,—her stockings cut from her feet,—while blood marked every step; but she saw nothing, felt nothing, till dimly, as in a dream she saw the Ohio side. (115)

Even the language of this passage (one of the few changes to the present tense in a five-hundred-page tome), its short phrases and interrupting dashes, create a panting tension that heightens the sexual threat. Leslie Fiedler points out that Eliza, caught by her pursuers, "might easily become the object not of blood lust, which is considered safe, but of quite specific sexual desire."[11] Where on her journey the transformation from maid to concubine would have taken place is beside the point, one might add; the terminus is only yet to be realized, for it has dogged her since her very introduction. In New Orleans—the market where George's sisters are sold, where buyers bid hundreds more for Emmeline's sensualized "curls" and where Legree's possessing gaze is actualized—the tension between Stowe's representation of the pure Eliza and the mulatta's constantly sexualized body can no longer be ignored by Stowe or her readers.

What, then, do we make of Eliza having been under such a gaze on the New Orleans market platform that she later escapes? After Mr. Shelby's death, his son relates that "in one of his trips to New Orleans [he] paid an extravagant sum for her, to be sure. I suppose on account of her extraordinary beauty" (488). If Eliza's status as sexual commodity rather than protected mulatta did not begin as she runs from the Shelbys' plantation but on her journey to it, how do we read her stay at the Shelbys? What differentiates her young master's gaze, as she stood in the same place later occupied by Legree's Emmeline, from the others'?

Stowe cannot purge the desiring gazes at the New Orleans market she reconstructs. Where, then, is this desire located in *Uncle Tom's Cabin*? Onto whom is it diffused? Does sexual prohibition play itself out as Shelby sells Eliza's son Harry, whose glossy curls resemble his own son George's (57, 156), the Shelby heir who bears Eliza's husband's name? The master's actions are a palimpsest, as Stowe insists they are, of other slave narrators' representations. Like Dr. Flint, the jealous owner who forbids his slave girl to see her free suitor,[12] like so many others in fact and fiction, Shelby can be read as punishing Eliza for her relation with another man by breaking their familial "union." Moreover, he also plays out a realized desire by selling Harry as if he had fathered the child and must, again like so many other such "fathers," rid the plantation of the evidence.

Complicated parentage in the Shelby-Harris ménage is everywhere evident. Not only does the curly-locked Shelby child bear Eliza's husband's name; Mrs. Shelby, the metaphorically wronged wife, also expresses these prohibited and so hidden relations. The mistress (and it is her ties with Eliza, not her husband's, which are emphasized) cannot believe that her husband would ever agree to sell Eliza's child. She articulates this by insisting to Eliza that "I would as soon have one of my own children sold" (63). The consanguinity Mrs. Shelby suggests, and the ease with which she articulates such a substitution, suggest that her words go beyond a mere verbal gesture to name the potential shared parentage of her and Eliza's sons.

Never, of course, does the language of sexuality touch Eliza explicitly; again, the slave's association with Mrs. Shelby protects her from more than implied contamination of the sexualized city New Orleans. Stowe draws the constructions of other such threats, however, in stronger strokes. George's reference to his defense of his wife Eliza illustrates such an elision. "I've had a sister sold in that New Orleans market," he steams. "I know what they're sold for" (245). Nor do even the cruder white men speak directly of *what* it is that is going to happen to Eliza. All alive with "enterprise," the trader Marks simply states instead, "We take the gal to Orleans to speculate on. An't it beautiful?" (122). In his language, profit overshadows sexual abuse. Yet when Stowe depicts other desired mulattas—Cassy, Emmeline, or George's mother—attention to such delicacy disappears. "We remark en passant, that George was, by his father's side, of white descent," Stowe writes. "His mother was one of those unfortunates of her race, marked out by personal beauty to be the slave of the passions of her possessor and the mother of children who may never know a father" (164). The "passions" of Eliza's "possessors," words which in this context suggest penetration in no uncertain terms, however, are always restrained.

Though Stowe acknowledges that "the public and shameless sale of beautiful mulatto and quadroon girls has acquired a notoriety" (503), she purges such contaminating evidence from her discursive reconstruction of Eliza. In her preface and conclusion, and insistently in A Key to Uncle Tom's Cabin, she claims narrative truth for her text and argues that the "characters ascribed to" the beautiful Shelby quadroon "are sketches drawn from life";[13] yet any threat of Eliza suffering the same fate as her quadroon sisters only enters the narrative *after* Eliza has left Mrs. Shelby's protective guidance.

Stowe insists that she is the documenter of truths about slavery; much has "come to her knowledge in conversation with former slaves now free in Ohio" (13) or from her copious reading. One of Stowe's closest familial sources was her Aunt Mary Foote, who married a West Indian planter and was greeted by his clan of mulatto children when she arrived at her new home. Disconsolate, she returned to the Beecher household and became very close to Harriet's older sister Catherine who, years later, lived with the Stowes while her sister composed much of Uncle Tom's Cabin.[14] Though her aunt died when Stowe was a toddler, this story was part of her childhood.[15] Neither does the knowledge Stowe gleans years later from her mulatta cook, whose Kentucky master had fathered all her children, filter into her depiction of Eliza. Stowe's cook's position—"You know, Mrs. Stowe, slave women cannot help themselves"[16]—finds voice in Harriet Jacobs's, Louisa Picquet's, and other Black women's narratives, not in Stowe's documentation of Kentucky. Rather, the Kentucky of Stowe's imagination houses the "mildest form of slavery" (62) where "folks spile [their] niggers" (61). She also excises other facts even as she claims her basis in historical truth. In an essay that establishes much of her literary borrowing, Robert Stepto notes that her story of the Kentucky slaves George and Eliza Harris "is roughly that of Henry and Malinda Bibb,"[17] to whom she refers directly in her Key. Yet Stowe substitutes Malinda's fate for another, purer one; in fact, Henry Bibb reentered the South to rescue his family only to discover that his wife had become his master's favorite concubine. The resonances echo when we consider Stowe's representation of "good" Mr. Shelby and his (wife's) favorite slave. In other words, Mrs. Shelby cannot create more than the idea of "pure" domestic space—an idea Stowe unsuccessfully inscribes in Uncle Tom's Cabin; nor can that space repel the sexual intrusions it simultaneously attracts. Instead, the Shelby plantation is a site of repressed sexual production. It is for this transgression that Mr. Shelby, its potential agent, dies, much like the master whom Stowe next introduces.

III

> Virtue! a fig!
> Our bodies are our gardens, to the
> which our wills are gardeners.
> —Iago, Othello

In contrast to the "domesticity" of the Shelby plantation, little about the St. Clare estate suggests purity, despite Eva's spotless white dress, the symbol of the sexually pristine. Situated in New Orleans—the very geographical icon of bared light bodies and lusting white "gentlemen"—the St. Clare estate almost everywhere betrays indulgence.[18] Gillian Brown notes that Miss Ophelia St. Clare is scandalized by "the promiscuous housekeeping" of her cousin's New Orleans estates.[19] Stowe describes the botanical gambol-grounds that frame the following two hundred pages. The house was

> built in the Moorish fashion—a square building enclosing a courtyard, into which the carriage drove through an arched gateway. The court, in the inside, had evidently been arranged to gratify a picturesque and voluptuous ideality. Wide galleries ran all around the four sides, whose Moorish arches, slender pillars, and arabesque ornaments, carried the mind back, as in a dream, to the reign of oriental romance in Spain . . . .
> The galleries that surrounded the court were festooned with a curtain of some kind of Moorish stuff, and could be drawn down at pleasure, to exclude the beams of the sun. (218)

Though Eva, who "seemed like a bird ready to burst from a cage, with the *wild eagerness* of her delight" (219, emphasis mine), has had her new slave on her mind, he is, as they approach the mansion, offstage. "Where's Tom?" she asks as they roll through the (Hortense Spillers might argue vaginal) archway; "On the outside," answers St. Clare. However, Tom's position is soon to change. As the travelers alight from the carriage, Stowe centralizes Tom. This "large, broad chested, powerfully made man" (75) climbs down "and looked about with an air of calm still enjoyment." "The negro," Stowe reminds us, "is an exotic of the most gorgeous and superb countries of the world, and he has, deep in his heart, a passion for all that is splendid, rich and fanciful." St. Clare's comment, "my boy, this [place] seems to suit you" (219), brings Tom, the outsider, inside. Tom's gaze is, momentarily, the legitimizing one for, as Spillers points out, "if the markings of landscape all signify the 'exotic' the strange the foreign, then what better gaze to preside over it than Tom's?"[20] It is precisely this "presiding," one could go on, that is as suggestive as it is temporarily granted. Tom is not just a textual site of the Oriental; he is its embodiment. Not only an "exotic" possession, he is *possessor* of the exotic. His presiding gaze, and "the Moorish fashion" that conjures up "the oriental Spanish romance," vividly echo a more famous Shakespearean figure whose unsanctioned desire and possession end in murder and death.

In Stowe's subtext, Tom, the garden, and Eva's "wild eagerness" are clearly sexualized, as Miss Ophelia's appraisal—"It looks rather . . . heathenish" (219)—only affirms. Eva's form, we are told, is "the perfection of childish beauty, without its usual chubbiness and squareness of outline" (201). Eva, then, is pointedly described as having already shed her baby fat, as possessing the figure of a miniature woman. Importantly, the avatar of the truly feminine, the senator's wife Mrs. Bird, is a "little woman, of about four feet in height" (133). She is, this Wife and Mother, with their attendant sexual status, the size of a child. Stowe's prose, though muted, suggests that "Little" Eva's prepubescence not be taken as the inhibitor of sexual signification. As Spillers argues,

> When Stowe places "Little Eva" and "Uncle Tom" in a new and revised "Garden of Eden," she might have aimed for a type of Eva as the mother of resurrected, reconstructed humankind, but there is nothing "pious" or "holy" about the altogether shocking outcome: The sacrificial lamb of *Uncle Tom's Cabin*—in the dual person of Eva the temptress and Tom the castrated—must be expended as *punishment* for crimes against the culture, rather than as *salvation* for the culture.[21]

One wonders at Stowe's description of the festooning curtains of "some kind of Moorish stuff" that "could be drawn down at pleasure, to exclude the beams of the sun." It is the reader who draws back the curtains to look, to imagine. The justifying comma that separates "could be drawn down at pleasure," from the clause which follows it only draws attention to its legitimizing presence. The curtains merely cover what Stowe's language doesn't.

As many otherwise differing critics agree, the presiding woman of the St. Clare estate is painted with the most vituperative strokes; her lack of motherly virtues makes the St. Clare estate, in Jean Fagan Yellin's most apt words, an "antihome."[22] If Marie St. Clare's absence is so loudly articulated, what, then, is her husband's attendant status? The syllogism is invited: if Marie is figured as antiwife, St. Clare is a bachelor in relief without the possibility of the reformation a true woman could bring. In the midst of New Orleans, then, what compels him to restraint? There is no reason, Spillers suggests, "why the fleshy beauties of the . . . place would not captivate the most cultivated appetitive capacities."[23] There are, of course, ready objects in the bodies of Jane and Rosa, two "coquettish" mulatta beauties circulating the St. Clare mansions. And there are the coral "ear-drops," which "spruce" Jane, the pretty chambermaid, wears, ever "twinkling," catching the eye (270–71).[24] Indeed, if earrings are described as "bewitching" (271), they are for Legree, the third and most explicitly licentious master, the sign of his own bewitching power, a dangling metaphor for sexual possession. He offers them to Emmeline, the young quadroon he has bought for a concubine, only if she is "a good girl" (402), an utterance the significance of which does not escape her. Jane and Rosa, like other mulattas bought to be maids-in-waiting (with all the fullness of double entendre attendant), occupy the slippery status between escapees of the sexual marketplace and objects of probable, if delayed, aggression.[25]

The festooning curtains "drawn down at pleasure" could, pulled back, reveal pairings to make Ophelia gasp yet again. One might ask, when considering Eva and Tom's garden gambols, upon what Eva's coquettish flower flirting and penchant for "shocking" gestures are modeled. The text suggests that, rather than the young St. Clare and a fleshy female beauty, Adolph, the owner's own *man*-in-waiting, would be curtained there. Once identified, the codes of Adolph's special status are in no way hidden. He is introduced among the throng of slaves running through the house to greet their master upon his return from the North:

> Foremost among them was a highly dressed young mulatto man, evidently a very *distingué personage*, attired in the ultra extreme of the mode, and gracefully waving a scented cambric handkerchief in his hand.
>
> "Back! all of you. I am ashamed of you," he said, in a tone of authority. "Would you intrude on Master's domestic relations, in the first hour of his return?" (219)

To what "domestic relations" could Adolph possibly refer? Indeed, this "heathenish" home, as Ophelia has just described it (219), houses no recognizable "domesticity" that fits nineteenth-century ideological definitions. Adolph himself, instead, is the focal point of such "relations":

> Owing to Mr. Adolph's systematic arrangements, when St. Clare turned round from paying the hackman, there was nobody in view but Mr. Adolph himself, conspicuous in satin vest, gold guard-chain, and white pants, and bowing with inexpressible grace and suavity.
> "Ah, Adolph, is it you?" said his master offering his hand to him. (219)

Stowe's construction of what will later become the stereotypical Black dandy does not displace the sexualized relation she constructs. If, as the hostile narrator of William Wells Brown's *Clotelle* contends, the "greater portion of colored [quadroon] women, in the days of slavery, had no greater aspiration than of becoming the finely-dressed mistress of some white man,"[26] then "Mr. Adolph" only needs a female-gendered pronoun accompanying his "graceful" air to fulfill Brown's depiction.

It is the gaze, constructed to place the object in the spotlight of inspection and desire,[27] that allows us to follow the almost "systematic arrangement" of the text's homoerotics. Adolph, who knows well the dynamics of fields of vision, recognition, and desire, manages St. Clare's homecoming so that there is "nobody in view but Mr. Adolph himself." He is represented as inviting his own object placement, as luring the spectator into a frame he consciously reproduces, in a gross if more "distingué" parody of the slave platform where a young girl is gazed upon and examined, and where the successful spectator finally is the buyer.[28]

Adolph's gazing (re)production inverts the gender generally associated with the sexualized slave market, and with feminist theories of the gaze, where the passive/object is female. The homoerotic relationship in question, however, can result in no biological issue and so no consequent economic reproduction of slave bodies to be circulated, gazed upon, and bought. Indeed, power is the primary commodity in circulation here. We see this after St. Clare dismisses a "whole assemblage" of welcoming slaves and

> his eye fell upon Tom, who was standing uneasily . . . while Adolph stood negligently leaning against the banisters, examining Tom through an opera-glass. . . .
> "Puh! you puppy," said his master, striking down the opera-glass; "is that the way you treat your company." (221)

This exchange again reveals Adolph's privileged status to construct visual frames. The intimacy that allows him this is revealed in the phrase "your company"; St. Clare addresses his slave as if the mulatto were the house's mister(ess).[29] It is through Adolph's "opera-glass" that the mulatto slave transforms himself from gazed-upon object to spectator. St. Clare clearly sees his man's visual gesture as an appropriative one. The master strikes the glass down, as he does likewise to Adolph's attempted transcendence of the class and racial status that informs the power behind, rather than the mere gesture of, the gaze. Indeed, it is St. Clare's sight that directs this scene; not only does he deny his mulatto gazing power over his "company," he puts Adolph back in his place as "Mr." of the house, as erotic spectacle.

Adolph's "opera-glass" magnifies the very dynamics of inspection and obsession with the intricacies of the sexual and economic reproduction of slavery; he seems occupied with national mythologies of Black male sexuality. St. Clare's contention that Tom "is worth two such puppies as you" (221) speaks beneath the pants of his two favored slaves;[30] he pronounces a judgment that engenders male, and specifically, white(ned) male, terror. It is Adolph rather than St. Clare, however, to whom these dynamics give rise, for whatever St. Clare possesses on his person, he *owns* Tom and so what the slave possesses. St. Clare has bought, both figuratively and literally, what stands for him as a fetishized fantasy of essentialized Black male sexual power;[31] the master can own the sex, while at the same time containing and indeed transferring to himself the power "attached" to it.

Adolph's visual query—What does this pure Black, broad-chested, powerfully made "behemoth" (222) of a man have that makes him worth all that?—is answered on the surface, at least, with—economic ability. Like his wife, Tom can manage excess; he "understands cost and come to" (259).[32] At the St. Clare plantation, as with slavery as an institution, economics is eroticized. Adolph's deprecation of "the passing of power out of his hands" on one level refers to his former mismanagement of finances. Yet it also references his slipping sexualized status (259). Tom's power of economic reproduction is the male substitution for what a traditional female in his place could do and was often forced to do and what Adolph most pointedly cannot do—produce "excess"; as with slave women, the economic and the sexual in this ménage collapse.

St. Clare himself fits into no convenient gender taxonomy, as critics' almost constant association of him with Lord Byron attests. Stowe's own attitudes about Byron frame her depiction of St. Clare. Alice Crozier argues that the poet was "the single greatest literary and imaginative influence on the writings" of Stowe.[33] Although this is certainly debatable, Byron was a living presence in the Beecher household, where family members were free to read and discuss him. Lyman Beecher devoted a sermon to the poet upon his death, and Harriet listened to her father preach that his superior capacity unrealized in Christ might lead to more stinging damnation; "His want of virtue and . . . of true religion" would lead him "to wander to the blackness of darkness forever!!"[34] Byron's spiritual state, and the physical indulgences that led him to it, remained a fascination for a much older Stowe. She formally exposed the poet's long-acknowledged incestuous relation with his half sister in *Lady Byron Vindicated* (1870), claiming that Lady Byron confessed this to her personally in 1856, though such rumors had circulated from the time of the couple's separation in 1816.[35]

Stowe disperses evidence of St. Clare's byronic nature throughout the text. He is "in his heart" a trope of nineteenth-century femininity, a "poetic voluptuary" (219) "who found it easier to indulge than to regulate" (259). Stowe genders him feminine, like his slave Adolph. In opposition to his twin brother, who is a cross between a "Roman" and a Southern gentleman, St. Clare in comparison has

> a Greek outline. . . . I [was] dreamy and inactive. . . . There was a morbid sensitiveness and acuteness of feeling in me of which he and my father had no kind of understanding and with which they could have no possible sympathy. (281)

For St. Clare, unlike the Greeks he resembles, there is no male community, no group of equals, within which he can define his self-identity. St. Clare's brother and father emphatically cannot provide understanding of and sympathy for his feminized qualities, for these emotions themselves would implicate them in a feminine economy to which Stowe places them in opposition.

. Marked as an outsider by the male community of his equals, St. Clare can elicit more understanding in the company of male slaves whose job it is, quite literally, to sympathize with the master's "deeper feelings" (363). In contrast to the external (and exaggerated) signs of femininity attached to Adolph, the descriptions of St. Clare, like those of Mrs. Shelby, emphasize interior subjectivity:

> In childhood, he was remarkable for an extreme and marked sensitiveness of character, more akin to the softness of woman than the ordinary hardness of his own sex. Time, however, overgrew this softness with the rough bark of manhood, and but few knew how living and fresh it still lay at the core. (208)

Tom, by any reading, is one of the few in the know. The possessor of a similar "feminized" interiority, he is, Elizabeth Ammons argues, "the supreme heroine of the book."[36] Stowe's ideal person, Ammons continues, is completely conventional: "pious, pure, non-competitive, unselfish, emotional, domestic and outwardly submissive"[37]—all traits that Tom, read straight, embodies. Yet the titular "heroine" cannot subsume maleness, just as "Mr." cannot be purged from Adolph. Gender inversions, as well as the means and objects of desire, complicate gender taxonomies in Stowe. Indeed, "the nineteenth-century's classic definition of the homosexual [is] a woman's soul trapped in a man's body. It follows that the homosexual is already a confined (trapped) subjectivity."[38] In Stowe's text, male bodies, whoever's souls they are said to house, cannot be erased. An easy gender switch, Tom as "heroine," though useful, does little to illuminate Stowe's configuration of male power and desire.

Eva, until her death, both expresses and is the expression of the desire over which Tom and St. Clare connect, byronic and incestuous resonances intact.[39] In a classic example of the erotic triangular paradigm Eve Kosofsky Sedgwick refigures,[40] Eva (the ostensible beloved) occupies Tom ("rival"), as St. Clare ("rival," father) looks on:

> A gay laugh from the court rang through the silken curtains of the veranda. St. Clare stepped out, and lifting up the curtain, laughed too. . . .
>   There sat Tom, on a little mossy seat in the court, every one of his button-holes stuck full of cape jessamines, and Eva, gayly laughing, was hanging a wreath of roses round his neck. (233)

While Spillers offers an incisive reading of the vaginal imagery in this passage,[41] she does not account for its parallel phallic gestures. If we read all the images Stowe presents, this scene does not express a purely heterosexual moment. Every one of Tom's receptive holes are quite full, for example, much to the pleasure of his voyeuristic master.

St. Clare's "desire for pleasurable looking," the scopophilia of this frame, moves full circle from the objects "caught unawares" to "the invitation," where St. Clare inserts himself where he previously had been only voyeur: Tom "lifted his eyes, when he saw his master, with a half-deprecating, apologetic air" (233).[42] Annette Kuhn's explication of the male-to-female gaze may be helpful here:

> In voyeurism . . . the power of catching its object unawares, may be pleasurable in itself, [yet] the object's unfathomable [excluding] desire

remains. . . . [While the object may seem unaware of the spectator's look] the risk of her indifference is mitigated by the fact that her body may at the same time be arranged as if on display for him. This implies an unspoken exhibitionism on the part of the object of the look.

The "come-on," Kuhn goes on, takes visual pleasure one step further,

> now openly to acknowledge the spectator by her direct look. . . . Exhibitionism wins out over voyeurism: the "come-on" look suggests that the woman is purposefully displaying her body for the spectator, that she knows he is there and is inviting him quite openly to take a good look.[43]

When St. Clare's look engages Tom's, the master/spectator has moved from being voyeur to being receiver of the "half-deprecating" "come-on." Eva's presence is superfluous as she is not an erotic object; nor is her gaze engaged. The flowers stuck in button holes act as the metaphor for the open, in this case male, body positioned for the gazer who "happens" upon the object erotically employed, only to have his desire affirmed and justified by the suggestive invitation of the now looking object, whose body is there, the returned look signifies, only for him.

Eva's death marks a crucial point on the trajectory of homoerotics in *Uncle Tom's Cabin*, though it, as always, competes with Stowe's religious discourse. Though Ophelia and Marie are in the room, they are cut out of the emotive close frame. St. Clare turns to Tom for comfort, not to Eva's mother or his own aunt:

> "O, God, this is dreadful!" he said, turning away in agony, and wringing Tom's hand, scarce conscious of what he was doing. "O, Tom, my boy, it is killing me!" Tom had his master's hands between his own; and with tears streaming down his dark cheeks, looked up for help where he had always been used to look. (353)

The hand-holding in this scene is not as telling as the language that qualifies it. There is something in the physical contact that borders on the illicit, that St. Clare would not do were he more than "scarce conscious." St. Clare's "my boy" has multiple meanings; it acts as an affectional replacement for the "my love" or "my dear" that would stand had Tom not been substituted at the woman's traditional bedside post. Yet the affectionate signs of such a substitution cannot efface a simultaneous reinscription of power—*boy* addressed to a Black man from a white man's mouth acts as a canceling epithet.

Eva's death is necessary for the working out of the homoerotics her presence threatens to eclipse, as well as for punishment for her role in the St. Clare ménage. In discussing Wilkie Collins's *The Woman in White,* D. A. Miller argues that "the project of confining the woman cannot succeed in achieving narrative quiescence of closure. Safely shut up . . . women cease being active participants in the drama that nonetheless remains to be played out . . . 'man to man.'"[44] Miller's analysis obtains in *Uncle Tom's Cabin.* Though Eva is consistently invoked to justify the ever more intimate relations between the two men, when she passes away their interaction is no longer mediated by her material presence. After Eva's death, only Tom's gaze "presides," only he sees St. Clare's soft core, revealed when the eye (or hand) strips back the rough bark:

> Tom, however, had a feeling at his own heart, that drew him to his master. He followed him wherever he walked, wistfully and sadly; and when he saw him sitting, so pale and quiet in Eva's room, holding before his eyes her little open Bible, though seeing no letter or word of what was in it, there was more sorrow to Tom in that still, fixed, tearless eye, than in all Marie's moans. (357)

As it did momentarily for Adolph, Tom's penetrating gaze, now sanctioned rather than slapped down by the master, seemingly allows him to move from the looked-at to the looker. Tom's own desire is implied here just as it was merely suggested in his first encounter with his owner:

> St. Clare, [c]arelessly putting the tip of his finger under Tom's chin, said good-humoredly, "Look up, Tom, and see how you like your new master." Tom looked up. It was not in nature to look into that gay, young, handsome face, without a feeling of pleasure. (207)

The response he felt at first sight is actualized in post-Eva scenes. Tom as desiring subject, as possessor of a penetrative gaze, implies an equality "between men" that his racial status and the repeated positioning suggested by Tom's looking up undermine. Back at the St. Clare estate,

> Tom, who was always uneasily following his master about, had seen him go to his library. . . . He entered softly. St. Clare. . . was lying on his face, with Eva's Bible open before him. . . . Tom walked up, and stood by the sofa. He hesitated; and while he was hesitating, St. Clare suddenly raised himself up. The honest face, so full of grief, and with such an

imploring expression of affection and sympathy, struck his master. He
laid his hand on Tom's, and bowed down his forehead on it. (358)

Stowe's religious apparatus becomes more emphatic in this section, as if in
competition with a contestational discourse. Eva's ever-open Bible is pointedly inaccessible. St. Clare sees "no letter or word of what was in it," and so
it is an ineffective counter to the warming physical contact between the two
men. The urgency of Tom's exhortations for St. Clare to find Christ implies an
immediate and opposite threat if he doesn't.

Stowe's imaginings fill in the traditional lacunae of the classic seduction
scene, where the young religious maiden, half-intrigued but reluctant, is se-
duced by a more knowledgeable man who finds it, in St. Clare's words, easier "to
indulge than to regulate" himself. St. Clare's and Tom's "discussions" regrind
the lenses through which one might read the silences around these "falls":

> Tom spoke with fast-running tears and choking voice. St. Clare leaned
> his head on his shoulder, and wrung the hard, faithful, black hand.
> "Tom, you love me," he said.
> "I's willin' to lay down my life, this blessed day to see Mas'r a
> Christian."
> "Poor, foolish boy!" said St. Clare, half raising himself. "I'm not
> worth the love of one good, honest heart, like yours." (359)

St. Clare goes on to read the Bible to Tom as his slave "knelt before him,
with . . . an absorbed expression of love, trust, adoration, on his quiet face."

> "Tom," said his master, "this is all real to you."
> "I can jest fairly see it, Mas'r."
> "I wish I had your eyes, Tom."
> "I wish, to the dear Lord, Mas'r had!"
> "But Tom, you know that I have a great deal more knowledge than
> you; what if I should tell you that I don't believe this Bible?" (360)

Ostensibly safe within a religious lexicon, Tom's and St. Clare's slippages
into a romantic discourse arise; the object of adoration, of desire (God, each
other), is often confused, until St. Clare moves to deny the biblical and so to
rearrange the sign system that has supposedly contained the explosiveness of
their speech.

As in seduction tales, the framing religious discourse, with its wan pro-
testations of the pious, does not overwhelm the more tempting alternatives;

indeed, it facilitates them. Only when seductive language is framed within religious discourse can it find expression and potential actualization. Tom's looking up for help, as he does at Eva's death bed, does not prove effective. St. Clare does not convert, and Eva's memory facilitates Tom and St. Clare's relations, as it did when she was materially represented. St. Clare

> attached himself to Tom more and more every day. In all the wide world, there was nothing that seemed to remind him more of Eva; and he would insist on keeping him constantly about him, and fastidious and unapproachable as he was with regard to his deeper feelings, he almost thought aloud to Tom. Nor would any one have wondered at it, who had seen the expression of affection and devotion with which Tom continually followed his young master. (363)

The grammatical running on of this passage suggests that separation and pause, indeed, are hard for its objects to negotiate. Tom is figured as a willing aural receptacle. His willingness, the mutuality of their desire, does not efface the power relations that overdetermine it, however.

This mutual attachment Stowe soon truncates. Well within the terrain of transgression, St. Clare, too, is killed off. He is stabbed in a "cafe" as he tries to separate two brawling, intoxicated "gentlemen" (374). In this homosocial setting where men gather together, it is phallic penetration, a knife in the side, that precipitates his end. No longer in the dominant position, St. Clare inserts himself between two "gentlemen," white men of a similar class whom he cannot regulate and define. The consequent inversion, St. Clare's penetrated body, causes his death.

St. Clare's lingering demise at home confirms this section's homoerotics. The first to see St. Clare's body brought back, Tom gives "a wild cry of amazement and despair" that alarms the others and brings slaves and family running. The physician turns "all these creatures" out of the death room:

> Adolph absolutely refused to go. Terror had deprived him of all presence of mind; he threw himself along the floor, and nothing could persuade him to rise. (375)

The whites present recognize Tom's special status, for there is no intimation that he is ever requested to exit. Instead, the narrative frame narrows in on Tom, the doctor, and the dying St. Clare:

> After a while, he laid his hand on Tom's, who was kneeling beside him, and said, "Tom! Poor fellow!"

"What, Mas'r?" said Tom, earnestly.

"I am dying!" said St. Clare, pressing his hand; "pray!"

"If you would like a clergyman—" said the physician. St. Clare hast-ily shook his head and said again to Tom, more earnestly, "Pray!" (375)

Tom and St. Clare's words of religion and prayer belie the physical signs of primary and illicit relations. The women, again, are silent and invis-ible. Around his bed, most immediately, are his turned-over mulatto and his new favorite, whose hand he holds onto, as he has since the last death scene. As Miller's reading of Wilkie Collins would suggest, once the female is absented, "the novel needs to supplement its misogynistic plot with a misanthropic one, in which it will detail the frightening, even calamitous consequences of unmediated relations between men" (131). St. Clare's death both enacts and anticipates the violent demise, at the hands of men, of men who love men.

Tom's death comes more slowly; his tortured body, as he descends into the hell of the Legree plantation, embodies the calamitous consequences Miller outlines. To Ammons, Tom is "the supreme heroine of the novel and literal victim unto death of the masculine social system Stowe attacks."[45] In such circumstances a heroine would have suffered sexual violation, as women do at the bachelor Legree's. The consequences of male relations, however, are also acted out upon Tom's body; Tom is rendered powerless, and the gazing power is put back in the master's hands. As Fiedler puts it, at Legree's

> all feelings associated with rape have been transferred to the final archetypal scene in which Tom has become the passive victim, and his ravisher . . . Legree. He is assisted by Sambo and Quimbo, represent-ing everything in white nightmares of black sexuality and aggression which Uncle Tom denies. "The two gigantic negroes now laid hold of Tom." . . . Legree "foaming with rage" and determined to assert his ultimate power as absolute master ("and isn't he MINE? Can't I do what I like with him?") consummates what is tempting to think of as con-nubial murder and rape.[46]

Judeo-Christian culture, even pre-Freud, recognizes the signs of sexual vio-lence Stowe employs in her scenes of beating.[47] The snakish whip brandished by strong hands in slave narratives often acts as metaphor for more explicit physical seduction and violation.[48] Tom's torture, metaphorical rape, and sub-sequent death, his "fall" to hell from ostensible "edenic" gardens, only pro-longs the consequences of his relations at St. Clare's, demonstrating that in

Uncle Tom's Cabin death is not merely redemptive; it is a sign of illicit sexual transgression.

Afterword

What my homoerotic reading of Tom and St. Clare perhaps does not bring home loudly enough is an examination of the politics of consent, always, as they are, overdetermined by power and in this case racially constituted. Perhaps I over-destabilize the very taxonomical constructions of master, slave, and desire that I interrogate. Postmodernism on a white horse can sweep us into a seductive subtext, and a radically romantic one, which might suggest that when desire displaces heterosexually gendered relations in the St. Clare household, it wipes away power inequities, if only momentarily. One can see it staged: "What color is love?" little Eva and her chorus query. "What's love," contemporary critics bellow back, "got to do with it?" In other words, one need not elide Tom's "movement" from reified sexual object to desiring subject to note that he is figured as *receptive* to St. Clare's attentions and that this names the range of both his potential literal and metaphorical locations. Under the rubric of consent, Tom's desires matter little. The position(ing)s to which he could consent are almost completely fixed. After all, though Tom is brought from the outside and narratively centralized, he never can wield his sexual "power" effectively enough to achieve what white masters often promise their lovers—freedom. The fairy tale hasn't been rewritten after all.

My primary interest is to trace how history, representational conventions, and power map themselves textually on the discursive and material bodies of Black people. The construction of sexuality that in this paper calls for a reading of repressed (homo)sexual desire is also of importance to me because Tom's case, or slave men's sexual vulnerability and white men's desire for them, is more representative than we generally acknowledge.[49] When we figure only relations between female slaves and white men under slavery as a field of sexual violence and contestation, we allow ourselves to construct and maintain ideological gaps and representational silences. The ramifications of these lacunae fit into a broader set of regulations: the resistance to seeing the male body as penetrable. Dominant society's blinding desire of course perpetuates the erasure of gay identity and rights. Yet, readers will note, fields of male desiring subjectivity under slavery are not my primary focus here. Because my triangle anchors more broadly on race and power, the logical political extension of this paper is an emphasis on the *discrete* yet simultaneous ideological working that renders invisible the penetrability of male bodies, and so other bodies that are vulnerable—those of African Americans, the poor, and children—and allows society to ignore actual and metaphorical penetrations.[50] Sexual abuse, or power's intercourse with consent, following this "logic," can be structured as a category where women can be its only "victims." The maintenance of the false opposition between female "penetrated" bodies and male "impenetrable" ones (the latter category so enmeshed in heterosexist classifications of gayness) allows attached signs—the passive, to-be-looked-at, "willing victim" who wanted it, invited it—to then invert dynamics of consent and power, and to collapse onto, into, the constructed Woman. It so allows men and women with power to perpetuate their abuses sexually. This project, then, hopes to be part of oppositional readings which fight that power.

Notes

Barbara Christian, Rhonda Cobham, Jacquelyn Goldsby, Jacquelyn McLendon, Andrew Parker, Genaro Padilla, Karen Sanchez-Eppler, and Richard Yarborough all commented on various drafts of this piece. As always, I greatly appreciate their feedback.

1. Mary Boykin Chesnut, a Southern plantation mistress, makes this comment in *Diary from Dixie* (Boston, 1949). The other famous one-line response to *Uncle Tom's Cabin*, though it may only be lore, is Abraham Lincoln's: "So you're the little lady who started the big war." See Eric Sundquist, "Introduction," *New Essays on Uncle Tom's Cabin* (New York, 1986), 23. Also see *Mary Chesnut's Civil War*, ed. C. Vann Woodward (New Haven, 1981).

2. My essay stops short of examining (homo)sexual abuse on the Legree plantation, primarily because Leslie Fiedler has done it so aptly; see "What Was Literature?" in *Critical Essays on Harriet Beecher Stowe*, ed. Elizabeth Ammons (Boston, 1980), 175.

3. The early colony's best-sellers *The Coquette* (1797) and *Charlotte Temple* (1794) are prominent examples. Hannah Foster, *The Coquette*, ed. Cathy N. Davidson (New York, 1986); and Susanna Rowson, *Charlotte Temple*, ed. Davidson (New York, 1986).

4. In her now famous essay, Barbara Welter explains that a "true woman" embodies the qualities of purity, piety, submission, and domesticity; "The Cult of True Womanhood," in *Dimity Convictions: The American Woman in the Nineteenth Century*, ed. Welter (Athens, Ohio, 1976), 21.

5. See Gillian Brown's "Getting in the Kitchen with Dinah: Domestic Politics in *Uncle Tom's Cabin*" in *Domestic Individualism: Nineteenth-Century American Politics of Self* (Berkeley, 1990).

6. Jane Tompkins, Elizabeth Ammons, Gillian Brown, Sandra Gilbert and Susan Gubar, Eric Sundquist, and Richard Yarborough all argue or agree that Eva is angelic

or that her and Tom's deaths are self-sacrificial. Hortense Spillers, in contrast, argues that "when Stowe places 'Little Eva' and 'Uncle Tom' in a new and revised 'Garden of Eden' . . . there is nothing 'pious' or 'holy' about the altogether shocking outcome: the sacrificial lamb of *Uncle Tom's Cabin*—in the dual person of Eva the temptress and Tom the castrated—must be expended as *punishment* for the crimes against the culture, rather than as *salvation* for the culture." My analysis builds upon Spiller's explication; see "Changing the Letter," in *Slavery and the Literary Imagination*, ed. Deborah E. McDowell and Arnold Rampersad (Baltimore, 1990), 39.

7. See Spillers, "Changing the Letter," 25–47; and Fiedler, "What Was Literature?" 174. Michel Foucault, *History of Sexuality* (New York, 1980), argues that sexual discourse was far from suppressed in the nineteenth century; instead, it was systematically encouraged. He does not address, however, the interstices of sexuality, race, and/or gender.

8. Karen Sanchez-Eppler, "Bodily Bonds: The Intersecting Rhetorics of Feminism and Abolition," in *The New American Studies*, ed. Philip Fisher (Berkeley, 1991), 240.

9. Harriet Beecher Stowe, *Uncle Tom's Cabin* (New York, 1962), 64. Further citations will be given in parentheses in the text.

10. Stowe provides numerous exhibitions of Shelby's wealth during the time he insists he is in crisis; see 82, 77, 79.

11. Fiedler, "What Was Literature?" 114.

12. See Harriet Jacobs, *Incidents in the Life of a Slave Girl*, ed. Jean Fagan Yellin (Boston, 1987), 39.

13. Harriet Beecher Stowe, *Key to Uncle Tom's Cabin* (New York, 1968), 502.

14. Kristin Herzog, *Women, Ethnics, and Exotics: Images of Power in Mid-Nineteenth-Century American Fiction* (Memphis, 1983), 114.

15. The stories and memories of Beecher women were part of her childhood. Harriet's mother, Roxanne, died when she was very young, yet stories of her goodness were vivid in her children's growing up. Likewise, though Mary Foote died when Harriet was a toddler, this story was kept alive in the Beecher household. See Jeanne Boydston, Mary Kelley, and Anne Margolis, eds., *The Limits of Sisterhood: The Beecher Sisters on Women's Rights and Women's Sphere* (Chapel Hill, N.C., 1988), and Joan D. Hedrick, *Harriet Beecher Stowe: A Life* (New York, 1994).

16. Sandra Gilbert and Susan Gubar, *The Madwoman in the Attic: The Woman Writer and the Nineteenth-Century Literary Imagination* (New Haven, 1979), 125.

17. Robert Stepto, "Sharing the Thunder: The Literary Exchanges of Harriet Beecher Stowe, Henry Bibb, and Frederick Douglass," in Sundquist, *New Essays*, 141.

18. Karen Halttunen's excellent discussion of seduction, the St. Clare garden, the Legree mansion, and Henry Ward Beecher's sermon can be found in "Gothic Imagination and Social Reform: The Haunted Houses of Lyman Beecher, Henry Ward Beecher, and Harriet Beecher Stowe," in Sundquist, *New Essays*, 113.

19. I borrow this term, and the title of this essay, from Gillian Brown. In Brown's critical economy, it is the St. Clare cook Dinah's kitchen, and slavery's penetration into the separation of home and market, that constitute promiscuity—not illicit sex itself. Still, Brown's language, like Ophelia's pronouncements of distaste, reveals the sexual grumblings of these lush estates; "Getting in the Kitchen with Dinah."

20. Spillers, "Changing the Letter," 27.

21. Spillers's stunning essay also addresses this precise passage and gives a fuller reading of Eva, Tom, and the politics of contamination; ibid., 39.

22. Jean Fagan Yellin, "Doing It Herself," in Sundquist, *New Essays*, 92. See also Minrose Gwin's *Black and White Women and the Old South: The Peculiar Sisterhood in American Literature* (Memphis, 1985); and Richard Yarborough, "Strategies of Black Characterizations," in *New Essays*. Leslie Fiedler in "What Was Literature?" William Faulkner, and Elizabeth Ammons are in unison in their analysis of the vituperative presentation of Marie St. Clare.

23. Spillers, "Changing the Letter," 37.

24. These "ear-drops" are mentioned no fewer than four times in three paragraphs, and again emphasized later when Topsy says she steals them, though in this incident the same earrings are in Rosa's ears (301). The consistent description is of the earrings, not who wears them; the two mulattas are interchangeable wearers of this signifying trope.

25. We have seen this with Eliza. William Wells Brown's *Clotelle* reveals the trajectory more clearly. Though he figures the position of maid-in-waiting as an escape from the direct and desiring male gaze throughout the novel, in his opening passage he asserts that "many a planter's wife has dragged out a miserable existence, with an aching heart, at seeing her place in the husband's affections usurped by the unadorned beauty and captivating smiles of her waiting maid" (6). Despite his insistence that the desired object is the agent of her own reification and rape (he might call it seduction, or invert even the power in the "seducing" relationship), that she can occupy the "place" of her mistress, his narrative belies his contention as it collapses its own opposition and demonstrates the easy slippage between the "safe" and the sexual.

26. William Wells Brown, *Clotelle, or, the Colored Heroine* (Miami, 1969), 6.

27. I borrow here Eve Kosofsky Sedgwick's definition of desire, which names "a structure; a series of arguments about the structural permutations of social impulses [which] fuel the critical dialectic"; *Between Men: English Literature and Male Homosocial Desire* (New York, 1985), 2.

28. See Annette Kuhn, *The Power of the Image: Essays on Representation and Sexuality* (Boston, 1985), 4. Obviously, film theory cannot be translated unmediated into other media. The gazed-upon object is a human body, not an image of the traditional female nude. Questions of voyeurism, and the realization of the spectator/consumer, then, are distinct. The successful buyer of art takes home an image; his possession is still

bodily inaccessible, so that the voyeur relationship remains intact. With the slave, instead, the desired "spectacle" can be taken home and materially violated, once bought. Of course, Stowe's representation of these relations reinscribes the original relation; readers remain in the private act of "viewing," and so the novel maintains its voyeuristic relations.

29. *Mistress* carries both the weight of lady-of-the-house and the sexual connotations of concubine. It would be reductive to fit male characters, feminized as they are, into female lexicons, instructive as the readings that situate Tom as heroine are. "Mr. Adolph," or "Mr. St. Clare" as Adolph often has himself referred to (271), and Tom, however, have male bodies with which we must contend. Despite its awkwardness, then, "mister" rather than "mistress" of the house articulates the homoerotic dynamics of this household's placements.

30. One classic though nonracialized example of such signifying occurs in Zora Neale Hurston's *Their Eyes Were Watching God* (Urbana, 1978). Janie's retort to her husband Joe Starks: "You big-bellies round here and put out a lot of brag, but 'taint nothin' to it but yo' big voice. . . . When you pull down yo' britches, you look lak de change uh life" robs "him of the illusion of irresistible maleness that all men cherish" (123). Stowe's rendition is weighted with racial mythologies played out between men.

31. See Kobena Mercer, "Imaging the Black Man's Sex," in *Photography and Politics II* (London, 1986), 64.

32. As "all the marketing and providing for the family" have been "intrusted to [sic]" Tom, he must figure quite well. Literacy, however, a commodity that within slave narratives tends to work best in a free labor market, is not the skill Stowe imagines Tom to have. Tom is constantly laboring over reading his Bible, and has George Shelby and Little Eva act as his translators of the written word. Left without help at Legree's, he gives reading up entirely. When he comes back to religion, he throws the Bible (and literacy) away as he becomes the living word, rather than a reader of the written one.

33. Alice Crozier, *The Novels of Harriet Beecher Stowe* (New York, 1969), 196.

34. Ibid.

35. Harriet Beecher Stowe, *Lady Byron Vindicated* (Boston, 1870). See "The Byron Controversy," in Ammons, *Critical Essays*, 174–86.

36. Elizabeth Ammons, "Heroines," in *Critical Essays on Harriet Beecher Stowe*, ed. Ammons (Boston, 1988).

37. Ibid., 153.

38. Catherine Gallagher and Thomas Laqueur, eds., *The Making of the Modern Body: Sexuality and Society in the Nineteenth Century* (Berkeley, 1987), xi. This definition did not emerge as "classic" until the late nineteenth century, though the dynamics which led to its configuration were in place much earlier.

39. See Spillers on Eva's announcement to St. Clare regarding Tom: "You have money enough, I know. I want him" (205); "Changing the Letter," 40.

40. Sedgwick, *Between Men*, see chaps. 1 and 2.

41. Spillers, "Changing the Letter," 41.

42. I use Kuhn's terminology here; she refers to film theory, not to *Uncle Tom's Cabin; Power of the Image*, 41.

43. Ibid., 41–42.

44. D. A. Miller, "Cage aux folles: Sensation and Gender in Wilkie Collins's *The Woman in White*," in Gallagher and Laqueur, *Making of the Modern Body*, 131.

45. Elizabeth Ammons, "Stowe's Dream of the Mother-Savior," in Sundquist, *New Essays*, 164.

46. Fiedler, "What Was Literature?" 175.

47. One of the most striking such scenes is Gracie Montfort's beating in Pauline Hopkin's *Contending Forces* (New York, 1988), 69. Stowe foregrounds the sexual contamination of whippings when the slave Rosa laments, "I don't mind the whipping so much, if Miss Marie or you was to do it; but to be sent to a *man*! and such a horrid man,—the shame of it, Miss Feeley!" (378).

48. Again see Fiedler: "Interethnic rape is . . . as central as interethnic flagellation, which [Stowe] eroticized to the point where it seems merely another version of sexual violation" (168). Despite this analysis, he later suggests that homoerotic relations, or in his language "this myth of the idyllic anti-marriage," appears repeatedly in American literature, but that Stowe's only "concession to her masculine readers" was the "minor sub-plot involving the tender relationship between Tom and young `Marse George'"; "What Was Literature?" 164.

49. Jacobs offers several instances of and allusions to sexual violence against men. Frances Foster notes that male narrators do not feel compelled to discuss their own sexuality even, one might add, in coded language or references. Their sexual vulnerability, then, seems to me one of those ornate silences that does not necessarily signify that the circumstances were "not there," to use Morrison's words again, even though they do not even engage in the strategies of undertell to signal this presence. See Frances Foster, "`In Respect to Females': Differences in the Portrayals of Women by Male and Female Narrators," *Black American Literature Forum* 15 (Summer 1981): 66–70.

50. The Milwaukee police's response to white serial killer Jeffrey Dahmer's Black neighbor's numerous complaints is a case in point. In one instance, the police *returned* to Dahmer's house Konerak Sinthasomphone, a fourteen-year-old Laotian boy, who was running down the street naked trying to escape. Though in this case, the police recognized the boy's penetrability by joking, "intoxicated Asian, naked male. Was returned to his boyfriend," they effaced his violability. There was evidence of violence, and of compulsion: the boy was reportedly bleeding from the buttocks; he was drugged; he had a hole drilled in his head that the police "did not notice"; and the complainant had stressed that he was underage. Yet these were explained away by Dahmer, who was the only person with whom the police spoke. When Dahmer was finally caught, the

national press emphasized the violated heads of these boys as much as their violated bodies, as if because many were gay the fact that they were drugged and raped were not an issue. Indeed, rape is a word that is *never* used to describe Dahmer's "sex acts" in any of the many *Time, Newsweek, New York Times, Washington Post,* or *Chicago Tribune* articles I have examined. Only Glenda Cleavland, one of the three black women who called in about Sinthasomphone, used the term when she called the police to ask "if the situation was being handled." When she learned that the instance was being dismissed as a love quarrel, she insisted that "this was a male child being raped and molested by an adult" (transcript of phone call to Milwaukee police, special to the *New York Times,* 31 July 1991). Yet, Dahmer's attempts to drill into the *heads* of his (mostly Black) male victims, to lobotomize them, as well as the much noted decapitations became the media's focus, as much as, or more than, the rest of their violated bodies.

Who Gets to Create the Lasting Images?

The Problem of Black Representation in Uncle Tom's Cabin

SOPHIA CANTAVE

◆　◆　◆

For late-twentieth-century teachers, the significance of Harriet Beecher Stowe as a white woman creating a national space for an "empathetic" discourse on the slave experience raises several questions. For instance, why didn't Mary Prince's exposé of slavery in the West Indies, *The History of Mary Prince* (1831), or Harriet Wilson's account of de facto slavery in the American North, *Our Nig* (1859), become the proverbial "shot heard around the world"? What enabled Stowe to write *Uncle Tom's Cabin* and begin a national and international literary exchange on slavery? The novel invented the modern idea of a "best-seller," and many of Stowe's characters became national stock types and icons. Even today, readers cry at the right places and express horror, relief, or disbelief where textually appropriate. Most important, Stowe's text allows whites to talk to other whites about the personal and national issues surrounding the slave experience and establishes the character types usually associated with African Americans. Indeed, throughout the second half of the nineteenth century and then the early twentieth century, Stowe's novel provided the nation with a shared cultural context for its discourse on slavery, offering reductive images, phrases, and symbols that quickly became the accepted norm.

For example, early in the twentieth century *Uncle Tom's Cabin* permitted the nameless narrator of James Weldon Johnson's *The Autobiography of an Ex-Colored Man* (1912) to talk finally to his mother about their racial identity. But what does it mean when two highly miscegenated characters use a white woman's novel as the basis for a discussion of their blackness in the United States? In contrast, *The History of Mary Prince*, though heavily edited, failed to galvanize the literate community or fill the racial imaginings of Americans. And the suppression of Harriet Wilson's *Our Nig* prevented it from shaping the national conceptions of the slave and nonslave experience.

When we use Stowe's novel in the classroom, I think it is important to ask who gets to make our national symbols and who gets to determine when a particular symbol or icon has outlived its usefulness. Although *Uncle Tom's Cabin* was essential in creating an earlier discourse on the slave experience, what is the usefulness of teaching the novel today? I reexamine that question. At the turn into the twenty-first century, I think modern readers want to bury the discourse Stowe began under the fiction that "we already know about slavery"—yet we do not know. To begin a broader discussion of American women's involvement in the "peculiar institution" as slaves, as slave owners, and as writers, readers need to go beyond the humiliating or embarrassing surface of the text and examine the issues that the existence of the novel raises. In this essay, I focus on Stowe's problematic status and symbols to ask where the United States slave experience, as Stowe writes it, should fit in a modern literary context—a question that should surely precede any teaching of the novel.

At first, a return to *Uncle Tom's Cabin* feels like a return to a crime scene with too many nagging questions left unanswered. Because of these questions, Stowe's novel should regain its place in contemporary classrooms and be taught for what it signifies about United States race relations 150 years after slavery. Few African Americans criticized Stowe's novel at the time of its initial publication. In the mid-nineteenth century, African American emancipation depended on acknowledging and supporting the national and international debate sparked by *Uncle Tom's Cabin*. Where all other writers "failed," Stowe succeeded. The significance of her success, and the instant commercialization of her subject, placed many of the African American abolitionists in an odd position. How does Frederick Douglass criticize a novel he feels beholden to? For the most part, Douglass praised the novel's efficacy and tirelessly referred to *Uncle Tom's Cabin* as the "master book of the nineteenth century" (Donovan 17). Of her text, Stowe said, "My vocation is simply that of a painter, and my object will be to hold up in the most lifelike and graphic manner possible Slavery, its reverses, changes, and the negro character, which I have had ample opportunities for studying. There is no arguing with *pictures*, and everybody is impressed by them, whether they mean to be or not" (Hedrick, *Stowe* 208). The power, efficacy, and timeliness of *Uncle Tom's Cabin* cannot be denied. But the unsettling issues surrounding Stowe's access and her relation to the "objects of her study" should not be denied either. At the turn into the twenty-first century, Stowe's novel continues to evoke uneasiness when readers consider blackness and, more important, slavery as the "canvas" that allowed her to write her most famous novel.

As is well known, Stowe's "sketches of slave life," as she popularly referred to her novel (Hedrick, *Stowe* 208), would eventually influence the development of the modern theater, the development of philanthropy as a business, and the marketing of "Uncle Tom" paraphernalia. Less well known is the fact that a viewing of *Uncle Tom's Cabin* served as the catalyst for Thomas Dixon's literary career. As part of his refutation of Stowe's version of Southern slavery, Dixon wrote *The Clansman* (1905), which later became the basis for D. W. Griffith's classic, racist movie, *The Birth of a Nation* (1915). In other words, the negative influence of Stowe's novel on the development of United States popular culture even in cases such as this, where Stowe's text is being attacked, must be considered. And the readily available "canvas of blackness" that allowed Stowe's sketches to come to life continues to enable the nation to solidify its power not only to relegate black people to the margins but also to regulate the discourses surrounding what constitutes human suffering and degradation. The slave experience, far from being understood, is trapped in multiple hegemonic constructions of power and nation as well as by self-imposed restrictions on language.

Many middle-class African Americans want to forget, or get past, the images of Topsy "just growing," of Sambo and Quimbo, of Sam and Andy, of Chloe and Uncle Tom himself. Members of the African American middle class shun what the black urban masses, largely the working poor, often vilify and reclaim with their popular usage of such terms as *niggers* and *hoes*, *players*, and *freaks* when referring to one another. Which national face should African Americans present as what they understand of their positionality and blackness in America? The slave experience, in the African American psyche, continues metaphorically to grope for the words to explain the silence, including the profusion of reactions to a white woman writing and creating a national discourse on slavery. These anxieties, in part, explain late-twentieth-century returns to the Middle Passage and its aftermath. Questions remain about black speaking subjects even as modern writers like Toni Morrison, Octavia Butler, Gloria Naylor, Charles Johnson, and others travel back in time in attempts to wrest control of black images from benevolent but racist white supporters and their detractors.

Josephine Donovan points out that Stowe, in explaining her construction of *Uncle Tom's Cabin*, said:

> "The writer acknowledges that the book is a very inadequate representation of slavery [because] slavery, in some of its workings, is too dreadful for the purposes of art. A work which should represent it strictly as it is would be a work which could not be read; and all works which ever mean to give pleasure must draw a veil somewhere, or they cannot succeed." In fiction, therefore, one can "find refuge from the hard and the terrible, by inventing scenes and characters of a more pleasing nature." (62)

In her successful attempt to make slavery readable, Stowe falls back on the comic interactions of blacks with other blacks and of blacks while in the presence of whites. By mixing the tragic and the laughable, *Uncle Tom's Cabin* gives white people and black people a way to read slavery together. This does not mean that African Americans did not then, and do not now, make use of comedy to explain parts of slavery. They had to and often did so for the benefit of their owners. Thus the joking relationship and the various uses of the comic exist as one of the earliest accepted signs of black subordination and one that slaves continuously manipulated. But the comic interactions as Stowe uses them do not so much subvert as reinforce the existing order.

This shared reading almost always insists that slavery, in its entirety, cannot be read and that slavery and the slave experience do not make for "good art." In some ways, this designation of slavery as unreadable and unfit for the purposes of high art continues, almost 150 years after the publication of *Uncle Tom's Cabin*. In assessing her novel, Stowe gives herself the power to decide on the purposes of art and when and where to draw the veil when writing on slavery. Thus, despite even her best intentions, *Uncle Tom's Cabin* betrays her overwhelming race and class privileges and the ways she herself helped to further limit African Americans' access to the dominant language and their own literary portrayal of the slave experience.

To do the necessary research for *Beloved* (1987), Toni Morrison went to Brazil to see various slave restraints like the iron collar and muzzle used to control and torture. The United States sterilized and reduced the slave narratives and slavery into formulaic stories that the nation as a whole felt more comfortable reading. Morrison confronts, in writing, what many of the early United States narratives could not when she writes about the devastating psychological trauma of slavery. She exposes the ease with which an exploding national discourse reduced the grossest human violations into instances of comic relief and shows how sentimental release acts as a potent signifier of white hegemonic control. For example, fearing competition where none existed before, Fuzzy Zoeller made a disparaging comment to an understanding white CNN newscaster about fried chicken littering a once exclusive golf tournament, a remark that immediately undercut the record-breaking achievement of Tiger Woods. Despite black excellence and achievement, such jokes, at key moments, perpetuate age-old images of nonwhite incompetence and buffoonery. In choosing to intersperse the comic alongside the tragic, Stowe inadvertently provided a way for white people, when threatened or challenged, to regulate black achievement, black national mobility, and black cultural expression. Even the relationships that black people form with one another are circumscribed by such strategies of the dominant culture and its definitions of blackness.

One way to illuminate these issues is by teaching *Uncle Tom's Cabin* side by side with Harriet Wilson's *Our Nig*, published just seven years after *Uncle Tom's Cabin*. Harriet Wilson, a severely marginalized black woman, began in her writing to make powerful connections with other black people about their shared economic and color oppression. Her disastrous marriage to a black man claiming to be a former slave goes beyond what Stowe imagines as the motivating force behind black female-male relationships. That is, Wilson's Frado leaves the best home she has ever known and her only moment of relative independence because she is drawn to a man who she believes shares her experiences. Aside from Frado's dead father and the man her mother runs off with, her husband makes the third black man to enter her life. Wilson makes a point of saying that Frado reacts to the bond created by their similar backgrounds. Ironically, however, Frado's husband lies about his slave experience and quickly abandons his new bride. Yet Wilson does not dwell on this lie. Instead, she hints that Frado's husband felt compelled to play the role of a former slave in order to get Northern abolitionists' sympathy and assistance. My point here has to do with the complexity of Wilson's perspective. Although Frado's marriage leads to her further physical deterioration, it shows Frado making choices that do not depend on white benevolence or white fictions of black desire. Yet because of her husband's dependence on white Northern sympathy, Frado indirectly suffers.

Wilson's multiple strategies of reappropriation and renaming help her subversively assert herself as a speaking subject. Even though heavily circumscribed and limited, she directs her appeals to her colored brethren, not the white masses. She asks her colored brethren to forgive her faulty prose and purchase her novel or, rather, her "sketches from the life of a free black, in a two-story white house, North." She says in her preface, "I have purposefully omitted what would most provoke shame in our good anti-slavery friends at home"(4). Wilson echoes almost the same sentiments as Stowe—that the worst of slavery has been omitted—but for different reasons. After her abandonment first by her mother and then by her husband, Wilson had to depend on the "good anti-slavery friends at home," the class that Stowe belonged to. Wilson's disclaimer says that she leaves out what would show Northern white abolitionists to be very much like their Southern white slaveholding counterparts. Wilson assumes much more subjectivity than the nation, in 1859, was prepared to accept or believe in a black speaker. If Stowe's detractors vehemently refuted "her blacks" as thinking subjects, *Our Nig*, written by a black woman in the North, gave white readers even more reason to dismiss Wilson's text altogether. At least with *Uncle Tom's Cabin*, later dramatic adaptations could exclude the heavily abolitionist tracts and overplay the comic moments that comfortably disrupt sections assigning blame or showing black agency since the joke always has a derogatory black reference that serves as the punch line. Students need to know that Topsy, on the stage, became an instant hit with the audiences in part because her reformation into a serious-minded missionary was conveniently left out. In contrast, Frado, far from being the butt of the jokes, instigates them and possesses more self-awareness than Topsy, who is primarily constructed as the antithesis of Little Eva.

Wilson offers her readers Frado's body both in its linguistic negation and as the epitome of Northern conceptions of blackness despite her light skin and white mother. Mrs. Bellmont, her keeper, delights in her complete control of Frado's body. She keeps on hand special blocks that she forces into the child's mouth in order to beat her with even greater abandon. Mrs. Bellmont cripples Frado's body without ever losing her status as a respectable member of her community. These spaces in Wilson's text of possible catharsis through the sadistic pleasure of physically or mentally violating black bodies present an unexplored area for students to think about. In contrast, Stowe emphasizes the sadism and ruthlessness of slave violation at the hands of white men, making Marie St. Clare the monstrous exception to the rule, while Mary Prince and Harriet Wilson delve deep into the pleasure white women derive from the physical energy expended in beating bodies even more marginalized than their own.

Harriet Wilson, writing her fictionalized autobiography only a few years after *Uncle Tom's Cabin*, gave considerable thought to her audience. She appealed to a black readership while simultaneously considering how white readers might receive her text. Wilson says in her preface, "I do not pretend to divulge every transaction in my own life, which the unprejudiced would declare unfavorable in comparison with treatment of legal bondmen" (4).

Because she lived in the North, Wilson left out the worst of what she experienced as a free black there, lest she alienate abolitionists. She wrote her autobiographical novel in an attempt to earn enough money to support herself and her son, who died before she sold one copy and her entire project slipped into obscurity. Conversely, Stowe as a writer committed to the abolitionist movement but also desiring a modicum of success in her endeavor, made the slave's experience readable, palatable for her expected audience. In *Uncle Tom's Cabin: Evil, Affliction, and Redemptive Love* Josephine Donovan says, "The slave narratives tended to focus on one person's unhappy experiences from that individual's point of view. Stowe realized that no one would read a novel that was relentlessly grim (indeed *Uncle Tom's Cabin* outsold all of the slave narratives and abolition novels put together)" (62). The fact that "*Uncle Tom's Cabin* outsold all of the slave narratives" underscores the significance of Stowe's literary and transgressive access to her potent subject matter that fueled the uninhibited imagination of the country. *Uncle Tom's Cabin* sold more copies than any American novel before or, for a long time, after it because Stowe's position as a white woman from a family of preachers enabled her to write not only with moral conviction but also with the necessary distance to calculate a specific textual effect. While being driven by a moral obligation to write against an institution she saw as diametrically opposed to Christianity, Stowe produced a text that surpassed even her wildest expectations.

But what has been the effect of this book on black people? An experiment lasting over fifteen years conducted by Albion Tourgee, a novelist, judge, and activist who spoke out against racial segregation, provides one answer. Tourgee had former slaves read or listen to readings of *Uncle Tom's Cabin* because he wanted "to determine to what extent [they] thought [*Uncle Tom's Cabin*] was an accurate portrayal of southern slavery" (Gossett, *American Culture* 361). "'Choosing the most intelligent colored people' available he 'found that most ex-slaves did not think Uncle Tom was too meek as later generations of black activists would. Instead they thought of him as unrealistically critical of his masters. Tom spoke out more frankly than a real slave might have dared to'" (Donovan 17). The few recordings of black responses to *Uncle Tom's Cabin* vacillate between evasive silences and complete acceptance of Stowe's words and reactions, suggesting that her depictions are better than what slaves could have produced. Donovan gives the example of a female former slave perfectly content with Stowe's words standing in for her own. "Sella Martin [...] in speaking of her difficulty in describing the horrors of being sold at the auction block, remarked, 'happily this [...] task is now unnecessary. Mrs. Stowe [has] thrown sufficient light upon the horrible and inhuman agency of slavery'"(17). Stowe also felt that it was *she* who should represent (and profit from) the telling of slave experiences, as her treatment of Harriet Jacobs's narrative illustrates. Instead of giving Jacobs the literary advice she sought, Stowe offered to include Jacobs's narrative in her *Key* to Uncle Tom's Cabin. The slave experience, with all its violations and humiliations, was the property of Harriet Beecher Stowe.

Yet according to one male former slave in Tourgee's study, Stowe "didn't know what slavery was so left out the worst of it" (Gossett, *American Culture* 361). To give even this cautious yet pointed critique was daring. He provides a reason completely different from the one Stowe gives for leaving out the worst of slavery. Attributing only this line to the speaker, Tourgee does not give any more space for the former slave to describe "the worst of it" beyond saying "the worst of it." Tourgee, though, provides his own analysis of speech and nonspeech patterns in slave communities. He says, "Perhaps the most striking feature characteristic of slavery was the secretiveness it imposed upon slave nature. [...] To the slave, language became in very truth an instrument for the concealment of thought, rather than its expression" (Donovan 17). Little wonder that language "became an instrument of concealment" in the face of overwhelming racial inequality and racial violence. Tourgee himself says, "Men do not argue with those who have the power of life and death over them" (Gossett, *American Culture* 361). Language itself continues to place black bodies as speaking subjects, then and now, at risk. In Uncle Tom's Cabin *and American Culture*, Thomas F. Gossett also discusses the conflicted responses of black people to Stowe's novel. Stowe wrote her novel at a time when African humanity, intelligence, and subjectivity were still being debated. Gossett says that many white readers criticized Stowe's portrayals of black people as being too complimentary. This sentiment, in combination with little or no access to the text, made it difficult for African American readers of that period to challenge the novel's reductiveness. After the publication of *Uncle Tom's Cabin*, African Americans who wanted to speak about blackness in America and be heard had to do it through Stowe or not at all.

Consequently, James Weldon Johnson's protagonist can begin a serious and thoughtful discussion of race only in the context of *Uncle Tom's Cabin*. Ironically, a man who sees himself as white and eventually decides to pass as white reads Stowe's novel in much the same way that sympathetic white readers read *Uncle Tom's Cabin*. The "thingness" of blacks, despite the richness of a culture little understood and searching for its expression, leads the Ex-Colored Man to live the life of "an ordinarily successful white man who has made a little money" (510). The risk involved in expressing himself as a black person causes him to " [sell his] heritage for a mess of pottage" (511), and the unspeakable act of lynching another human being remains uncontested. Significantly, the lynching occurs at the moment the Ex-Colored Man finishes his documentation of black music and cultural expression in the South and begins contemplating the future publication of his findings. Confronted with such a display of power—the lynching of a black man by a group of respectable citizens—a miscegenated black man chooses whiteness and the suppression of any and all claims to black subjectivity and authorship.

In considering issues of authorship and vocality, the following question also needs to be raised in the classroom: When can black people speak and in what words that do not already replicate in some way the dialectic of past ownership and subordination? Even as modern writers anxiously go back to write and say the things that enslaved or freed blacks could not say, what are the words and images that will not leave them at risk and produce yet again another silencing in the present age? Too little has been done with the contemporary resurgence in pop culture of "niggers," "boys," "players," "freaks," and "hoes," all old images with old origins. The comic, the hypersexualized, and the desexualized remain as the most readily available symbols of African Americans in the United States. In place of words, Stowe and a minstrel tradition older than the one she helped formalize give black expression wholly over to hand gestures, mimicry, stoicism, and other nonspeech acts.

Given this reduction of black expression to the guttural, the comical, and the lewd, the dominating theoretical framework for analyzing black literature and black culture, in the early twentieth century, focused on psychic doubling, veils, tricksterism, and masks. All these approaches centered on black performance and the stifling relation of black bodies to a power structure that did not see itself as oppressive or feel culpable in demanding these performances of race. The current discourse on race allows for too many gaps, too many silences, while whole discussions about race and racial equity continue to take place without the participation or presence of black people. Stowe's discarded subtitle, *The Man That Was a Thing*, accurately describes the role of black people when white people gather to discuss whom they will and will not allow entry into their coveted circles. African American struggles to wrest control of our national images, icons, and symbols from the white power structure must continue as part of the fight against objectification and erasure.

African American discourse, even in urban slang, still manages to conceal, evade, and leave much, sometimes too much, unsaid. The silent ironies of early African American discourses, though ensuring African American survival despite physical and psychic violation, need to "call Stowe out of her name." To do this "calling out" (and make Stowe's text useful in the classroom) students must question the novel's runaway success and influence not only in the United States but also around the world. Similarly, students must also question the complex social, cultural, and political context, at this fin de siécle, that keeps Stowe's text from being read by both black and white readers. The resistance to the kinds of remembrances that *Uncle Tom's Cabin* provokes about the nation's slave past provides other ways to discuss issues of African American textual silence, erasure, and the continuing appropriation of black images. In rethinking black people's reaction to this encroachment, what happens when irony is lost on its audience, when silence, double subversions, reversals get buried so deep they become undecipherable and completely disconnected from their original negation? African American literary discourse began with multiple capitulations to a white reading public that made discussing and writing about the worst of slavery unacceptable. In addition to the frayed and moldy bills of sale, the "owners" of the slave experience and its symbols also own and regulate the national discourses on slavery. *Uncle Tom's Cabin* may have wanted to show how slave owners could overcome the reification and reduction of human beings to the status of things but this reduction and reification are precisely what happen in the novel and particularly in the Tom shows it inspired. For teachers today, the novel exists as an uncomfortable but necessary place to begin critical discussions about the racial dynamics of literary access, power, and popular culture.

As the writer who helped shape the national discourse on slavery, Stowe provided the parameters of that discourse, establishing where slavery can and cannot go in the popular imagination and as high literature. These stifling limitations explain, in part, why two subversive black women's texts, Wilson's *Our Nig* and Prince's narrative, received little or no literary attention at the time of their original publication. In many ways, 150 years after Stowe published her novel, African Americans still do not have the words to say what the worst of slavery really was, or rather, African Americans did not create the terms that define the slave experience in the national consciousness. African Americans who step outside the accepted parameters of slavery's discourse risk shutting down discussions, arousing white defensive or apologetic barrages and black desires to acquiesce and make nice in the face of such responses. All these responses take away from speaking honestly and critically about power inequities even in some of the most common social interactions. In acquiescing, in giving up the national discursive space to white culture, unspeakable things remain unspoken, especially in the academy where one's vocality, erudition, and authorship matter. "Being nice," helping to keep one's colleagues comfortable, results in the loss of too much ground. All these issues in one way or another come into play in Stowe's novel. *Uncle Tom's Cabin*, precisely because of its literary success and its continuing, though unadmitted, influence on United States cultural history, needs to reenter current, critical discussions of race to shed light on some of the nagging issues that are still too difficult to name.

Historically, *Uncle Tom's Cabin* provided a framework for the United States and the European nations to discuss the "peculiar institution" and their positions within that institution. Stowe's novel in a late-twentieth-century classroom context should highlight issues of appropriation, privilege, national accountability, and the intricate workings of power in the United States. After the publication of *Uncle Tom's Cabin*, almost all slave narratives by black people became a part of Harriet Beecher Stowe's *Key to* Uncle Tom's Cabin. That is, the telling of the slave experience became a strangely white affair, being told in ways that let white audiences be moved to tears and still find the work enjoyable. Yet the former slaves' responses to the novel seem to tell a different story, one about the absence of their words and what it means to accept someone else's language. Stowe's own admission, that slavery as it existed did not make for good art, supports my belief that what the nation as a collective understands about race relations it does not write or readily discuss except, possibly, in the joking relationship. The national fiction of understanding and knowing slavery exists as a complex cultural production depending on black and white people to play their parts. The very idea of Stowe giving her words to a former slave woman disturbingly points to the issues at stake in questions of authority and ownership. The quote of the nameless male former slave who lamented the absence of "the worst of slavery" in literature represents what remains forever out of reach when black people fail to resist and question master/mistress narratives, even ones that are done with the best intentions.

Denying African Americans the opportunity to tell their story without comic interjections left whole things unsaid. Early on, African Americans, the majority of whom were unable to write freely in their own words about their experiences, did not create the lasting images of the slave experience. Simultaneously, Stowe refused to write the worst of slavery. African Americans, unable to tell the worst of slavery directly, packed multiple meanings in generic evasive responses that lessened the linguistic and physical risks involved in speaking in a repressive society. The unspoken, the unspeakable, became its own signifier. Arguing these points in the classroom does not mean that black people did not imagine themselves in relation to other blacks, other people of color, or that black people were not instrumental in advocating for changes that established legal precedents for other groups to follow. It does mean that African American cultural production and discourses need to move from the margins, where they are easily appropriated and reauthored, to the center.

Locating Stowe in her historical moment and outside it, a century and a half later, provides the setting for a discussion of the politics involved in her discursive access to her black subjects and the continuing use of black bodies as fodder for the nation's intellectual, cultural, economic, and political revisions and reassessments. To read the criticism on Stowe, even that which goes beyond questioning her literary status, is to confront over and over again the "thingness" of the African American slave body. Despite Stowe's own marginalization as a woman in her own period, the "thingness" of African American bodies and the pervasive acceptance of a culture based on human ownership made the figures of Uncle Tom, Topsy, Eliza, Cassy, Dinah, Sam, Andy, Sambo, and Quimbo available to her. These images of African Americans persist in their original and updated forms, as efforts to denounce the persistence of the mammy figure in the late 1980s illustrate. After threatened boycotts, the makers of Aunt Jemima pancakes responded to the criticism of their logo by unveiling a new version of the mammy figure. Since removing the logo was out of the question, the Quaker Oats Company decided to remove Aunt Jemima's head scarf and give her a perm. Thus the new "Aunt Jemima" cut short any and all efforts to denounce continued use of the mammy figure. Silence, shame, embarrassment, and powerless indignation filled the space where anger and continued activism belonged. African Americans, in Stowe's time and now, do not own the images and symbols of African American culture, long wedded to big business and commercial success. Only a perm separates a mammy of the slave era from one in the late twentieth century.

To have this myriad of black bodies at the nation's collective disposal bespeaks a power that white culture rarely admits to owning. In the late twentieth century, Uncle Tom/Sam is Clarence Thomas, Eliza/Chloe/Cassy is Anita Hill, and George Harris is potentially a young O. J. on the rise. These black figures act as catalysts for national debates on racial parity, equity in the justice and law enforcement systems, sexual harassment, spousal abuse, and the responsibilities of government agencies to the working poor. Renewed attacks on affirmative action, white culture's only begrudging capitulation to the intricate and exclusive workings of white privilege, reassert white culture's power to decide what constitutes African American access and redress for past inequities. In these displays of power, white hegemony reasserts its control by limiting not only the extent of black people's access but also their creative and competitive potential.

Without any particular acknowledgment or any sense of appropriation, expression of the slave experience became Stowe's own. It is this ownership, this appropriation of African American images, phrases, and culture by white culture, that continues to threaten the legitimacy of African American literature in the academy and that needs to be interrogated in the classroom. Blackness remains, at the turn into the twenty-first century, one of the few subjects that does not go beyond genteel academic or social discussion. In discussing blackness and making it readable for a predominantly white power structure, Stowe says, the jokes, the moments of comic relief at the expense of black people, are indispensable. Thus, as Toni Morrison argues, unspeakable things do remain unspoken and the worst of the slave experience continues to search for its words ("Unspeakable Things").

Works Cited

Dixon, Thomas, Jr. *The Clansman: An Historical Romance of the Ku Klux Klan.* New York: Doubleday, Page, 1905.

Donovan, Josephine. *Uncle Tom's Cabin: Evil, Affliction, and Redemptive Love.* Boston: Twayne, 1991.

Gossett, Thomas F. *Uncle Tom's Cabin and American Culture.* Dallas: Southern Methodist UP, 1985.

Griffith, D. W., dir. *The Birth of a Nation.* 1915. New York: Kino on Video, 1992.

Hedrick, Joan. *Harriet Beecher Stowe: A Life.* New York: Oxford UP, 1994.

Jacobs, Harriet A. *Incidents in the Life of a Slave Girl, Written by Herself.* Ed. Jean Fagan Yellin. Cambridge: Harvard UP, 1987.

Johnson, James Weldon. *The Autobiography of an Ex-Colored Man.* 1912. Ed. Henry Louis Gates Jr. New York: Avon, 1965.

Morrison, Toni. *Beloved.* New York: Plume, 1987.

Morrison, Toni. "Unspeakable Thing Unspoken: The Afro-American Presence in American Literature." *Within the Circle: An Anthology of African American Literary Criticism from the Harlem Renaissance to the Present.* Ed. Angelyn Mitchell. Durham: Duke UP, 1994. 368–98.

Prince, Mary. *The History of Mary Prince.* Ed. Henry Louis Gates Jr. New York: Mentor, 1987.

Stowe, Harriet Beecher. *A Key to Uncle Tom's Cabin.* Boston: Jewett, 1853.

Stowe, Harriet Beecher. *Uncle Tom's Cabin; or, Life among the Lowly.* Boston: Jewett, 1852.

Wilson, Harriet E. *Our Nig; or, Sketches from the Life of a Free Black.* 1859. Ed. Henry Louis Gates Jr. New York: Vintage, 1983.

Up to Heaven's Gate, Down in Earth's Dust

The Politics of Judgment in Uncle Tom's Cabin

JOSHUA D. BELLIN

◆　◆　◆

IN HER INTRODUCTION TO the 1878 edition of *Uncle Tom's Cabin*, Harriet Beecher Stowe wrote that "the story can less be said to have been composed by her than imposed upon her."[1] But this illusion of authorlessness or powerlessness—she would come to claim that God had written the book—is at odds with the passionate declaration with which Stowe is said to have commenced her novel, at her sister-in-law's urging: "I will write something. I will—if I live!"[2] These two moments in the mythos of *Uncle Tom's Cabin* illuminate two conflicting energies within the novel itself: the power of the individual human will and the powerlessness of the individual in a universe controlled by God. In its attack on slavery, *Uncle Tom's Cabin* fluctuates between these two alternatives, dramatizing not only the struggle of humans seeking to respond to and resist the slave system, but also the struggle of humanity seeking to negotiate and comprehend its proper role in God's design.

Structurally, *Uncle Tom's Cabin* mirrors its deeply divided sympathies. This doubleness arises from and is driven by Stowe's relentless pairing of characters, events, and views. Stowe produces, among countless pairs, two St. Clares in Augustine and his twin, Alfred; two Christs in Tom and Eva; two little children in Eva and Topsy; two plots in Tom's journey South, deeper into enslavement, and the Harrises' journey North, closer to freedom; and two models of response to slavery, the active, violent resistance of George Harris, and the passive, saintly acceptance of Uncle Tom. Jane Tompkins writes that "every character in the novel, every scene, and every incident, comes to be apprehended in terms of every *other* character, scene, and incident."[3] While essentially correct, this assessment muddies the strategy of Stowe's narrative. *Uncle Tom's Cabin* is not a morass of "cross-references"[4] but a carefully poised and counterpoised structure of opposed pairs. If *Uncle Tom's Cabin* is divided, it is divided by design, by Stowe's unyielding control of her text—almost, one might say, by divine plan.

And yet, in the end, this divisiveness appears to get the better of Stowe; and *Uncle Tom's Cabin*, unable to reconcile its contradictory impulses, is pulled apart: "up to heaven's gate in theory, down in earth's dust in practice," as Augustine St. Clare says of himself.[5] It is critical to note the context in which this pronouncement is spoken, as well as its speaker, for herein, I feel, lies the key to *Uncle Tom's Cabin*. St. Clare, the most profoundly divided character in the novel, the only character capable both of grasping the deepest causes of slavery and of doing something about it, has just predicted a *dies irae*, a mustering of the oppressed masses. Yet to Stowe the *dies irae* means much more: it means, quite literally, the Coming of the Lord, the Day of Judgment, the "wrath of Almighty God!" (629). In St. Clare one sees the clearest expression and aim of Stowe's oppositional scheme. St. Clare is both spokesman for and symbol of the novel's deepest pattern: the separation, on the Day of Judgment, of the damned from the saved, the oppressor from the oppressed, those (like Haley and Legree) who have dwelled "down in earth's dust" from those (like Tom and Eva) who have lived up at "heaven's gate." In short, *Uncle Tom's Cabin* is a book that, for all its lamentation over the separating of families, celebrates—indeed, is predicated upon—the Day when *"Parents and children there shall part!"* (530). But the novel itself seemingly succumbs to its self-conscious divisiveness; though purportedly addressing the daily reality of slavery, *Uncle Tom's Cabin* ultimately abandons any scheme for active resistance and contents itself with judgment while waiting fervently for The Judgment. And yet, I contend, it is the novel's resolution of this internal conflict—a resolution which seems to discard resistance in favor of judgment—which enabled *Uncle Tom's Cabin*, paradoxically, to empower and motivate a nation in the period before the Civil War. *Uncle Tom's Cabin* resolves, or appears to resolve, the most profound dilemma of the day; it achieves for its audience, through its struggles with human fallibility and moral grayness, a certitude which makes its own position of judgment seem very like the Judgment of God.

To understand *Uncle Tom's Cabin*'s remarkable power one must perceive its sensitivity to and manipulation of the religious rhetoric which surrounded the slavery issue. The novel gathers the threads of a debate which had raged within the churches and consciences of the nation: what was the proper Christian response to slavery? Reluctant at first to enter the lists, the religious leaders of the North came to be some of the most vocal champions of the antislavery cause. Their solutions to the dilemma, however, varied greatly, and it is in the variety of their responses that one can see emerging the central debate in Stowe's novel.[6] The dilemma, as Timothy Smith writes, boiled down to a single painful question: "Through all these churchly debates over political and ecclesiastical measures, finally, ran the thread of an essentially religious paradox—whether Christians might do violence in pursuit of charitable ends. The dilemma was as old as the faith itself, Jesus having been, in a sense, crucified upon the arms of it. In Gethsemane he had bidden Peter to sheathe his sword. How then could his disciples march off to holy war, singing 'John Brown's body lies amold'ring in the grave'?"[7]

For some religious figures, such as Stowe's brother Henry Ward Beecher, the potential cost of active resistance—the threat of violence—was simply too great: "Our policy for the future is plain. All the natural laws of God are warring upon slavery. We have only to let the process go on. Let slavery alone."[8] For others, most notably Theodore Parker (who was, in fact, a member of the "Secret Six" who conspired with John Brown), the "natural laws of God" demanded nothing less than active defiance of the corrupt laws of man. In "The Function of Conscience" (1850), Parker issues this mandate to the nation:

> It is plain to me that it is the natural duty of citizens to rescue every fugitive slave from the hands of the marshal who essays to return him to bondage; to do it peaceably if they can, forcibly if they must, but by all means to do it. . . . I am not a man who loves violence. I respect the sacredness of human life. But this I say, solemnly, that I will do all in my power to rescue any fugitive slave from the hands of any officer who attempts to return him to bondage. . . . One thing more I think is very plain, that the fugitive has the same natural right to defend himself against the slave-catcher, or his constitutional tool, that he has against a murderer or a wolf. The man who attacks me to reduce me to slavery, in that moment of attack alienates his right to life, and if I were the fugitive, and could escape in no other way, I would kill him with as little compunction as I would drive a mosquito from my face. It is high time this was said.[9]

In Beecher and Parker, one sees the essential distinction which Stowe was to embody in Uncle Tom and George Harris: while the former submits to earthly law, trusting in God to work his salvation and the salvation of his fellows, the latter—the very figure of the desperate fugitive whom Parker envisions— takes the law into his own hands, believing that it is his God-ordained right to resist the perversion which men call law. *Uncle Tom's Cabin* thus positions itself at the center of a religious debate with far-reaching implications: the separation of Church and State; the religious leader's responsibility to individual souls versus his responsibility to institutions; the significance of grace versus works in the individual's salvation; and, finally, the Church's historical commitment to pacifism versus the present call to arms.

Two events—one national, the other international—sharpened this debate. As Parker's words make clear, the passage of the Fugitive Slave Law in 1850 led some religious figures to re-evaluate the necessity of Christian political action. In her "Concluding Remarks" to *Uncle Tom's Cabin*, Stowe conveys her own dismayed and determined reaction to the Compromise of 1850:

> since the legislative act of 1850, [says Stowe, speaking in her characteristic third person] when she heard, with perfect surprise and consternation, Christian and humane people actually recommending the remanding escaped fugitives into slavery, as a duty binding on good citizens,—when she heard, on all hands, from kind, compassionate and estimable people, in the free states of the North, deliberations and discussions as to what Christian duty could be on this head,—she could only think, These men and Christians cannot know what slavery is; if they did, such a question could never be open for discussion. And from this arose a desire to exhibit it in a *living dramatic reality*. (621–22)

Stowe's use of the word "duty," in both its secular and its religious contexts, calls to mind Parker's conceptualization of Duty as "the natural and personal obligation to keep the law of God as my conscience declares it," which he contrasts with Business, "the conventional and official obligation to comply with some custom, keep some statute, or serve some special interest." In case of any conflict between the two, Parker asserts, "the natural duty ought to prevail and carry the day before the official business; for the natural duty represents the permanent law of God, the absolute right, justice, the balance-point of all interests; while the official business represents only the transient conventions of men, some partial interest."[10] The Fugitive Slave Law, by forcing the individual to take part actively in the evil of slavery, necessitated, in Parker's view, an equally active resistance. For Stowe, then, as for all Northerners, the Slave Law weakened what was already a tenuous position of moral aloofness: inaction on the one hand—failure to re-port a fugitive—became, in the eyes of the law, a crime against one's country; while inaction on the other—failure to protect a fugitive—became, in the eyes of God, a sin against one's fellow and one's conscience. Though resistance may have seemed un-Christian, nonresistance began to seem the same.

In addition, the European events of the late 1840s dramatized the dangers both of resistance and of neutrality. As Larry Reynolds demonstrates, "the fact and spirit of revolution that permeated Europe during the years 1848–49 engaged the attention of the American people and stirred the imaginations of American writers."[11] Uprisings in France, Austria, Prussia, Italy, and other nations during these years brought the specter of revolution before America's eyes; the news of oppressed people attempting to shake off their masters must have struck a responsive chord, both fearful and hopeful, within antebellum Americans. The European revolutions—which were overwhelmingly short-lived, bloody, and unproductive—not only underscored the tragic necessity of resistance but also suggested the enormity of the problem and the inefficacy of mere human action. Complicating this picture were the millennial expec-tations of some Christians, including Stowe; many hoped that the rumblings in Europe—fail though they might in human hands—would prove to be the precursor of a revolution guided by divine hands. As Alice Crozier writes: "Mrs. Stowe sees herself as setting down the events of her time in order that her contemporaries and descendants might understand the role of these events in the total scheme of human history from the Fall to the Final Judgment. Thus, she speaks with the prophets of old, reminding the nation of its historical com-mitments, recording its present struggles, warning of the impending wrath of the Almighty if the nation should betray its covenant and its destiny."[12]

This millennial spirit involved Stowe, and her contemporaries, in apparent contradictions; for the role of human action becomes problematic at best if all is but a stage in the Divine Plan. Thus, though Stowe seems to have caught the revolutionary bug—her description of George Harris fending off the slave-catchers, as Reynolds notes, invokes the Hungarian revolutionaries—she cannot wholeheartedly embrace his valiant and violent efforts.[13] Here again, the contrast with Uncle Tom is pointed and persistent; the escalating mayhem of George Harris's escape finds its counterpart in the increasing purity and power of Uncle Tom's pacifism: "Mas'r, if you mean to kill me, kill me; but, as to my raising my hand agin any one here, I never shall,—I'll die first!" (508). Uncle Tom's nonresistance, that is, assumes a cosmic force which Stowe will not grant George Harris's merely temporal rebellion.

Bridging these two moments—the explosive rage of George Harris and the saintly mortification of Uncle Tom—is Augustine St. Clare, the man in whom Stowe will bring together these oppositions, the battlefield upon which the struggle of the novel's opposing tendencies will be fought. The revolutionary power of *Uncle Tom's Cabin* lies in its ability to reconcile these forces, to tame action by uniting it with judgment and to vitalize judgment by uniting it with action. Paradoxically (but, as I will show, necessarily), *Uncle Tom's Cabin* goes about this project of unification through a sustained act of separation.

One need not look far in *Uncle Tom's Cabin* for evidence of oppositions; indeed, one need look no farther than the first page. Stowe writes: "Late in the afternoon of a chilly day in February, two gentlemen were sitting alone over their wine." But in the next paragraph, she introduces the note which will sound throughout the text: "For convenience sake, we have said, hitherto, two *gentlemen*. One of the parties, however, when critically examined, did not seem, strictly speaking, to come under the species" (41). The series of qualifications before condemning the slave-trader Haley may indicate reticence on Stowe's part, but nonetheless judgment has been pronounced, and henceforth Haley will prove unregenerate, as if Judgment has, indeed, already been pronounced at the Throne. As Tompkins says, characters in *Uncle Tom's Cabin* "do not change or develop. . . . They are not defined primarily by their mental and emotional characteristics—that is to say, psychologically—but soteriologically, according to whether they are saved or damned."[14] The cross-references between characters, as Tompkins says, often change; Eva is paired with everyone from Tom to Topsy to Ophelia to Marie. But in every case, the pairing constructs itself as an opposition of two essentially different qualities. Here James Baldwin's "Everybody's Protest Novel" is instructive: "The failure of the protest novel lies in its rejection of life, the human being, the denial of his beauty, dread, power, in its insistence that it is his categorization alone which is real and which cannot be transcended."[15]

Though Baldwin's condemnation of *Uncle Tom's Cabin*, and particularly of Stowe, is excessive, he has grasped the central problem of the book: in its concern with the "last things"—and its consequent reading of all human experience in terms of the Divine Plan—*Uncle Tom's Cabin* flirts dangerously with reducing slavery to an abstraction, a metaphysical puzzle. Thus Tom's very real suffering at Legree's hands becomes a "glorious resurrection," to use Frederick Douglass's phrase for his fight against his own master;[16] thus George Harris's potentially revolutionary rage must be defused by that "eloquent preacher of the Gospel," Eliza (611); thus George Shelby, though vowing to do "*what one man can*" to fight slavery (593)—and though possessing the position and means to do much—seems to feel that the most one man can do is change hats, becoming a benign boss rather than a benign master.[17]

Thus Stowe—with her eye on the prize, the "crown without the conflict" (429)—continually skirts the question of resistance in the here and now. No less an authority than William Lloyd Garrison recognized this; in his review of *Uncle Tom's Cabin* in the 26 March 1852 *Liberator*, he asks rhetorically:

> We are curious to know whether Mrs. Stowe is a believer in the duty of non-resistance for the white man, under all possible outrage and peril, as well as for the black man; . . . or whether she impartially disarms all mankind in the name of Christ, be the danger or suffering what it may. . . . That all the slaves at the South ought, "if smitten on the one cheek, to turn the other also"—to repudiate all carnal weapons, shed no blood, "be obedient to their masters," wait for a peaceful deliverance, and abstain from all insurrectionary movements—is every where taken for granted, because the VICTIMS ARE BLACK. . . . But, for those whose skin is of a different complexion, the case is materially altered. When they are spit upon and buffeted, outraged and oppressed, talk not then of a non-resisting Savior—it is fanaticism! Talk not of overcoming evil with good—it is madness! Talk not of peacefully submitting to chains and stripes—it is base servility! Talk not of servants being obedient to their masters—let the blood of the tyrants flow! How is this to be explained or reconciled? Is there one law of submission and non-resistance for the black man, and another law of rebellion and conflict for the white man? When it is the whites who are trodden in the dust, does Christ justify them in taking up arms to vindicate their rights? And when it is the blacks who are thus treated, does Christ require them to be patient, harmless, long-suffering, and forgiving? And are there two Christs?[18]

These are powerful words, and they speak directly to the issues with which *Uncle Tom's Cabin* struggles. Racially motivated or not—and there are indications, as I will discuss later, that it is—Stowe does indeed disarm all mankind in the name of Christ; judgment supplants deeds as the novel's primary medium of interaction with the world. Like Mrs. Shelby, who pronounces "God's curse on slavery" (84), *Uncle Tom's Cabin* is largely concerned with judging and clearly uneasy with acting. This is why, when Stowe finally asks the question which the novel has dramatized—"what can any individual do?"—her answer is, "There is one thing that every individual can do,—they can see to it that *they feel right*" (624). "Right feeling," then, becomes a visible sign of Election: one has judged rightly and will be so judged on the Final Day. Right feeling, in short, becomes a way of separating the "sheep from the goats" (447), of dividing the good from the bad.

Yet, as I have suggested, Stowe's novel is not so simple as all that. Nor do I mean to imply that Stowe is "playing God." Rather, she is recruiting God in a deeply felt crusade. And in order to succeed in this crusade she must complicate her novel's deceptively simple design, must allow its logic to be threatened from within. Thus, during the two-hundred-some pages occupying the middle segment of the novel, she introduces Augustine St. Clare.[19] In St. Clare, Stowe's most contradictory, most fully realized character, one sees the problems Garrison detected rising to the surface, setting off a struggle which determines the fate not only of St. Clare but of the novel itself. This struggle is put plainly by St. Clare: "what can a man of honorable and humane feelings do, but shut his eyes all he can, and harden his heart?" (328). Stowe herself was troubled by this question: "In many years of her life the author avoided all reading upon or allusion to the subject of slavery, considering it too painful to be inquired into . . . the subject was so dark and painful a one, so involved in difficulty and obscurity, so utterly beyond human hope or help, that it was of no use to read, or think, or distress oneself about it."[20]

In St. Clare, as in Stowe, a terrible conflict rages; the paralysis engendered by the enormity of the problem—and by the seeming insignificance of what "one man can do" about it—collides with the imperative to *do something*. Eva's death, according to Philip Fisher, is a model for this dilemma: "The mysterious illness that carries [Eva] away is a symbol of . . . unendurable knowledge in the absence of the power to act."[21] What can one man (or woman) do, St. Clare/Stowe seems to ask, but depart this impossible world, like Eva, or sit helplessly by her bedside, like her father?[22]

Yet, as Fisher goes on to say, Stowe—in the best sentimental tradition—has stacked the deck to achieve this crippling feeling of an "absence of the power to act":

> The two time schemes of sentimental stories involve moments when action is impossible: once an outcome is inevitable it is too late to act or to intervene, and, secondly, once an action is in the deep past and has left irreversible damage, even the consequences cannot be lessened. . . . where death is used as the analogy for social, remediable suffering, our general helplessness . . . is underlined and the will to act is weakened if not denied. The feeling of suffering becomes more important than action against suffering. Tears become more important than escapes or rescues.[23]

Or, as I have said, judgment becomes more important than action. As in the Rousseauvian model of compassion which Fisher cites—the imprisoned man watching a wild beast tearing a child from its mother's arms—the viewer's response is limited to feelings, not actions.[24] One of these feelings, and the obvious goal of sentimental fiction, is compassion. Another, which neither Rousseau nor Fisher explores, is judgment. For if we feel compassion for mother and child, do we not also feel rage against the beast—especially if, as in Stowe's case, it is not an irrational beast but a nation of thinking individuals?

However, we will feel this only if we are imprisoned—or believe ourselves to be so. If not, we may rush outside seeking to affect the outcome of the struggle. But if, like Stowe, we feel that the outcome is "utterly beyond human hope or help," then we have imprisoned ourselves. Thomas Gossett feels that "the strain of Calvinism in [Stowe] may have induced her to believe that slavery could not be abolished unless God willed it to be. If He had decided the time had not come, then all the anguish in the world could not change the fact."[25] This is partially true; Stowe *did*, if *Uncle Tom's Cabin* is any indication, believe that slavery could be abolished only by God. But Stowe's religious fervor and conviction were such that she truly believed in the power of "right feeling," the power, if not to affect anything in the here and now, then to hasten the coming of the Lord. Thus Gossett errs when he asserts that St. Clare's *dies irae* means only "that if nothing is done to better the condition of the poor there will be a whole series of revolutions."[26] Certainly, in the wake of the European revolutions, Stowe was preoccupied with the threat of violence in this country; as St. Clare says, in words that barely disguise his creator's anxiety, "educated [the slaves] will be, and we have only to say how. Our system is educating them in barbarism and brutality. We are breaking all humanizing ties, and making them brute beasts; and, if they get the upper hand, such we shall find them" (391). But the *dies irae* cannot be read merely as a temporal revolution, initiated purely by human will; indeed, the horror Stowe clearly feels at the prospect of human—and especially black—violence goes some way toward explaining why she must temper these uncontrollable powers by subsuming them in the Divine Plan. St. Clare's "series of revolutions" is, in this sense, a literal, worldly representation of the Final Judgment, the anticipation of which pervades Stowe's novel.

It is important to remember in this context that St. Clare, the man who recognizes the likelihood of temporal revolution, also quotes at length from the text of eternal revolution: "When the Son of man shall come in his glory, and all his holy angels with him, then shall he sit upon the throne of his glory: and before him shall be gathered all nations; and he shall separate them one from another, as a shepherd divideth his sheep from the goats. . . . Then shall the king say unto him on his left hand, Depart from me, ye cursed, into everlasting fire . . ." (447–48).

But St. Clare does not stop at this vision of divine retribution; he continues, linking the text to virtuous action in the profane world: "I was an hungered, and ye gave me no meat: I was thirsty, and ye gave me no drink: I was a stranger, and ye took me not in: naked, and ye clothed me not: I was sick, and in prison, and ye visited me not. . . . Inasmuch as ye did it not to one of the least of these my brethren, ye did it not to me" (448). Further, St. Clare—whose gospel has been "shut our eyes and ears, and let it alone" (328)—expands this charitable, "good works" mandate to include the necessity of social resistance. Inspired by the vision of Judgment, he speaks of "throwing the whole weight of his being against this monstrous system of injustice that lies at the foundation of all our society; and, if need be, sacrificing himself in the battle" (451). Thus St. Clare goes far beyond "feeling right," far beyond performing small, personal acts of Christian kindness; he speaks of taking part himself in the temporal *dies irae*, in the revolution.

This is the turning point of the novel. It is the point at which judgment and action must either merge or part ways. The St. Clare/Stowe symbiote seems on the verge of splitting; Stowe's creation, previously crippled by inactivity like his creator, seems ready to put judgment aside and, rushing out, tear the child from the jaws of the beast. St. Clare, who has not yet been "typed" as either damned or saved, who combines the compassion Stowe attributes to women with the vigor she attributes to men—who is capable, therefore, not only of right feeling but of right *acting*—has arrived at a moment of decision. St. Clare has seemingly been given a choice, precious few of which exist in this novel. In St. Clare, one sees the possibility of deconstructing *Uncle Tom's Cabin*'s rigid typology of opposed pairs; St. Clare could, conceivably, fuse qualities previously defined by their separateness, thereby dismembering the hegemony of judgment in the novel. One feels that St. Clare could do something—if he lives.

But St. Clare dies, killed in his first ineffectual attempt to fight. With his death, Tom—and the novel—commence an inevitable downward spiral away from light and hope in this world. Amy Schrager Lang argues that St. Clare's death reflects Stowe's failure or unwillingness to transcend gender types; if St. Clare could carry right feeling (province of the woman) into right acting (province of the man), then Stowe's rigid rule of "spheres" would be abrogated.[27] I feel that the problem is more pervasive than this. St. Clare cannot live because *Uncle Tom's Cabin* cannot ultimately sustain the radical, generalized contradictoriness he embodies. Poised between heaven and earth, unwilling to simplify the tragic complexity of life, St. Clare is dangerous *because* untyped. Were he let loose in the novel's painstakingly wired circuitry, he could wreak havoc upon the binary system upon which judgment in *Uncle Tom's Cabin* is based. St. Clare's understanding of social/economic oppression is potentially ruinous to "right feeling," for he has shown himself capable of excavating the horror beneath the North's—or any individual's—self-deceiving morality. Thus Stowe allows his disturbing vision its moment, but she veers away from its full implications. St. Clare learns to feel right, then goes out and dies, speaking his mother's name on his death bed. For the novel to preserve itself, this is all he *can* do. His soul has been rehabilitated; he has seen the error of his ways and now may pass on to his well-earned rest.

This critical juncture in *Uncle Tom's Cabin* thus serves ultimately to support its ideological machinery. Indeed, so fully is the novel's moral/narrative strategy developed that the St. Clare episode—despite its radicalizing potential—retrospectively takes on, like everything else in the novel, a logic, a reason for its placement: St. Clare occupies the center of the novel because it is in him that the two alternatives he represents may be set in opposition to one another, examined, and then the one cast into the fire and the other embraced. Significantly, he exists between the "heaven" of Tom's life in Kentucky and the "hell" of Legree's Louisiana plantation; St. Clare, like the ice over which Eliza crosses to safety, serves as a bridge which breaks apart once crossed, dissolving the connection between the sinner and the saved, the profane and the divine, the Now and the Eternal. Once he is dead, St. Clare's life takes on a theoretical taint. One feels that he was where he was and who he was *in order that* the dilemma of judgment versus action might be played out and resolved, as I have said, decisively in favor of the former.

And yet one senses that St. Clare has not simply been set up to be knocked down; his passionate insights into the nature of economic oppression and his dark vision of global strife are too real to be dismissed. They are so important to an understanding of *Uncle Tom's Cabin*'s ultimate political stance that I will quote at length from St. Clare's lecture—or sermon—to Ophelia:

> This cursed business, accursed of God and man, what is it? Strip it of all its ornament, run it down to the root and nucleus of the whole, and what is it? Why, because my brother Quashy is ignorant and weak, and I am intelligent and strong,—because I know how, and *can* do it,—therefore, I may steal all he has, keep it, and give him only such and so much as suits my fancy. . . . Talk of the *abuses* of slavery! Humbug! The *thing itself* is the essence of all abuse! . . . I declare to you, there have been times when I have thought, if the whole country would sink, and hide all this injustice and misery from the light, I would willingly sink with it. . . . I have been ready to curse my country, to curse the human race! (331–32)

Alfred who is as determined a despot as ever walked, . . . stands, high and haughty, on that good old respectable ground, *the right of the strongest*;

and he says, and I think quite sensibly, that the American planter is "only doing, in another form, what the English aristocracy and capitalists are doing by the lower classes"; that is, I take it, *appropriating* them, body and bone, soul and spirit, to their use and convenience. (340)

One thing is certain,—that there is a mustering among the masses, the world over; and there is a *dies irae* coming on, sooner or later. The same thing is working in Europe, in England, and in this country. My mother used to tell me of a millennium that was coming, when Christ should reign, and all men should be free and happy. And she taught me, when I was a boy, to pray, "thy kingdom come." Sometimes I think all this sighing, and groaning, and stirring among the dry bones foretells what she used to tell me was coming. But who may abide the day of His appearing? (344)

As I have said, St. Clare's condemnation of the human race and his anticipation of the revolution are simply too powerful to be dismissed; this is the one place in *Uncle Tom's Cabin* in which Stowe's intellectual and emotional energies—normally at war—converge, supporting each other with devastating strength. But this is precisely why St. Clare's words are, if not dismissed, then pushed into the background, exposed as the idle theorizing of a pampered, leisured man who describes himself as a "piece of driftwood" and a "contemptible *non sequitur*" (343).[28] Painfully aware that the darkness St. Clare unmasks is anything but a non sequitur, Stowe is unwilling to explore this darkness fully; instead she prefers, as in her fervently written deathbed scenes, to skip over this world and welcome the world to come. Like St. Clare, Stowe is engaged in a struggle with herself, up to heaven's gate in theory (which she wishes were practice), down in earth's dust in practice (which she wishes were theory). Thus, to Stowe, St. Clare's theories are not theories at all; they are a cry from a world of suffering and a prophecy of violence unmitigated by the softening love of Christ. They are like Augustine's dreaded *real*: "But the *real* remained,—the *real*, like the flat, bare, oozy tide-mud" (241). Mud is Simon Legree's element, from the "red, muddy, turbid" river (487) which carries the slaves to his plantation to the fetid swamp surrounding the plantation itself. Legree's dwelling is not just a symbolic hell but a symbolic earth as well: here, "down in earth's dust" (or mud), we see a world which St. Clare pronounces "as empty as an egg-shell" (435) and which the novel gives us little reason to find any more promising. The chapter introducing Legree's domain is entitled "Dark Places" (488), and this might be an image of the novel's final worldview.

In a fine essay, Cushing Strout discusses Stowe's wavering between a premillennial Calvinism that predicted a wrathful God descending upon the

earth to wipe it clean and a postmillennial vision that prophesied the establishment of a Golden Age on earth before the Judgment.[29] That *Uncle Tom's
Cabin* wavers too is apparent in its first half; but after the death of Eva and
St. Clare the hope of the temporal golden age vanishes, along with the hope
(and the fear) of a temporal means of bringing it about. Perhaps Eva's brief
time on earth—in particular, her deathbed scene—is meant to represent
this golden age, the best and final hope of humanity. For from this point
on *Uncle Tom's Cabin* seems to support St. Clare's indictment of the world as
"empty"; the novel, one feels, would declare only too gratefully, along with
the chapter heralding St. Clare's death, "This Is the Last of Earth" (429). Later
Stowe quotes Ecclesiastes 4:1—"*I praised the dead that are already dead more than the
living that are yet alive*" (510). A great weariness descends upon Stowe's fictive
world, figured by the tragic Cassy,[30] and the novel itself seems to hurry des-
perately toward a final judgment.

I therefore disagree with Baldwin that *Uncle Tom's Cabin* is "activated by what
might be called a theological terror, the terror of damnation."[31] Rather, it is
activated by a profound theological *despair*—and by an equally profound *mortal*
terror. Stowe, like St. Clare's saintly mother, seems to have " [given] up, in
despair. It never will be known, till the last account, what noble and sensitive
natures like hers have felt, cast, utterly helpless, into what seems to them an
abyss of injustice and cruelty, and which seems so to nobody about them"
(337). Nor has Baldwin gotten the tone of the novel quite right when he says,
"The virtuous rage of Mrs. Stowe is motivated by nothing so temporal as a
concern for the relationship of men to one another . . . but merely by a panic
of being hurled into the flames, of being caught in traffic with the devil."[32]
True, *Uncle Tom's Cabin* does not concern itself primarily with "the relationship
of men" (or of women, for that matter); it concerns itself with people's relationship to God. But it is the terror of *living*, of facing a world in which unendurable atrocities must be endured and in which worse atrocities may loom in
the future—rather than the terror of dying—that infuses the novel.

And yet, this seems at odds with the revolutionary power which *Uncle Tom's
Cabin* possessed, its ability to galvanize a nation. Whether one accepts or dis-
cards as apocryphal Lincoln's famous remark—"So this is the little lady who
made this big war"—the novel did enjoy remarkable popularity and potency
at the time it was written. Tompkins, writing of *Uncle Tom's Cabin*'s transfor-
mative ability, feels that "Eva initiates a process of redemption whose power,
transmitted from heart to heart, can change the entire world,"[33] but this
redemptive power, within the novel itself, is directed more toward preparing people for *another* world. The following exchange between the St. Clares
expresses this: "'St. Clare, how will she ever get along in the world?' said

Marie. 'The Lord knows,' said St. Clare, 'but she'll get along in heaven better than you or I'" (277).

Within *Uncle Tom's Cabin*, St. Clare's alternative of social reform ceases to be a viable response after his death. The figures of secular revolution, George Harris and George Shelby—read here George Washington—give way to figures of sacred revolution, Tom and Eva. George Shelby arrives too late to save his beloved Tom, while George Harris vanishes into the Dark Continent. And, though Stowe promises that "the world will yet hear from him" (612), what the reader hears at novel's end is Stowe's voice, urging us all to feel right and prophesying "the *day of vengeance*" that looms in the near future (629).

Hence, Stowe's answer to her novel's frightening power was both simple and predictable: God had written the book. However, this tells us nothing about the novel as written. Disturbing though it might be to hear Stowe uttering such remarks as "I am His Chosen one, and I shall reign with Him when all the stars have done blossoming,"[34] we can agree with Gossett that "the novel fortunately makes no such claim for itself."[35] Rather, I feel that the novel's paradoxical ability to elicit social action derives from its ultimate indictment of this world and from its anticipation of the world to come. One could argue, with Baldwin, that *Uncle Tom's Cabin* frightens its reader into the fold; but this insight, while valuable, is insufficient. Stowe is no Jonathan Edwards; her novel does not conjure images of eternal flames and wrathful Gods frying sinners on a whim. Rather, she persuades her readers with two images: the image of a deadly world so far gone that only divine judgment can set things right, and its complement, the image of heaven as pictured by Tom and Eva. At novel's end, as I have said, judgment assumes an absolute ascendancy. Yet the intensity of the novel's struggle to achieve this position lends "right feeling" a superhuman power, making judgment seem not simply one alternative of a neatly matched pair, but an absolute, even divine mandate—a promise of Love over Chaos—which is not a choice at all. *Uncle Tom's Cabin*, having played out the drama of action versus judgment, having portrayed the two as if they were separate and incorruptible, is capable then of transforming fatalism to hope and judgment to a clarion call.

In "Fate" (1860), Ralph Waldo Emerson makes a similar move from despair to what he calls a "fatal courage."[36] And in two earlier essays, he demonstrates how such a move is possible. In his deeply personal meditations on "Experience" (1844), Emerson anticipates the despair which gripped the nation before the Civil War: "Nothing is left us now but death. We look to that with a grim satisfaction, saying, There at least is reality that will not dodge us."[37] However, in "Man the Reformer," written in 1841, Emerson also captures the promise, a fatalistic optimism that transcends wishful thinking or the glory of self-immolation:

> the believer not only beholds his heaven to be possible, but already to begin to exist,—not by the men or materials the statesman uses, but by men transfigured and raised above themselves by the power of principles. To principles something else is possible that transcends all the power of expedients. . . . This great, overgrown, dead Christendom of ours still keeps alive at least the name of a lover of mankind. But one day all men will be lovers; and every calamity will be dissolved in the universal sunshine.[38]

This sunny vision—which substitutes hazy "principles" for active resistance—gains its power, it should be noted, only when juxtaposed with the despair of "Experience." Having emerged from the crucible of his sorrow, Emerson is able to pronounce his coda with all the confidence and authority of a prophet: "Patience and patience, we shall win at the last."[39] Stowe's own words are remarkably similar: "Patience! patience! ye whose hearts swell indignant at wrongs like these. Not one throb of anguish, not one tear of the oppressed, is forgotten by the Man of Sorrows, the Lord of Glory. In his patient, generous bosom he bears the anguish of a world. Bear thou, like him, in patience, and labor in love; for sure as he is God, 'the year of his redeemed *shall* come'" (211).

Thus Stowe, like Emerson, transforms judgment (or "principles") into a beneficent, loving power, and right feeling into God's Will. In this way, she is able to shoo the crippling forces of doubt while safely controlling the unpredictable forces of violence. Her timing was exquisite; she wrote during a period when, as Edmund Wilson says, "the Civil War was looming as something already felt but not yet clearly foreseen: an ambiguous promise and menace, the fulfillment of some awful prophecy which had never quite been put into words."[40] The nation, like Rousseau's imprisoned man, like St. Clare, and like Stowe herself, must have felt paralyzed by its inability to act and must have been attuned to any relief from its burdens. The relief Stowe provided was one of moral surety; she told her audience, torn by conflicting self-interests and fearful of the bloody results of making the wrong decision, that there was a simple right and wrong, a clear, absolute guide for how to feel and act. Hers was a promise that, with patience and a devotion to God's judgment, we would win at the last.

Thus, *Uncle Tom's Cabin* both arises from the apocalyptic fears of the time and makes the most of them, offering a reassuring alternative to apocalypse, even if that alternative is predicated on apocalypse: it offers readers the opportunity to judge themselves and to decide whose side they are on, the right side or the wrong. In choosing the right, Stowe promises her readers, they will have aligned themselves with the Will of God. They can rest assured, in Emerson's words, "that a higher law than that of our will regulates events; that our painful labors are unnecessary and fruitless; that only in our easy, simple, spontaneous action are we strong, and by contenting ourselves with obedience we become divine."[41] Easy, simple, spontaneous: Emerson's configuration, like Stowe's, portrays action and choice as nonaction and nonchoice, nonaction and nonchoice as action and choice. Within this circle, the individual will is merged with the divine Judgment, and history becomes inevitability. As Strout says: "*Uncle Tom's Cabin* is . . . the expression of a specific religious imagination in its desperate attempt both to meet and to escape the dilemmas of American culture in the antebellum years . . . . [Its popularity] is proof . . . of the pressure Americans felt—and still feel—to exaggerate their guilt, while minimizing their political responsibility, through a vision of history which wavers between a nightmare of doom and a dream of utopia."[42]

Stowe's "religious imagination," that is, found a responsive chord in the religious imaginations of her fellows not simply because it attempted to escape the dilemmas of the antebellum years but also because it attempted to show that escape was not really escape but obedience to the will of God. It attempted, that is, to portray these dilemmas as if they were not dilemmas but absolute moral realities. As Henry Ward Beecher wrote on the eve of the Civil War, "Whether men have acted well or ill, is not now the question; but simply this: *On which side will you be found?* . . . We have gone to the end. There is no need of compromise in this matter, then. It is a plain, simple matter. It is never mystified except when bad men have bad ends to accomplish, and bring up a mist over it."[43] Beecher, like his sister, succeeds in demystifying the dilemma by mystifying it, by removing it from the realm of human fallibility to the realm of black-and-white, divine Right.

Thus, in the end, Stowe's novel is not self-contradictory at all. Its seeming divisiveness serves a purpose: the polar oppositions, by shoving action off the stage, enable Stowe to transform judgment into an active principle, to subsume action within judgment as a manifestation of a program long settled by divine Will. Choice-making comes to seem simple, instinctive, even preordained; horror is contained by Mercy. To the soldiers of the Civil War, "political responsibility" was less important than the conviction that what they were doing was right. Marching into battle, they desired the illusion that there was a clear moral battleground and that choosing the right side did not involve an agonizing internal struggle—indeed, that choice was not involved at all—but that joining

the right side was as natural and inevitable as the apocalypse itself. By containing horror, then, *Uncle Tom's Cabin* contributed to unleashing horror.[44] Like all
propaganda—which it resembles in its heated emotional appeals, single-minded
intensity, and simplified resolution of its own inner turmoil—*Uncle Tom's Cabin*
succeeds where merely rational approaches might fail. By removing the individual's "political responsibility," it elicits decisive political action. By promising the
"crown without the conflict," it makes the conflict manageable, acceptable, even
desirable. And by sitting in judgment itself, it makes judgment seem ultimately
unnecessary. The issues having been resolved beforehand—long beforehand,
by Divine Plan—one does not need to trouble oneself with the quest for a socially
responsible course of action. Trusting that one's actions—no matter what they
may be—are sanctioned, decreed, suspended within a design larger than oneself,
all that one needs to do is act.

Notes

1. Quoted in Charles Foster, *The Rungless Ladder: Harriet Beecher Stowe and New England Puritanism* (Durham: Duke University Press, 1954), 29.

2. Quoted in Johanna Johnston, *Runaway to Heaven: The Story of Harriet Beecher Stowe* (Garden City, N.Y.: Doubleday, 1963), 199.

3. Jane Tompkins, *Sensational Designs: The Cultural Work of American Fiction, 1790–1860* (New York: Oxford University Press, 1985), 136. Tompkins, focusing on Stowe's millennial feminism, provides a much-needed reassessment of the revolutionary nature
of Stowe's novel.

4. Tompkins, *Sensational Designs*, 136.

5. Harriet Beecher Stowe, *Uncle Tom's Cabin or, Life Among the Lowly*, ed. Ann Douglas
(New York: Penguin, 1981), 344. All further quotations from the novel are from this
edition and are cited in parentheses in the text.

6. On antebellum Christian responses to slavery, see Charles Cole, *The Social Ideas of the Northern Evangelists, 1826–1860* (New York: Octagon, 1977), 192–220; Timothy Smith, *Revivalism and Social Reform: American Protestantism on the Eve of the Civil War* (Baltimore: Johns Hopkins University Press, 1980), 178–224; and Conrad Wright, "The Minister as Reformer," in *The Liberal Christians: Essays on American Unitarian History*, ed. Wright (Boston: Beacon, 1970), 62–80.

7. Smith, *Revivalism and Social Reform*, 198.

8. Quoted in Cole, *The Social Ideas of the Northern Evangelists*, 203.

9. Theodore Parker, "The Function of Conscience," in *"God Ordained This War": Sermons on the Sectional Crisis, 1830–1865*, ed. David Chesebrough (Columbia: University of South Carolina Press, 1991), 47–48.

10. Parker, "The Function of Conscience," 41.

11. Larry J. Reynolds, *European Revolutions and the American Literary Renaissance* (New Haven: Yale University Press, 1988), 5. Reynolds discusses the influence of the revolutions in France (52–53) and Hungary (153–57) on Stowe's novel.

12. Alice Crozier, *The Novels of Harriet Beecher Stowe* (New York: Oxford University Press, 1969), 6–7.

13. Reynolds, *European Revolutions*, 155–56.

14. Tompkins, *Sensational Designs*, 135.

15. James Baldwin, "Everybody's Protest Novel," in his *Notes of a Native Son* (New York: Dial, 1955), 22. This passionate essay is indispensable for the study of Stowe's novel.

16. Frederick Douglass, *The Narrative and Selected Writings*, ed. Michael Meyer (New York: Modern Library, 1984), 81.

17. For a discussion of George Shelby, see Amy Schrager Lang, *Prophetic Woman: Anne Hutchinson and the Problem of Dissent in the Literature of New England* (Berkeley: University of California Press, 1987), 193–214. Lang writes that George "acts purely privately, engaging neither in lawless opposition to slavery nor in political action of any kind" (212). The much-ignored young master—who, after all, gets tagged with the heavy title of "The Liberator"—also receives some attention in Eric Sundquist, "Introduction," in *New Essays on Uncle Tom's Cabin*, ed. Sundquist (New York: Cambridge University Press, 1986), 1–44.

18. William Lloyd Garrison, "Review of *Uncle Tom's Cabin*," *The Liberator*, 26 March 1852, 2.

19. See John Ward, *Red, White, and Blue: Men, Books, and Ideas in American Culture* (New York: Oxford University Press, 1969), 73–92, for a cogent discussion of St. Clare. Ward writes: "St. Clare stands precisely between the poles defined by Tom and George Harris. Incapable of action, like George, unredeemed by faith, like Tom, St. Clare is the mouthpiece for the central dilemma of the book" (82). Ward feels that this dilemma concerns "whether it is possible to be a moral human being in society" (81).

20. Quoted in Constance Mayfield Rourke, *Trumpets of Jubilee: Henry Ward Beecher, Harriet Beecher Stowe, Lyman Beecher, Horace Greeley, P. T. Barnum* (New York: Harcourt, Brace & Co., 1927), 101.

21. Philip Fisher, *Hard Facts: Setting and Form in the American Novel* (New York: Oxford University Press, 1985), 107.

22. In *The Rungless Ladder*, Foster cites Stowe's reaction to her own infant son's death: "It was at his dying bed and at his grave that I learned what a poor slave mother may feel when her child is torn away from her. In those depths of sorrow which seemed to me immeasurable, it was my only prayer to God that such anguish might not be sufferedin in vain. . . . I felt that I could never be consoled for it, unless this crushing of my own heart might enable me to work out some great good to others . . ." (27).

St. Clare, too, seeks to transform his sorrow into some "great good"; but, as I will show, he is ultimately unable to do so.

23. Fisher, *Hard Facts*, 108, 110.

24. Fisher, *Hard Facts*, 105.

25. Thomas F. Gossett, *"Uncle Tom's Cabin" and American Culture* (Dallas: Southern Methodist University Press, 1985), 306–7.

26. Gossett, *"Uncle Tom's Cabin" and American Culture*, 389.

27. Amy Schrager Lang, "Slavery and Sentimentalism: The Strange Career of Augustine St. Clare," *Women's Studies* 12 (1986): 31–54. Lang provides a persuasive account of St. Clare's function in the text and of Stowe's gender typology and feminism.

28. It is remarkable that this novel of nonresistance goes out of its way to indict St. Clare for his nonresistance. Forced into passivity so that Stowe may revile his lack of gumption, forced into action so that she may lament his foolhardy lack of caution, St. Clare is in the unfortunate position of having to play out his creator's conflicting beliefs. Thus it is significant that he dies not in the fight against slavery but in a tawdry barroom brawl. This gratuitously cynical and disparaging detail is a mechanical and unfitting end for St. Clare, and it reveals the lengths to which *Uncle Tom's Cabin* must go to protect its ideology.

29. Cushing Strout, *"Uncle Tom's Cabin* and the Portent of Millennium," *Yale Review* 57 (1968): 375–85.

30. In Cassy, too, we see a figure who, like St. Clare, could combine attributes Stowe normally compartmentalizes: the aggressiveness of the white man and the maternal instinct of the black woman. Significantly, Stowe shies away from the "kill the master" plot which is brewing; Cassy escapes with her surrogate daughter Emmeline and is soon leeched of her dangerous tendencies. She journeys to Africa, where, under the care of the woman whom she discovers to be her daughter Eliza, she "yielded at once, and with her whole soul . . . and became a devout and tender Christian" (607). Thus, Stowe's favorite constellation of traits—woman, mother, black, Christian—has been fulfilled. It is worth noting that Stowe must introduce a pure *deus ex machina*—the mysterious, preposterous Madame de Thoux—in order to fulfill it.

31. Baldwin, "Everybody's Protest Novel," 17.

32. Ibid.

33. Tompkins, *Sensational Designs*, 131.

34. Quoted in Rourke, *Trumpets of Jubilee*, 110.

35. Gossett, *"Uncle Tom's Cabin" and American Culture*, 97.

36. Ralph Waldo Emerson, "Fate," in *Selected Writings*, ed. Donald McQuade (New York: Modern Library, 1981), 683.

37. Emerson, "Experience," in *Selected Writings*, 328.

38. Emerson, "Man the Reformer," in *Works*, Vol. 1 (Boston: Houghton Mifflin & Co., 1883), 238, 242.

39. Emerson, "Experience," in *Selected Writings*, 348.

40. Edmund Wilson, *Patriotic Gore: Studies in the Literature of the American Civil War* (New York: Oxford University Press, 1962), 88.

41. Emerson, "Spiritual Laws," in *Selected Writings*, 178.

42. Strout, "*Uncle Tom's Cabin* and the Portent of Millennium," 385.

43. Henry Ward Beecher, "Against a Compromise of Principle," in "*God Ordained This War*," 73, 75. Beecher's conception of the conflict is, however, considerably more naive than his sister's. Beecher writes: "In the North every shape and form of society in some way represents liberty. In the South every institution and element of society is tinged and pervaded with slavery" (73).

44. Desert Storm, with its biblically evocative name and its theme song, "(God is Watching Us) from a Distance," is the most recent time America has drafted God into military service. The suppression of Desert Storm's horror—one hundred thousand Iraqi dead, American casualties which the networks chose not to show returning home in bodybags—facilitated the horror, encouraging us to think of it as a Holy War against dark-skinned defilers of Liberty.

Freeing the Slaves and Banishing the Blacks

Racism, Empire, and Africa in Uncle Tom's Cabin

ELIZABETH AMMONS

◆ ◆ ◆

> For two hundred and twenty-eight years has the colored man toiled over the soil of America, under a burning sun and a driver's lash— plowing, planting, reaping, that white men might roll in ease, their hands unhardened by labor, and their brows unmoistened by the waters of genial toil, and now that the moral sense of mankind is beginning to revolt at this system of foul treachery and cruel wrong, and is demanding its overthrow, the mean and cowardly oppressor is mediating plans to expel the colored man entirely from the country. Shame upon the guilty wretches that dare propose, and all that countenance such as a proposition. We live here—have lived here—have a right to live here, and mean to live here.
>
> —Frederick Douglass, *The North Star*, 26 January 1849

*U*NCLE TOM'S CABIN (1852) ends with George and Eliza Harris and their children, plus George's sister, mother, and half brother, as well as Topsy—all free at last and safely residing in Canada—departing for Liberia as colonists. With Tom dead, a martyr to the system of U.S. slavery that Harriet Beecher Stowe has attacked for almost four hundred pages, the author sends these free blacks "back" to Africa, despite abolitionists' vehement and well-known objections to the very idea of African colonization. Why?

This essay examines how antislavery perspectives, mainstream white racism, Christian evangelicalism, and unwavering belief in the righteousness of Western imperialism come together in *Uncle Tom's Cabin* to create a narrative conclusion that at best compromises and at worst undercuts the novel's liberatory claims.[1]

During the decade that led to Stowe's antislavery novel, Western imperial powers invaded what seemed to be every corner of the earth in the name of capitalism, Christianity, and "civilization." In 1842, the Treaty of Nanking forced Hong Kong into the British Empire, and the Boers stole land in southern Africa to create the slaveholding Orange Free State. Two years later, the Treaty of Tangier ended the war in Morocco by solidifying French colonial power in northern Africa, and in 1846 the first Anglo Sikh War concluded with the British victorious and the East India Company secure in India. In 1848, the United States, having invaded Mexico, annexed what is now Texas, New Mexico, California, Utah, Nevada, Arizona, and parts of Colorado and Wyoming. In response to such imperial aggression, militant resistance and revolutions erupted. In New Zealand, Maori people repeatedly rose up against the British. In Hungary, local inhabitants rebelled against Austrian rule. In China, the beginnings of what would become the Tai P'ing Rebellion stirred. In the United States, American Indians fought to repel white theft of indigenous lands.

To illustrate even more specifically the turbulence and shifting global context in which Stowe conceived *Uncle Tom's Cabin,* consider 1848. Karl Marx and Friedrich Engels published the *Communist Manifesto* in London. The first women's rights convention in the United States was held at Seneca Falls, New York. The second Sikh War of resistance to British rule began in India, while riots broke out in Ceylon in response to new taxes levied by the British occupiers there. The Treaty of Guadalupe Hidalgo approved the U.S. confiscation of half of Mexico, and revolutions advocating constitutional rule by the middle classes occurred in so many places in Europe—France, Spain, Italy, Prussia, Hungary—that 1848 became known as the year of revolutions. The discovery of gold in California started the rush that would see sixty thousand people from all over the world, including China, go there by the end of the next year. Britain stole yet more land in southern Africa, the first English settlers headed out to invade and possess New Zealand, and the potato famine in Ireland, exacerbated by British colonial rule, went into its third year, killing tens of thousands of people and turning even larger numbers into desperate emigrants.[2]

Uncle Tom's Cabin clearly shows Stowe knew about many of these world events. Asked by Ophelia to read the future, Augustine St. Clare observes: "One thing is certain,—that there is a mustering among the masses, the world over; and there is a *dies irae* coming on, sooner or later. The same thing is working in Europe, in England, and in this country" (202). Reiterating the point to his brother, Alfred, he draws analogies between slave unrest in the United States and the French Revolution, the Haitian Revolution, and contemporary rebellions in Italy and Hungary. He reminds Alfred that the masses "took *their* turn once, in France," and continues ironically with reference to the successful slave rebellion in Haiti in 1804: "It makes a terrible slip when they get up . . . —in St. Domingo [Haiti], for instance" (233). To Alfred's boast that he is willing to "sit on the escape-valve, as long as the boilers are strong," Augustine replies by alluding to the French Revolution and then contemporary turbulence in Europe: "The nobles in Louis XVI's time thought just so; and Austria and Pius IX [in Italy] think so now; and, some pleasant morning, you may all be caught up to meet each other in the air, *when the boilers burst*" (233–34). Around the globe, Stowe's novel emphasizes, oppressed people are throwing off tyrannical masters.

Most directly invoked in the novel is the Hungarian Revolution, which receives direct mention in Stowe's description of George Harris's militance.

> If it had been only a Hungarian youth, now bravely defending in some mountain fastness the retreat of fugitives escaping from Austria into America, this would have been sublime heroism; but as it was a youth of African descent, defending the retreat of fugitives through America into Canada, of course we are too well instructed and patriotic to see any heroism in it; and if any of our readers do, they must do it on their own private responsibility. When despairing Hungarian fugitives make their way, against all the search-warrants and authorities of their lawful government, to America, press and political cabinet ring with applause and welcome. When despairing African fugitives do the same thing,—it is—what *is* it? (172)

As Susan Belasco Smith points out, Stowe's brother Henry Ward Beecher published a long article on the Hungarian Revolution in the *Independent* in 1851, a portion of which ran in the *National Era* in the same issue as chapter 19 of *Uncle Tom's Cabin.* Not surprisingly, as Smith puts it, "To Stowe, busily writing the middle chapters of *Uncle Tom's Cabin,* the Hungarian revolution could . . . serve as a convenient analogy to the situation in the United States" (81).

Given Stowe's references to the Haitian Revolution, the French Revolution, and various struggles for freedom in Europe, particularly the Hungarian Revolution, her support for emigration to Liberia in *Uncle Tom's Cabin* strikes a discordant note. Why should people living in the United States, the supposed haven from oppression—witness her own reference to Hungarian refugees— leave to find a freedom that, ironically, involved depriving others of theirs?

From the beginning, Liberia was controversial. Founded by the American Colonization Society in 1822 for settlement by free African Americans and manumitted slaves, the West African colony was preceded by other colonization and "repatriation" ideas and attempts. As Benjamin Brawley explains in what remains an excellent summary of pre-Liberia thinking in the United States, prominent white Americans proposed Sierra Leone, the West Indies, and the North American Southwest and Northwest as resettlement sites for American blacks. Since the late 1700s, Britain had been shipping poor blacks to West Africa, especially refugees who had fought on the side of the British in the Revolutionary War and then fled to England, only to find themselves abandoned and impoverished.

In the United States, whites advocated black emigration not to remove indigents but to banish potential insurgents. Afraid that escaped or freed slaves would lead armed rebellions, the General Assembly of Virginia in 1805, for example, asked the federal government to designate a part of the Louisiana Purchase "to be appropriated to the residence of such people of color as have been, or shall be, emancipated, or may hereafter become dangerous to the public safety" (Brawley 122). Four years earlier, President Thomas Jefferson had written to the governor of Virginia, James Monroe, for whom the capital of Liberia would later be named: "Africa would offer a last and undoubted resort, if all others more desirable should fail" (Brawley 121). In 1811, Jefferson continued to hope for a colony in Africa that could serve as both refuge and dumping ground for African Americans. "Nothing is more to be wished than that the United States would themselves undertake to make such an establishment on the coast of Africa." Problems existed, however, as Jefferson conceded:

> But for this the national mind is not yet prepared. It may perhaps be doubted whether many of these people would voluntarily consent to such an exchange of situation, and very certain that few of those advanced to a certain age in habits of slavery, would be capable of self-government. This should not, however, discourage the experiment, nor the early trial of it. (Brawley 122–23)

Evidently, public support for the idea and black people's willingness to emigrate amounted to minor details for Jefferson.

Inspired by the example of Sierra Leone, founded by the British in 1791 as a destination for debtor blacks, "recaptives" (Africans liberated from captured slave ships), and free blacks and escaped slaves living in the British colony of Canada, Liberia was primarily the idea of racist white Americans who wished to remove African Americans. The American Colonization Society (ACS), founded by Southern slaveholders, aimed "to rid the country of free blacks by colonizing them in Africa" (J. Smith 2). As one ACS member said of the growing class of free blacks in the United States: "I dread for [Virginia] the corroding evil of this numerous caste, and I tremble for a danger of disaffection spreading through their seduction, among our servants." Others maintained,

"African colonization . . . is our only security from social and political death" (J. Smith 2).

If Southern planters wanted to exile threatening free blacks, many white Northerners and some African Africans expressed support for colonization because it would Christianize Africa. As the editors of *African-American Exploration in West Africa* point out, "The 1810s had seen the birth of the American Foreign Missionary Society, and the idea of colonization attracted several white Christians who argued that their mission to civilize, moralize, and evangelize in Africa could best be served by African-American preachers. Indeed, such an idea even provided a religious explanation for the phenomenon of slavery that they now abhorred but which society embraced: in slavery, God was creating civilized black evangelicals who would call Africa to Christianity" (Fairhead et al. 8). In a study of black and white Methodist missionaries in Liberia from 1820 to 1875, Eunjin Park likewise notes the white belief that black missionaries would best succeed in converting Africans, as well as the conviction among black missionaries themselves that Liberia offered the opportunity both to proselytize and to "advance far beyond the second-class ecclesiastical roles they had been allowed in America" (xx). Although they would be disappointed in that aspiration, African American missionaries believed Liberia was a place where they could get out from under white control as they converted fellow blacks to Christianity.

For other advocates of Liberian colonization, both black and white, pragmatism ruled. Unable to obtain justice in the United States, free blacks, they argued, might follow in the tradition of the New England Pilgrims and seek freedom far from home. The 1847 Declaration of Independence of Liberia— a nation with a red, white, and blue starred-and-striped flag and its very name meaning liberty—emphasized the parallel by deliberately echoing the Declaration of Independence of its 4,500 African American immigrants' homeland. The document reads in part:

> We, the people of the Republic of Liberia, were originally inhabitants of the United States of North America.
>
> In some parts of that country, we were debarred by law, from all the rights and privileges of men; in other parts, public sentiment, more powerful than law, frowned us down.
>
> We were everywhere shut out from all civil office.
>
> We were excluded from all participation in the government.
>
> We were taxed without our consent.
>
> We were compelled to contribute to the resources of a country which gave us no protection.

We were made a separate and distinct class, and against us every avenue of improvement was effectually closed. Strangers from all lands, of a color different from ours, were preferred before us.

We uttered our complaints; but they were unattended to, or met only by alleging the peculiar institution of the country.

All hope of a favorable change in our country was thus wholly extinguished in our bosoms, and we looked with anxiety abroad for some asylum from the deep degradation.

For the black people who emigrated, Liberia testified from the beginning to the U.S. failure to grant them the same rights and freedoms as whites.

Some African Americans found the passage of the Fugitive Slave Act in 1850 pivotal in making them proponents of colonization. Just as the legislation precipitated the writing of *Uncle Tom's Cabin* by forcing Stowe, like other Northern whites, to recognize her own personal, direct involvement in slavery, so it forced free blacks to face the fact that they could never be safe anywhere in the United States as long as slavery existed. By requiring all free people of every race, North or South, to turn over escaped slaves directly to slave agents, the Fugitive Slave Act put free blacks in the United States at constant risk of kidnap and enslavement. Although that possibility had always existed, now it escalated dramatically because the new law bypassed the judicial system—itself little enough protection—by mandating the return of alleged fugitives to slave catchers. Without even the recourse of the courts, free blacks lived in constant fear of kidnap and sale. As black abolitionist Martin Delany declared:

By the provisions of this bill, the [free] colored people of the United States are positively degraded beneath the level of the whites. . . . We are slaves in the midst of freedom waiting patiently, and unconcernedly— indifferently, and stupidly, for masters to come and lay claim to us. . . . The slave is more secure than we; he knows who holds the heel upon his bosom—we know not the wretch who may grasp us by the throat. (Melish 267)

Because of the Fugitive Slave Act, as Joanne Pope Melish explains in *Disowning Slavery,* emigration no longer seemed defection, no longer represented abandonment of enslaved fellow blacks who had no choice about leaving or remaining in the United States. Instead, emigration could represent "the escape of one group of slaves who, having transformed themselves by this act into 'freemen,' might work successfully to achieve the emancipation of the others" (267).

Yet even in the shadow of the 1850 Fugitive Slave Act and the domestic terrorism it authorized against all African Americans, Liberian colonization never gained great popularity among black people in the United States. From the time the ACS was founded, the idea of African American emigration met resistance. In the 1820s, the activist David Walker in Boston angrily responded to the idea of emigration: "America is more our country than it is the whites— we have enriched it with our blood and tears . . . and will they drive us from our property and homes which we have earned with our blood?" (Fairhead et al. 9–10). By 1860, out of a population of 4.4 million African Americans in the United States, 99 percent of them born in the U.S. and 448,000 of them free people living in both the North and the South, only 13,000 had chosen to emigrate to Liberia. Statistics for 1820–33 show that of those emigrating, the vast majority did so not as free people but in order to gain freedom; their manumission from slavery depended on their agreeing to leave the United States. By 1852, the year *Uncle Tom's Cabin* came out, "only 40 percent of immigrants had been free before immigration. . . . The choice was between being a slave in the U.S. or a free citizen in Liberia" (Fairhead et al. 10). Most colonists who went to Liberia were enslaved African Americans whose only hope for freedom lay in expatriation.

Not surprisingly, bitter debate churned around the idea of Liberian emigration. Like David Walker and like Frederick Douglass, quoted in my epigraph, the majority of African Americans opposed colonization as a racist scheme to remove Americans whose heritage and labor justified their citizenship every bit as much as, if not more than, that of anyone else in the United States. Philadelphia Bethel Church leaders in 1816, for example, called colonization "a circuitous route" back to slavery, a plot to banish free blacks "into the wilds of Africa" (Liebenow 19). Martin Delany called Liberia a "poor miserable mockery—a burlesque on a government . . . a mere dependency of Southern slaveholders" (Sundiata 3), and in his introduction to William Nesbit's scathing 1855 narrative, *Four Months in Liberia: or African Colonization Exposed,* he praised Nesbit's "graphic portrayal of the infamy of that most pernicious and impudent of all schemes for the perpetuity of the degradation of our race, the AMERICAN COLONIZATION SOCIETY. I say *most* pernicious, because it was originated in the South, by slave-holders, propagated by their aiders and abettors, North and South, and still continues to be carried on under the garb of philanthropy and Christianity, through the medium of the basest deception and hypocrisy." At the end of this introduction, Delany explicitly labels Liberia a conscious plot of whites to exterminate African Americans: "The wretches who selected the tide-swamp of the coast of Guinea, instead of a healthful location in Africa, as a colony for the colored people of America, knowingly and designedly established a national Potter's Field, into which the carcass of every emigrant who ventured there, would most assuredly moulder in death" (Moses 81, 85–86). Although he, like most African Americans, supported emigration to other parts of West Africa, Delany categorically rejected Liberia.

White abolitionists also vigorously opposed Liberian colonization. William Lloyd Garrison attacked the idea repeatedly in *Thoughts on African Colonization* (1832) and, as Brawley summarizes, charged the ACS in an editorial one year earlier

> first, with persecution in compelling free people to emigrate against their will and in discouraging their education at home; second, with falsehood in saying that the Negroes were natives of Africa when they were no more so than white Americans were natives of Great Britain; third, with cowardice in asserting that the continuance of the Negro population in the country involved dangers; and finally, with infidelity in denying that the Gospel has full power to reach the hatred in the hearts of men. (126–27)

Garrison's partner on the Baltimore antislavery newspaper the *Genius of Universal Emancipation,* Benjamin Lundy, though supportive of voluntary emigration to places such as Haiti, likewise condemned ACS mandatory immigration schemes as racist. In 1829, he declared: "The odious distinctions between white and black have been created by tyrants . . . for the express purpose of acquiring and preserving their *unjust authority*. . . . That is the Alpha and Omega of it" (Mayer 73). The United States needed to abolish slavery and address white racism, not banish blacks, Lundy argued.

In Cincinnati, where Stowe lived from 1832 to 1850 and formed many of the ideas that went into *Uncle Tom's Cabin,* opposition both to slavery and to the ACS exploded in 1834 at the Lane Seminary, where Stowe's husband, Calvin, taught and her father, Lyman Beecher, was president. Although Stowe credited her father with inspiring her own antislavery views, as she explained in a letter to Frederick Douglass in 1851 (Charles Stowe 152), President Beecher equivocated on abolition in the 1830s and advocated gradualism. Against his wishes, the divinity students conducted an eighteen-day antislavery meeting, and under the leadership of Theodore Dwight Weld, a student, almost every seminarian came out in support of immediate abolition. Moreover, many committed themselves to continued activist roles in the antislavery movement and volunteered as teachers in the local black community. When the seminary's trustees and President Beecher, himself a member of the ACS, ordered the students to disengage—they were not to take a stand on slavery or work in the local African American community—most of them went on strike and left the institution, never to return. So impressive was the students' activism that James Gillespie Birney, a white Kentuckian who had freed his slaves and who would later be lynched by a Cincinnati mob for his antislavery views, publicly resigned his membership in the ACS, where he had held office, and joined the American Anti-Slavery Society (Mayer 189–90).

Opposed by almost all African Americans and abolitionists as a racist plot to evacuate African Americans from the United States, Liberian colonization nevertheless did attract some black supporters. Emigrationists such as Edward Blyden and Bishop Henry McNeal Turner subscribed to the argument that colonization offered American blacks freedom from oppression, along with the opportunity to participate in the great work of spreading Christianity, the missionary task of "African redemption" (Sundiata 3). Other Liberian settlers voiced much the same reasoning. Lott Carey of Richmond, Virginia, declared, "I am an African. I wish to go to a country where I shall be estimated by my merits, not by my complexion; and I feel bound to labour for my suffering race" (Liebenow 20). In 1855, explicitly countering the denunciations of Delany and Nesbit, the Rev. Samuel Williams recalled in *Four Years in Liberia* the injustice of being denied the vote in the United States and referred to Liberia as "our beloved little republic," stating with contentment: "Liberia is my home and I expect to end my days in it" (Moses 147, 177). Writing back to the United States in the 1870s, Scott Mason echoed that sentiment: "The Colored man is never free, and never will be until he plants his foot on the land of his forefathers," and Alonzo Hoggard wrote, "I am well satisfied here in this place. I have no more use for America" (Belcher et al. 1).

Other immigrants, however, found Liberia a betrayal. The climate hosted fatal diseases to which Americans had no immunity, the land would not support crops they knew how to cultivate, the geography confined them to a thirty- to forty-mile coastal strip, and the African people did not want to be colonized, which often resulted in armed conflict. In 1855, Nesbit called the ACS's descriptions of Liberia "egregious falsehoods" and added: "The whole country presents the most woe begone and hopeless aspect which it is possible for a man to conceive of" (Moses 88). Decades of colonial occupation did not produce significant change. Returning to the United States in the early 1930s, the former immigrant Elizabeth McWillie stated that many Americo-Liberians were "so fed up on Liberia that they would kiss a Mississippi cracker if he could only get them away from there." Another colonist wrote to L. K. Williams of the National Baptist Convention in 1934: "I have never in my life seen black people hate other black people as this Administration and the so called leading people in Liberia hate the American Negroes; they do not want any American Negroes out here in large numbers" (Sundiata 112). A century of colonial rule, regardless of the invaders' skin color, had not made Africans love their conquerors.

The relationship between Liberia and the United States was ambiguous from the start. Never an official U.S. colony, Liberia nevertheless functioned as one and yet—because its transplanted Americans were black—also found itself ignored and abandoned by the U.S. government. The early colonial settlers reproduced European imperialism, setting themselves up as a ruling elite and maintaining that the native population would benefit from their enforced exposure to Western civilization and Christianity. Late in the nineteenth century, the Firestone Rubber Company established a long period of economic imperialism, blessed and protected by both the Americo-Liberian and U.S. governments, and Western economic imperialism helped block the black emigration project of Marcus Garvey's anti-European Universal Negro Improvement Association in the 1920s, which, unlike ACS efforts, had wide support in the U.S. black community. Not until 1980 did Americo-Liberian elite one-party rule end.[3]

Further and equally important, within the African American immigrant community in Liberia, imported ideas about class and color inculcated by the systems of slavery and racism in the United States created deep divisions. Delany as early as the 1850s lambasted this implantation of U.S. racism and classism into Liberia, saying, "these people, the true Liberians, have mainly been themselves the servants and slaves of the whites, and, consequently, have acquired all of the folly and vices of their former wicked and unprincipled masters, considering themselves their equals, the more nearly they ape after them" (Moses 83). Conflicts between dark-skinned and light-skinned colonists in Liberia cut various ways, with imported racist privileging of fair-skinned blacks creating economic, political, and social advantages for them at the expense of darker skinned American Liberians, while the latter, in a twist on the racist-inspired science of the day deployed by leaders such as Blyden, boasted that they survived diseases better because they did not bring with them from North America an "unhealthy mix of Caucasian and Indian blood" (Fairhead et al. 20). As the editors of *African-American Exploration in West Africa* explain, color-based racism, imported from the United States and then locally modified, shaped Americo-Liberian colonial identity and life throughout the nineteenth century and well into the twentieth (Fairhead et al. 18–23).

For the colonized Africans, Liberia meant oppression. Quickly, they came to identify African American colonization with European and American imperialism and racism. J. Gus Liebenow summarizes the irony:

> Liberia was founded so that those who—on the basis of skin color alone—had been denied the rights and privileges of full participation

in American society could enjoy the benefits of freedom in the continent of their ancestors. Yet, in the experience of securing the blessings
of liberty for themselves, their treatment of the tribal people during the
tutelary period under the American Colonization Society (1822–1847),
as well as during the tenure of the First Republic (1847–1980), resulted
in the systematic denial of liberty to others who were forcibly included
within the Republic. (5)

Liebenow observes: "It was not unusual to hear tribal people refer to Americo-
Liberians as Kwee, or 'white' people, or to have them call Monrovia [the capital of Liberia] 'the America place'" (23). As in any colonial regime, imported
systems of class and racial subordination produced hatred.

A dictated letter to the ACS in 1910 provides an indigenous perspective on
this history of colonization. King Gyude and a group of chiefs of the Grebos
explained that their predecessors welcomed the first black American settlers
in 1834, "pitying their condition and rejoicing in their anticipation that by their
settlement among us the benefits of Christian enlightenment and civilization
would be disseminated among the youth of our land." However, the authors
assert, the newcomers "soon began to despise us, placing us in their room
and they in their masters', just in the same fashion as in their slavery days in
America." Then in 1856, while *Uncle Tom's Cabin* was being devoured throughout the Western world, the Americo-Liberian rulers burned the homes of the
Grebo people and expelled them from their ancestral land, initiating a long, bitter history in which, according to the king and chiefs, "the Liberian colony . . .
has operated as a source of oppression and demoralization to our people"
(Richardson 31–32).

Conceived by Southern planters, not supported by most African Americans, opposed by abolitionists, and rapidly and repeatedly resisted by Africans,
Liberia was always a contested idea. Why, then, does Harriet Beecher Stowe
endorse colonization in *Uncle Tom's Cabin?*

Stowe places her support for Liberian emigration in the mouth of George
Harris (374–76), her smartest, angriest, most militant black—which, of course,
goes a long way toward explaining her support for an idea that abolitionists
from Douglass to Garrison roundly condemned. Deportation conveniently
solves the problem of dealing with demands for racial equality in America.
If at the end of *Uncle Tom's Cabin* George Harris remained in the United States,
or even just across the border in Canada, how would Stowe contain his militant voice, not just for emancipation but also for black equality? Imagine
Tom living rather than dying, and the point becomes obvious. Tom would
never pose a problem because he has learned well the obedient behaviors of

a servant and, even more important, subscribes to a philosophy of Christian nonviolence and forgiveness. George Harris, however, does present difficulties. Educated, enraged, determined not to acquiesce in American racism, he represents a character potentially out of the author's control: an articulate advocate for racial equality in the United States. Similarly, Topsy, "civilized" and educated, represents a threat, as do an independent Eliza, the Harris children, Cassy, and, quickly mentioned at the very end, Cassy's son, an educated "young man of energy" (377). Consequently, Stowe, in the tested tradition of the ACS, packs them all off to Africa, the place for dangerous, ambitious, free American blacks.

Part of the explanation for this lies in the fact that *Uncle Tom's Cabin,* to the surprise of many readers, is simultaneously antislavery and racist. Stowe unequivocally condemned and opposed slavery. Although she knew and could persuasively render the arguments and rationalizations of pro-slavery whites, which is one thing that makes the novel powerful (pro-slavery positions find credible representation in white characters ranging from bold, horrific slaveholders such as Simon Legree and Marie St. Clare to weak yet no less contemptible ones such as Mr. Shelby and Augustine St. Clare), Stowe's opposition to all pro-slavery positions never wavers. She was a staunch supporter of abolition. Yet antislavery did not for Stowe, or, indeed, for most white abolitionists, mean antiracist. *Uncle Tom's Cabin* argues for an end to slavery but not to white supremacy, which is why the novel endorses colonization. Removing educated, assertive, free blacks from the United States means removing the problem of whites having to participate in a social change even more profound than the abolition of slavery: the social change of white people relinquishing (willingly or not) the unearned white privilege, power, and conferred dominance on which the whole U.S. system of racism depends.

Stowe's particular brand of racism reflected the mainstream, white, nineteenth-century outlook that George M. Fredrickson has labeled "romantic racialism." Nineteenth-century racialism in general, unlike racist white theories of the day that denied full human status to people of color, locating them above animals but below whites, granted humanity to people of all races but then asserted that every race had its own essential, inherent characteristics. These supposedly inborn racial traits and dispositions were predetermined for each designated racial group (a set of categories impossible to maintain, as I will explain) and allegedly showed up in different types of intelligence, physicality, temperament, spirituality, artistic ability, and so forth. Thus each race, though all created and beloved by God, had its special virtues, vices, and, most important, ranked location in the ongoing drama of Western civilization. At the top because supposedly most talented as leaders, thinkers, and explorers—and therefore, in a nice tautology, naturally and divinely ordained to lead, think, and explore—were Anglo-Saxon whites. Below them came hierarchically ranked groups of other whites and then people of color, also arranged hierarchically. Except for keeping whites at the top, the whole scheme, not surprisingly, constantly shifted and proved unstable because the basic concept of race itself—the idea of definite boundaries establishing definable, distinct races—could not be maintained. No matter how hard nineteenth-century science tried to name, measure, quantify, and thus control "race," it proved impossible to fix as a biological reality.[4] Nevertheless, invented by whites to justify and maintain their own supremacy, racialism asserted itself as an objective reflection of reality, invoking science and God to prove its veracity.

As one type of racialism, or the belief that each race is essentially and inherently different, romantic racialism differed in claiming not to rank races hierarchically. Each race (again, a completely slippery category) had its own characteristics, true, but none, it was argued, was better or worse. Rather, different races' different characteristics made each better in some ways and worse in others. As Fredrickson explains, romantic racialism posited race as a system of relativism rather than hierarchy and therefore attributed certain putatively positive racial characteristics to blacks: "Although romantic racialists acknowledged that blacks were different from whites and probably always would be, they projected an image of the Negro that could be construed as flattering or laudatory in the context of some currently accepted ideals of human behavior and sensibility" (101–2). Significantly, those flattering or laudatory characteristics were docility, submissiveness, gentleness, humility, kindness, affectionateness, and selflessness, traits conventionally associated in Victorian society with powerless people such as women and children. Antislavery advocate William Ellery Channing, for instance, defined "the African" in 1835 as "affectionate, imitative, and docile." A year later, fellow white abolitionist Charles Stuart "praised the black slaves for being so 'eminently gentle, submissive, affectionate and grateful'" (Fredrickson 103).

The obvious fit between romantic racialism's construction of blacks as humble, gentle, submissive, and selfless and mainstream nineteenth-century Protestantism's construction of the ideal Christian as humble, gentle, submissive, and selfless led many white abolitionists, Stowe included, to argue that African Americans were not only "natural" Christians but, indeed, superior ones, models for all people to follow. "The romantic racialist position," Fredrickson emphasizes, "was to deny unequivocally that these traits constituted inferiority, and its logical extreme was to argue, as Methodist Bishop Gilbert Haven did during the Civil War, that the Negro was the superior race—'the choice blood of America'—because his docility constituted the ultimate in

Christian virtue" (102). One person who made precisely that argument thirty years earlier and almost certainly had an influence on Stowe was Alexander Kinmont, who delivered a series of romantic racialist lectures in Cincinnati in the 1830s, when Stowe was living there, and then published his speeches in 1839 as *Twelve Lectures on the Natural History of Man.*[5]

As a romantic racialist, it made perfect sense to Harriet Beecher Stowe to vigorously condemn discrimination against blacks and insist that all human beings deserve equal treatment in the eyes of the law, as section after section of her *Key to* Uncle Tom's Cabin illustrates. If all stand equal before the throne of God, she reasoned, it is blasphemy to use human laws to condone enslavement of blacks. Yet at the same time, like other progressive whites of her day, including those in the antislavery movement, Stowe's view of African Americans as essentially different led her to routinely condescend toward and patronize black people, as can be seen even in her correspondence with and about Frederick Douglass, a man she admired (see Charles Stowe 149–53, Fields 214–15). Her declarations about the spiritual and even legal equality of all people regardless of race did not, in other words, mean that she viewed all races as the same.

Stowe's romantic racialism shows up in *Uncle Tom's Cabin* most obviously, of course, in Tom. His inherent selflessness, patience, piety, and humility, which make him simultaneously Christlike and maternal (Ammons, "Heroines"), as well as childlike, are always essentialized as racial traits. The text abounds in biologistic racial descriptions such as: "Tom, who had the soft, impressible nature of his kindly race, ever yearning toward the simple and childlike" (127). Or of blacks in general: "the instinctive affections of that race are peculiarly strong. Their local attachments are very abiding. They are not naturally daring and enterprising, but home-loving and affectionate" (83). Or: "the African, naturally patient, timid and unenterprising" (84). Fitting right in with this essentializing rhetoric about Tom and other black characters and equally important, although perhaps less noticed, are George Harris's romantic racialist reasons for emigrating to Liberia. Envisioning colonization, he describes Anglo-Saxons and Africans in explicitly raced terms drawn directly from romantic racialist ideology:

> I think that the African race has peculiarities, yet to be unfolded in the light of civilization and Christianity, which, if not the same as those of the Anglo-Saxon, may prove to be, morally, of even a higher type.
>
> To the Anglo-Saxon race has been intrusted the destinies of the world, during its pioneer period of struggle and conflict. To that mission its stern, inflexible, energetic elements, were well adapted; but, as a Christian, I look for another era to arise. On its borders I trust we stand;

and the throes that now convulse the nations are, to my hope, but the birthpangs of an hour of universal peace and brotherhood.

I trust that the development of Africa is to be essentially a Christian one. If not a dominant and commanding race, they are, at least, an affectionate, magnanimous, and forgiving one. (375–76)

In classic romantic-racialist rhetoric, George labels Anglo-Saxons innate leaders, pioneers, soldiers, and conquerors, that is, strong, virile, and powerful. Blacks, by contrast, are loving, generous, and forgiving—perfect Victorian Christian women or children, take your pick, but in no case powerful, angry adults.

The problem with romantic racialism's claim of different but equal, of course—like *Plessy v. Ferguson*'s claim of separate but equal fifty years later—is that the ideology is not, in fact, about equality. It is about re-encoding dominance and subordination by praising and essentializing alleged black contentment with a subordinated position in the United States. If African Americans are inherently humble, simple, loving, and genetically prone to Christian self-sacrifice, whites need not worry about black retaliation for hundreds of years of injustice, black demands for reparations, or black challenges to white supremacy in the present. Instead, white people can wring their hands at their own inborn hard-heartedness and hyperactive leadership skills while they enjoy their unearned privilege and wait for the new millennium, at which point meek, childlike black people shall usher in a new world order of brotherly love in which all is forgiven.

African Americans attacked this racist ideology from the beginning. David Walker and Frederick Douglass, as their words quoted earlier testify, grounded their angry condemnations of colonization in insistence on black people's full, earned entitlement to live in the United States as free, equal citizens who have literally, with blood and muscle, built the nation. They maintain African Americans are not children. Nor do they happily or docilely acquiesce in their own oppression. Walker and Douglass write as angry, militant adults. Their Christianity—like Martin Delany's, who said of *Uncle Tom's Cabin*'s representation of black people: "Mrs. Stowe knows nothing about us"[6]—does not teach submission, either to slavery *or* to white supremacy. To be sure, some African Americans subscribed to romantic racialist thinking. Because it was a dominant race theory of the day, it is not surprising that William G. Allen stated in an 1852 letter to the editor of *Frederick Douglass' Paper:* "That the bona fide African race has peculiarities, I admit; and I admit, farther, that if these peculiarities are drawn out without intermixture, they will develop a civilization very good indeed; indeed, so good as to be almost good for nothing." Although

Allen's articulation of romantic racialist premises can be seen as ambiguous— is he serious or is he being ironic in his vision of "almost good for nothing" African civilization?—he clearly, even if reluctantly (the two inclusions of "I admit"), endorses the view that different races differ inherently. That view does not, however, in any way diminish his attack on white racism, including that of many abolitionists, or his unequivocal argument in favor of interracial unions, a multiracial United States, and universal equality in the world, for which he invokes "the great law of equal brotherhood."[7]

If Stowe's endorsement of black emigration reflects her racism, and it definitely does, it can also and paradoxically be argued that it suggests respect for African Americans' full equality as fellow Christians, world missionaries, and, therefore, potentially glorious imperialists. Even those who opposed Liberian colonization in the nineteenth century did not oppose it because it was wrong to inflict Western religion, social codes, and economic systems on people who already had their own cultural practices and beliefs. For blacks and whites alike, imperialism was not the issue; exiling African Americans was. Therefore, it is important to ask: Is it possible to think of Stowe's endorsement of Liberian colonization both as a racist move to deport American blacks *and* as an idealistic imperialist project (hard as it might be for us to put those terms together) with black people rather than whites in the lead? The opposition of leaders such as Douglass and Garrison, the history of Liberia, and progressive condemnation of imperialism today make it difficult to find anything positive in Stowe's support for African American colonization of Liberia. Nevertheless, Stowe does assign to black Americans the same respected nineteenth-century status enjoyed or aspired to by many white Americans, that of pioneer or settler, which is to say, imperialist. She includes African Americans as primary actors in *the* nineteenth-century Western drama of colonizing the globe in the name of Christianity and Western civilization.

Indeed, Allen in his letter to *Frederick Douglass' Paper,* while criticizing Stowe's decision to exile black characters at the end of *Uncle Tom's Cabin,* embraces colonialism itself. "I have no objection to the christianization of Africa. God speed the missionaries who go thither for so high and holy purpose—Those also, be they white or colored, who go to build republics upon her shores, go to perform a work, great, grand, and glorious—God speed them also" (3). Likewise, to remind ourselves that, like Stowe, most Americans in the past viewed colonialism positively or, at the very least, uncritically, consider the respected twentieth-century African American historian Benjamin Brawley's description of Liberian settlers:

If we compare them with the Pilgrim Fathers, we find that as the Pilgrims had to subdue the Indians, so they had to hold their own against a score of aggressive tribes. The Pilgrims had the advantage of a thousand years of culture and experience in government; the Negroes, only recently out of bondage, had been deprived of any opportunity for improvement whatsoever. (191)

The idea that Americans might take pride in not living up to the Pilgrim Fathers' brutal example reflects my, not Brawley's, view.

In the final analysis, however, there is no rationalizing the racism of Stowe's Liberian solution, which readers, black and white, have rightly criticized from the beginning.[8] Reacting to attacks, Stowe herself, in a letter to the American and Foreign Anti-Slavery Society, regretted sending George Harris to Africa (Levine 536), and clearly, even as she wrote *Uncle Tom's Cabin*, she knew her position required strenuous defense. The text attempts to head off charges of collusion with the ACS—and, we must also note, adds insult to injury—by assigning the job to George Harris, an African American rather than a white character. Colonization is not about whites' racism, this strategy implies. Equally important, Stowe has Harris consciously rebut the standard anticolonization arguments of her day. He concedes that "the scheme may have been used, in unjustifiable ways, as a means of retarding our emancipation" and acknowledges that emigrants could be seen as turning their backs on fellow African Americans. In response, he maintains that a sovereign black nation in Africa would have power to speak "in the council of nations" worldwide: "A nation has a right to argue, remonstrate, implore, and present the cause of its race,—which an individual has not" (375). Most important, his motive for leaving the United States is the same as that of Liberian immigrants I have quoted. George renounces the United States—"I have no wish to pass for an American, or to identify myself with them" (374)—and, Afrocentrically, chooses Africa as his home. While his rhetoric is Victorian, the sentiment anticipates Marcus Garvey and W. E. B. DuBois. George says, "I go to *my country*,— my chosen, my glorious Africa!" (376).

But then Stowe tips her hand entirely. Immediately following George's proud, impassioned denunciation of U.S. racism, she dispatches every educated black American in her book to Africa (377). George's rhetoric simply establishes the pretext for removing all powerful black opponents of racism in *Uncle Tom's Cabin*. Completing the picture, she next shows us the uneducated, newly freed blacks on the Shelby plantation so grateful to their magnanimous young white master that they vow never to leave the plantation (379). Stowe wants slavery to end and racial inequality to remain. There is no other conclusion.

Chattel slavery, capitalism, missionary Christianity, racism, and Western imperialism represent facets of one core ideology. Each institutionalizes

inequity—protects and guarantees a system of dominance and subordination: master over slave, rich over poor, chosen over damned, white over
people of color, West over the rest of the world. Each system of power supports the others, and each requires Americans not to see the connections.
One hundred and fifty years after its publication, the most lasting cultural
work of *Uncle Tom's Cabin* may not be its antislavery arguments, important
as they are, or even its enduring racist legacy, pernicious as that remains.
Instead, the book's most lasting importance may lie in its brilliantly typical
but instructive failure to recognize the impossibility of arguing against slavery but for colonialism, racism, missionary Christianity, and world capitalism. Stowe's dispatch of freed slaves to Africa at the end of *Uncle Tom's Cabin*
upset abolitionists in the nineteenth century because of its racism, its banishing of blacks from the United States. Equally troubling in the twenty-first
century, one hopes, is its fundamental and unquestioning endorsement of
American imperialism.

Notes

1. Some portions of this discussion appeared in short form in my earlier essay,
"*Uncle Tom's Cabin*, Empire, and Africa," in Ammons and Belasco, eds., *Approaches.*

2. Useful surveys of world events can be found in compendiums such as Freeman-
Grenville or R. Stewart; also see Takaki.

3. For detailed discussion, see Liebenow, Shick, and Sundiata.

4. For two useful treatments of nineteenth-century U.S. race thinking, see Gould
and Gossett, *Race.*

5. Both Fredrickson (104) and Gossett, Uncle Tom's Cabin *and American Culture*
(chapter 5), discuss this.

6. Gossett, Uncle Tom's Cabin *and American Culture,* 174.

7. See Allen, *Frederick Douglass' Paper,* 20 May 1852: 3.

8. See, e.g., Gossett, Uncle Tom's Cabin *and American Culture,* chapter 10.

Works Cited

Allen, William G. "Letter to the Editor." *Frederick Douglass' Paper.* 20 May 1852, 3.

Ammons, Elizabeth. "Heroines in *Uncle Tom's Cabin*." *American Literature* 49 (1977): 161–79.

Ammons, Elizabeth, and Susan Belasco, eds. *Approaches to Teaching Stowe's* Uncle Tom's
Cabin. New York: Modern Language Association of America, 2000.

Belcher, Max, Svend E. Holsoe, Bernard L. Herman, and Rodger P. Kingston. *A Life and Land Remembered: Americo-Liberia Folk Architecture.* Athens: University of Georgia Press, 1988.

Brawley, Benjamin. *A Social History of the American Negro: Being a History of the Negro Problem in the United States; Including a History and Study of the Republic of Liberia.* New York: Macmillan, 1921.

Fairhead, James, Tim Geysbeek, Svend E. Holsoe, and Melissa Leach, eds. *African-American Exploration in West Africa: Four Nineteenth-Century Diaries.* Bloomington: Indiana University Press, 2003.

Fields, Annie. *Life and Letters of Harriet Beecher Stowe.* Boston: Houghton Mifflin, 1898.

Fredrickson, George M. *The Black Image in the White Mind: The Debate on Afro-American Character and Destiny, 1817–1914.* New York: Harper & Row, 1971.

Freeman-Grenville, G. S. P. *Chronology of World History: A Calendar of Principal Events from 3000 BC to AD 1973.* London: Collings, 1975.

Gossett, Thomas F. *Race: The History of an Idea in America.* New York: Oxford University Press, 1997.

Gossett, Thomas F. *Uncle Tom's Cabin and American Culture.* Dallas, TX: Southern Methodist University Press, 1985.

Gould, Stephen Jay. *The Mismeasure of Man.* London: Penguin, 1984.

Levine, Robert S. "*Uncle Tom's Cabin* in *Frederick Douglass' Paper:* An Analysis of Reception." *American Literature* 64 (1992): 71–93. Rpt in H. Stowe, *Uncle Tom's Cabin,* ed. Ammons, 523–42.

Liebenow, J. Gus. *Liberia: The Quest for Democracy.* Bloomington: Indiana University Press, 1987.

Mayer, Henry. *All on Fire: William Lloyd Garrison and the Abolition of Slavery.* New York: St. Martin's Press, 1998.

Melish, Joanne Pope. *Disowning Slavery: Gradual Emancipation and "Race" in New England, 1780–1860.* Ithaca, NY: Cornell University Press, 1998.

Moses, Wilson Jeremiah. *Liberian Dreams: Back-to-Africa Narratives from the 1850s.* University Park: Pennsylvania State University Press, 1998.

Park, Eunjin. "*White*" Americans in "*Black*" Africa: Black and White American Methodist Missionaries in Liberia, 1820–1875.* New York: Routledge, 2001.

Richardson, Nathaniel R. *Liberia's Past and Present.* London: Diplomatic, 1959.

Shick, Tom W. *Behold the Promised Land: A History of Afro-American Settler Society in Nineteenth-Century Liberia.* Baltimore: Johns Hopkins University Press, 1977.

Smith, James Wesley. *Sojourners in Search of Freedom: The Settlement of Liberia by Black Americans.* New York: University Press of America, 1987.

Smith, Susan Belasco. "Serialization and the Nature of *Uncle Tom's Cabin.*" *Periodical Literature in Nineteenth-Century America,* eds. Kenneth M. Price and Susan Belasco Smith. Charlottesville: University Press of Virginia, 1995.

Stewart, Robert. *The Illustrated Almanac of Historical Facts from the Dawn of the Christian Era to the New World Order.* New York: Prentice, 1992.

Stowe, Charles Edward. *Life of Harriet Beecher Stowe Compiled from Her Letters and Journals.* Boston and New York: Houghton, Mifflin, 1890.

Stowe, Harriet Beecher. *Uncle Tom's Cabin* (1852), ed. Elizabeth Ammons. New York: W. W. Norton, 1994.

Sundiata, I. K. *Black Scandal: America and the Liberian Labor Crisis, 1929–1936.* Philadelphia: Institute for the Study of Human Issues, 1980.

Takaki, Ronald. *A Different Mirror: A History of Multicultural America.* Boston: Little, Brown, 1993.

Selected Bibliography

◆ ◆ ◆

Ammons, Elizabeth, ed. *Critical Essays on Harriet Beecher Stowe*. Boston: G. K. Hall, 1980.

Ammons, Elizabeth, and Susan Belasco, eds. *Approaches to Teaching Stowe's* Uncle Tom's Cabin. New York: Modern Language Association, 2000.

Blackburn, Robin. *The Making of New World Slavery*. New York: Verso, 1997.

Davis, David Brion. *Inhuman Bondage: The Rise and Fall of Slavery in the New World*. New York: Oxford University Press, 2006.

Donovan, Josephine. Uncle Tom's Cabin: *Evil, Affliction, and Redemptive Love*. Boston: Twayne, 1991.

Fields, Annie. *Life and Letters of Harriet Beecher Stowe*. Boston: Houghton Mifflin, 1898.

Gossett, Thomas F. *Race: The History of an Idea in America*. 1963. Reprint, New York: Oxford University Press, 1997.

Gossett, Thomas F. Uncle Tom's Cabin *and American Culture*. Dallas, TX: Southern Methodist University Press, 1985.

Hedrick, Joan D. *Harriet Beecher Stowe: A Life*. New York: Oxford University Press, 1994.

Jordan-Lake, Joy. *Whitewashing* Uncle Tom's Cabin: *Nineteenth-Century Women Novelists Respond to Stowe*. Nashville, TN: Vanderbilt University Press, 2005.

McDowell, Deborah, and Arnold Rampersad, eds. *Slavery and the Literary Imagination*. Baltimore: Johns Hopkins University Press, 1989.

Meer, Sarah. *Uncle Tom Mania: Slavery, Minstrelsy and Transatlantic Culture in the 1850s.* Athens: University of Georgia Press, 2005.

Stowe, Charles Edward. *Life of Harriet Beecher Stowe Compiled from Her Letters and Journals.* Boston and New York: Houghton Mifflin, 1890.

Stowe, Harriet Beecher. *Dred: A Tale of the Great Dismal Swamp,* ed. Robert S. Levine. 1856. Reprint, Chapel Hill: University of North Carolina Press, 2000.

Stowe, Harriet Beecher. *A Key to* Uncle Tom's Cabin. Boston: John P. Jewett, 1853. Reprint, New York: Arno, 1968.

Stowe, Harriet Beecher. *Uncle Tom's Cabin: Authoritative Text, Backgrounds and Contexts, Criticism,* ed. Elizabeth Ammons. New York: W. W. Norton, 1994.

Sundquist, Eric J., ed. *New Essays on* Uncle Tom's Cabin. Cambridge: Cambridge University Press, 1986.